Southgate Circus
Library
High Street N14
886 3728

RIDGE AVENUE
LIBRARY,
RIDGE AVENUE,
LONDON, N21 2RH
Tel: 360 5662

LONDON BOROUGH OF ENFIELD
LIBRARY SERVICES

This book to be RETURNED on or before the latest date stamped unless a renewal has been obtained by personal call, post or telephone, quoting the above number and the date due for return.

THE FOURTH ARM

By the same author

Elizabeth's Army (1966)
Army Royal: Henry VIII's Invasion of France 1513 (1969)
The English Occupation of Tournai 1513–1519 (1971)
The German Occupation of the Channel Islands (1975)
Greece 1940–1941 (1976)

The Fourth Arm
Psychological Warfare 1938-1945

CHARLES CRUICKSHANK

DAVIS-POYNTER
LONDON

First published in 1977 by
Davis-Poynter Limited
20 Garrick Street London WC2E 9BJ

Copyright © 1977 by Charles Cruickshank

All rights reserved. No part of this publication may be reproduced, stored in a retrieval system, or transmitted, in any form or by any means, electronic, mechanical, photocopying, recording or otherwise, without the prior permission of the publishers.

ISBN 0 7067 0212 3

Printed in Great Britain by
Bristol Typesetting Co Ltd
Barton Manor, St Philips, Bristol

Contents

PREFACE		*page* 7
ONE	Going into business	9
TWO	Organization and Management	28
THREE	Articles of association: Propaganda policy	44
FOUR	Market research: Intelligence	59
FIVE	The product: Propaganda themes	69
SIX	Delivering the goods: Propaganda techniques	87
SEVEN	Special delivery	113
EIGHT	Hard sell: Propaganda in military operations	134
NINE	Customer reaction: The effect of propaganda	159
TEN	Conclusion: Profit or loss?	176
APPENDIX	Manuscript sources	188
SELECT BIBLIOGRAPHY		191
INDEX		193

Preface

This book is written almost entirely from the contemporary papers listed in the Appendix. At the beginning of my research I consulted survivors of the Political Warfare Executive staff, including some of the rash (or is the collective noun 'a caution'?) of ambassadors which spread from the devious paths of political warfare at Woburn Abbey and Bush House to splendid embassies around the world, in whose powerful corridors deviousness is shunned and only the truth is spoken; but I found (as I had done when researching earlier books on the Second World War) that no-one remembers accurately what happened thirty or more years ago. Therefore I am not indebted for a single fact to anyone other than the authors of contemporary official letters, minutes, memoranda and records of meetings. There is no need to enter the usual disclaimer, after thanking the many people who did help, that all the errors and omissions in the following pages are mine and mine alone.

I must, however, acknowledge most generous guidance from Ellic Howe, who was in charge of PWE's black printing unit; and from Cecil de Sausmarez, of Sausmarez Manor, Guernsey, a member of that Island's legislature, who served with distinction in PWE, whose contribution to the rehabilitation of Belgium is remembered with gratitude by many Belgians, and who, along with Winston Churchill, received the Golden Spurs of the City of Courtrai after the war. Mr de Sausmarez's help in elucidating some of the more obscure PWE papers has been invaluable.

The Political Warfare Executive papers are, perhaps inevitably, in a mess. There are 545 'pieces' – ie boxes or covers each containing one or more files. There was no formal registration of papers in the early days of the propaganda department and the researcher is now faced with a multiplicity of 'do-it-yourself' filing systems which have nothing in common, except the extreme difficulty of making head or tail of them.

C.G.C.

I
Going into business

The Munich Rehearsal
For a decade after the disbandment in 1918 of the Crewe House organization,[1] which carried on propaganda against Germany in the last months of the First World War, the British government engaged in no overseas propaganda, except for publicity through the Foreign Office News Department. It re-entered the field indirectly with the establishment in 1929 of the Travel and Industrial Development Association, which publicized British industry and resorts; and in 1934 of the British Council, whose charter to sell the British way of life made it a genteel propaganda machine. In 1938 the BBC started broadcasting in foreign languages.

Compared with the propaganda output of Germany and Italy this was less than nothing, certainly to Sir Robert Vansittart, a prophet of doom whose forebodings about the rise of the Nazis were as unwelcome to British Ministers – almost all with their head in the sands of appeasement – as the unprofessional way he put his views to them. Vansittart, one of history's great own worst enemies, was replaced as head of the Foreign Office at the beginning of 1938 by Sir Alexander Cadogan, and put out to grass with the title of Chief Diplomatic Adviser.

It was difficult to find anything for him to advise about; but the Foreign Secretary (Mr Anthony Eden[2]) suggested that he should co-ordinate British overseas publicity. This would give him something to do, and would show that the government was not neglecting these matters.[3]

Sir Horace Wilson, the Prime Minister's principal adviser, warned his master that propaganda was not a good substitute 'for calmly getting on with the business of Govt. including a rational foreign policy', but Chamberlain nevertheless acted on Eden's suggestion.[4] A committee was set up with innocuous terms of reference: 'to prevent overlapping, and by exchange of information among the bodies engaged in various forms of publicity abroad, to co-ordinate their programmes

---
[1] An inadequate description of this organization is in *Secrets of Crewe House* (London, 1920), by Sir Campbell Stuart, its deputy head.
[2] Later Lord Avon.
[3] PREM 1/272, ff. 55-8.
[4] *Ibid* ff. 53-4.

A*

and activities'[5] – tailor-made to keep officials busy without giving them much chance of putting forward tiresome new policies.

The propaganda-conscious Germans took the new committee much too seriously. The *Völkischer Beobachter* reminded its readers of the 'masterly British propaganda' of 1918 which would now be renewed under the hated Vansittart. Hitler himself affected to see a threat in the work of the committee and had to be reassured by the British ambassador, Sir Nevile Henderson.[6] The Nazis might pour out oceans of anti-British propaganda without a murmur of protest from Westminster, but the merest threat of a droplet in reply had to be defended to the Führer.

Vansittart's committee duly met; and on 28 May 1938 he sent a report direct to the Prime Minister. He had written it himself, throwing to the winds the restrictive terms of reference. He made some recommendations not examined by the committee, and others to which they had objected. He proposed that the activities of all the existing publicity bodies should be extended. He also wanted a new Films Council, a clutch of fifteen new press attachés in key embassies, the upgrading of Rex Leeper,[7] head of the Foreign Office News Department, and the appointment of Lord Lloyd, unpaid Chairman of the British Council, as President of the Travel Association, with £5,000 a year for doing both jobs.[8]

In a covering letter he asked – virtually ordered – the Prime Minister to read the report, and to approve it forthwith. He added that if the recommendations did not speak for themselves he hoped that the Prime Minister would make himself available one day in the following week so that he (Vansittart) might enlarge on them.[9]

Chamberlain was taken aback. He noted: 'It is really a very astonishing document to receive from a Civil Servant'. In acknowledging it he told Vansittart that he must wait to hear what the Foreign Secretary (now Lord Halifax, Eden having resigned on 20 February over the policy of appeasement) had to say about it. In the event Halifax did not comment and the Treasury waited in vain for his officials to provide reasoned argument. All that happened was that Leeper – who had a vested interest because of the recommended upgrading of his job – said his Department accepted the recommendations in toto.[10] Warren Fisher, head of the Treasury, noted unkindly: 'Mr. Leeper is already overpaid, tho I wd. be prepared to pay him more as a pension.'[11]

[5] Hansard(Commons) vol. 331, col. 671.
[6] FO 371/21711, ff. 2-5.
[7] Later Sir Rex Leeper.
[8] PREM 1/272, ff. 28-51.
[9] *Ibid* ff. 26-7.
[10] *Ibid* f. 3.
[11] *Ibid* f. 15.

The Treasury castigated the Foreign Office for its irresponsibility. They also stated the case against overseas propaganda, quite apart from its cost. In recent years it had poisoned the international atmosphere. Even if in praising oneself one did not decry others, the unflattering implication was there. When Hitler had occupied Austria a few days earlier, the press acclaim of Britain's diplomatic effort for peace was bitterly resented in Germany because it implied that the Führer had been on the point of going to war. Hitherto Britain had been careful to avoid direct government propaganda. The BBC, Travel Association, and British Council were all autonomous bodies; but now the government was being asked to enter the propaganda field in its own person. Appeasement and a forward policy in propaganda were irreconcilable. There were, of course, also financial objections. If Vansittart's argument was accepted the level of expenditure on this dubious service would be determined by Germany, which meant that the sky would be the limit.[12]

The author of this memorandum recognized that the policy *was* appeasement, and stated his official view that an overseas propaganda campaign might work against that policy. He may have felt as passionately as did Vansittart that appeasement was wrong, but nevertheless accepted that Ministers and not civil servants made policy – right *or* wrong.

The Treasury's examination of the case dragged on for the rest of the year. The final outcome was that everything that Vansittart had asked for was allowed, but on a much-reduced scale. His original plan would have cost half a million pounds a year, but only a fifth of that amount was approved by the Treasury.[13] The inference is that if he had put his ideas forward in the ordinary way and not like a bull in a china shop he might have got all that he wanted without delay. It is doubtful whether this would have made much difference in the long run to Britain's wartime performance; but at least it would have provided a few months' longer experience of the new arrangements, which would have helped when it became necessary to establish a more sophisticated propaganda organization.

Before the dust from this skirmish had settled the Munich crisis of September 1938 arrived. It seemed to many who believed that the German people were not all solidly behind the Nazi regime that propaganda might save the day. Officials and private individuals pressed for a campaign to show the Germans that Britain was their friend and Hitler their enemy. Vernon Bartlett, journalist and Member of Parliament for Bridgwater, told the Foreign Office that propaganda would be much more important in a new war against Germany than it had been in the last. There was strong opposition to the Nazis,

[12] PREM 1/272, ff. 17-18.
[13] FO 395/605, f. 420.

the quality of food in Germany was poor, the overtrained youth were no longer inspired by their new uniforms, the older people did not relish the thought of another war so soon, and press and radio propaganda had been so overdone within Germany that they would cease to have any effect. Germany could be defeated on the home front even while her armies were still winning victories over less well-prepared countries.[14]

Another expert on international affairs, Stephen King-Hall,[15] saw the problem in the same light. Britain faced a war of ideas. Her objective must be to destroy the Nazi regime, the strength of which lay in its control of information. The average German had now attained everything he was willing to make sacrifices for. The great mass of the people were ripe for a propaganda attack from outside, which to King-Hall meant the dissemination of truth. The struggle would be between democracy and totalitarianism, between free and controlled thought. Britain's first weapon must be propaganda, regardless of the cost.[16]

Unsolicited advice was also proferred from within Whitehall. An officer of one of the Military Intelligence Branches pointed out that when Napoleon's escape from Elba in 1815 was reported to the Congress of Vienna the allied nations instantly proclaimed him an outlaw. 'I suggest that if it comes to war the same idea should be followed, and that war should be declared, not against the German people, but against Hitler and the Nazi leaders.' This would be good for Britain's image all over the world and might have decisive results in Germany.[17]

These views may seem to be naive, perhaps based on unrepresentative soundings, since British travellers in Germany tended to rub shoulders with moderate Germans rather than with out-and-out Nazis. Some Germans shared them, however. Dr Hermann Rauschning, former President of the Senate of Danzig, later said that up to the time of Munich Britain could have used propaganda 'to mobilise the general unwillingness of the German people to fight, and create something in the nature of a general strike against war'.[18]

In the midst of the Munich crisis the Director General designate of the embryo Ministry of Information, Sir Stephen Tallents,[19] devised a propaganda attack to be launched against Germany as soon as the Prime Minister's latest appeasement efforts had failed. His main idea was to drop leaflets over Germany – ten million nightly as far afield

[14] FO 898/1 (27.9.38).
[15] Later Lord King-Hall.
[16] FO 898/1 (28.9.38).
[17] *Ibid* (20.9.38).
[18] FO 898/4, ff. 101-2.
[19] He was succeeded in June 1939 by the Earl of Perth (CAB 16/127, f. 25).

as Berlin – from aircraft and small balloons. The latter had dropped 100,000 leaflets a day over the German lines in 1918.[20]

The messages prepared for the leaflet bombardment reflect the belief that the German people were significantly divided. For example:

> Hitler and his lot mean everlasting war. What is the result of his five years' rule? This five years' mockery has come to a grisly end. Now you are paying the bill for this demented government. We attack you with a heavy heart . . .
> German people! We are not fighting you but your Leader. We know you have been deceived and defrauded by him . . . If you can release yourselves from his Leadership, which sets the world in flames so as to conquer it, we promise you a decent peace and the way to an honourable future . . .
> German Mothers! Hitler butchers your and our children simply in order to gratify his megalomaniac desire for power. It is all the same to him – he has no childen . . .[21]

In the event no leaflet was dropped. The holocaust was deferred for twelve months. Tallents wrote on 4 October 1938: 'Last week's dress rehearsal . . . taught us various lessons, but the sharpest and most urgent of them was the need for properly co-ordinated arrangements for the conveyance of information to enemy countries';[22] and he urged that when the Ministry of Information was set up it should be enabled to operate an enemy publicity branch almost at a moment's notice.[23] With the enthusiasm of a crusader he set about improving the arrangements – having first discounted the argument that British propaganda in 1918 was effective only because enemy morale was by then shattered.

He pointed out that thanks to radio and air transport it was now easier to carry information to whole enemy populations, and not just to men in the fighting lines; and in a strict dictatorship where news was rigidly controlled the impact of truth from outside would be greater.[24] Radio had its limitations, however, since people could not be compelled to listen. Broadcasts must be carefully timed, and not, as happened on 26 September 1938, accidentally programmed to coincide with a Hitler speech from the Sport Palast, to which the whole of Germany naturally gave priority. Leaflets also had their limitations. They could be used only after war had started, and might be hindered by bad weather. They took time to prepare, although in 1918 – thanks to a special War Office printing unit in Boulogne –

[20] FO 898/1 (7.11.38).
[21] Ibid (27.9.38).
[22] Ibid (4.10.38).
[23] CAB 16/127, f. 61.
[24] FO 898/1 (7.11.38).

they had been delivered to the dropping balloons forty-eight hours after their messages had been approved in London. This was important since the September experience suggested that in dropping leaflets speed was of the essence.[25]

He went on to say that new methods of delivering propaganda might be developed. Rockets with a capacity of thirty leaflets had been used on the Italian front in the last war; and it was said that rockets carrying a thousand over one and a half miles had been used in the Spanish Civil War. With the co-operation of the War Office and the Secret Service, subterranean channels could be devised for the transmission of information.[26]

Thus far Tallents was on safe ground. No one was much concerned about schemes for rocketting leaflets at the Germans. But he then went on to propose two things. First, an organization to study public opinion in potential enemy countries; and second, the preparation of propaganda material for use at short notice when the need arose. The Defence Departments, shocked by the lack of preparedness in this area, whole-heartedly supported these proposals.[27]

This immediately brought the Foreign Office into the fray. The study of public opinion in foreign countries was *their* responsibility. In the morning of 14 December 1938 the Foreign Secretary presented to the Cabinet a memorandum on overseas publicity. If Europe had to choose between a Pax Germanica and a Pax Britannica, the issue might well be settled by the success of British propaganda; Britain should refrain from criticizing the Germans but rather inform them about her own affairs and outlook; and her campaign must not be niggardly. Halifax then put forward specific proposals. The ten-minute BBC news in German *might* be increased to fifteen. The Germans *might* be asked to allow a Briton to broadcast to Germany on British affairs, if they were afforded reciprocal facilities in Britain. Advantage *might* be taken of contacts between British and German businessmen. An office of the Travel Association *might* be set up in Berlin. The British Council *might* produce a monthly in German, called say *Digest of British Achievement*. Time *might* be bought on Radio Luxembourg for programmes in German sponsored by a British travel agent.[28]

This pitiful package of barrel-scrapings is a classic example of the defence of departmental responsibilities at the expense of public policy. Tallents had seen the need to do something positive which the Foreign Office was not doing. To defend their empire the Foreign Office had to pretend that it was already being done. It is to be hoped

[25] CAB 16/127, ff. 259-67.
[26] *Ibid*
[27] *Ibid* f. 273.
[28] CAB 24/281, ff. 107-9; 23/96, ff. 384-8.

that those who put the package together for the Foreign Secretary did not seriously believe that it would influence the German view of Britain one iota, but recognized that it was no more than a card in the inter-Departmental game of Beggar-my-neighbour.

Cabinet discussion of the Foreign Office proposals brought them only a little nearer to earth. The Chancellor of the Exchequer (Sir John Simon)[29] who would have to foot the bill, had his doubts. He was sceptical about reciprocal radio talks, as were some of his colleagues. The Foreign Office News Department came in for some criticism because its guidance had not always been in harmony with government policy. The British Council and Travel Association were also suspect. Lord Lloyd, now head of both (as recommended by Vansittart) had been a severe critic of the government.

It is difficult to decide which proposal would have contributed least to Halifax's Pax Britannica. The prize probably goes to the use of businessmen to spread the gospel in Germany. The stalwarts of the Federation of British Industry were to be issued with suitable literature so that they might 'speak on the right lines' to the Germans they encountered. Alas, no-one suggested making *this* ploy reciprocal. The vision of Teutonic businessmen – armed with suitable literature, no doubt a pocket edition of *Mein Kampf* – 'speaking on the right lines' to their British counterparts might have led some members of the Cabinet to see how fatuous the idea was; and to go on to ask themselves whether the other proposals made any better sense.

As it was, the Cabinet approved the package in principle, subject to further discussion the following week. They wanted to think again about reciprocal broadcasts; and they thought that instead of asking the Federation of British Industry to unleash a swarm of right-minded businessmen upon the German scene, the Foreign Office should seek out suitable captains of industry for conversion into instant diplomatists.[30]

The deferment of Cabinet approval must have been a disappointment to Foreign Office officials, for an inter-Departmental meeting had been arranged for the afternoon of the same day, no doubt in the hope that by that time they would have a Cabinet decision in their favour which would enable them to put Tallents firmly in his place. They need not have worried, however. Tallents represented a Ministry yet unborn and had no Minister to fight for him. In putting forward his proposals he argued, with the support of the Vice-Chief of the Air Staff, Air Vice-Marshal R. E. Peirse,[31] that the only way of getting the British point of view across to Germany in September would have been to drop leaflets. The whole of the preparatory work –

---

[29] Later Viscount Simon.
[30] CAB 23/96, ff. 384-8, 425-7.
[31] Later Air Marshal Sir Richard Peirse.

drafting leaflets, planning their printing and distribution – had to be started from scratch, and the Foreign Office had not been able to give the slightest help.

Leeper agreed; but he explained that in the meantime his News Department had been expanded. The same difficulties would not arise again. He went on to pour cold water on Tallents's idea that propaganda should be prepared in advance. It would be out of date before the ink had dried. When the need arose the Foreign Office would be able to cope, using material already in their possession.[32] His trump card, however, was simply that publicity in foreign countries was a Foreign Office responsibility, and that was that. The debate ended swiftly when Warren Fisher concurred. Nevertheless, since under the rules no inter-Departmental meeting may end with the total defeat of one side, a new sub-committee was set up to examine the conduct of propaganda in foreign countries in the event of war.

The German desk at the Foreign Office, which was perhaps closer to reality than the News Department, proposed that extracts from Chamberlain's speeches should be circulated in Germany. The observations of the hierarchy on this proposition, in ascending order of rank, show how policy is made – or marred – in Whitehall:

> *Third Secretary:* 'This may not do much good, but can we afford to neglect any opportunity?'
> *First Secretary:* 'I thoroughly agree . . .'
> *Counsellor:* 'Why should not the Anglo-German Fellowship be asked to co-operate?'
> *Deputy Under-Secretary:* 'Our Printing Department could produce the pamphlets without extra expense'.
> *Permanent Under-Secretary:* ' I am in favour . . .'
> *Foreign Secretary:* 'I am in favour of this, but think PM should see . . .'

The PM saw, and turned the idea down. There was no need to do anything. Appeasement had already saved the day.[33]

The phoney war, and after

In September 1938 Sir Campbell Stuart, the Canadian second-in-command of British propaganda in 1918, was invited by the Prime Minister to set up a new propaganda department. This was kept a close secret, in particular from Sir Stephen Tallents who was under the impression that wartime propaganda would be looked after by the proposed Ministry of Information. No sooner had Stuart collected together a small staff than Chamberlain met Hitler at Munich. 'Peace in our time' made propaganda superfluous and Stuart was instructed

[32] CAB 16/127, ff. 75-81.
[33] FO 371/21791, ff. 219-21.

to down tools. He was even told that it would be dangerous to do more than 'think ahead'. However, when it became plain in the spring of 1939 that Hitler was still bent on war, whatever the archdupe of the century might have thought after Munich, Stuart was asked to revive his plans.³⁴

With the blessing of a small Ministerial committee he produced stocks of propaganda literature for the early days of a war, using as his base Electra House on the Embankment, the office of the Imperial Communications Committee of which he was chairman. Horace Wilson once again told the Prime Minister that he was sceptical about the value of propaganda leaflets, especially immediately after the declaration of war when the individual German would be too excited to pay any attention to them. He admitted, however, that propaganda might have its uses later on.³⁵ It was arranged that if war did come Stuart's staff should move to Woburn Abbey in Bedfordshire where they would be able to perform their intellectual conjuring tricks safe from bombs and prying eyes; and this plan was duly carried out.

For ten months the Department of Propaganda in Enemy Countries – EH for short – had primary responsibility for propaganda. It carried on where its predecessor of 1918 had left off, working on the same principles and using the same techniques, except that it had an important new medium at its disposal – radio. At first it reported to the Minister of Information (Lord MacMillan) but in the middle of October 1939 it was transferred to the Foreign Office.³⁶ Then at the beginning of June 1940, it was returned to the Minister of Information, now Mr Duff Cooper.³⁷

When Churchill became Prime Minister in May 1940 he wanted something more dynamic than broadcasting and leaflet-dropping. On 16 July he approved the establishment of the Special Operations Executive 'to co-ordinate all action by way of subversion and sabotage against the enemy overseas', and put the Minister of Economic Warfare (Dr Hugh Dalton) in charge. Dalton divided SOE into two branches: SO 1, which took over the secret propaganda element of EH, with Leeper in command; and SO 2 which was responsible for sabotage. The open propaganda element of EH was temporarily left with the Ministry of Information, since at first Dalton would have his hands full building up the sabotage side of SOE.

This had unforeseen consequences. Since SOE was a secret unit the Minister of Economic Warfare could not answer in public for its activities. Therefore, when in due course Dalton took over open

[34] PREM 1/374, ff. 24-9.
[35] Ibid ff. 4-6.
[36] INF 1/859 (20.10.39).
[37] FO 898/1 (1.6.40) Campbell Stuart left the propaganda department in August 1940. (Duff Cooper later became Lord Norwich.)

propaganda broadcasting, Duff Cooper as Minister responsible for the BBC would have to answer in parliament for his colleague's policies. This was a relatively unimportant technicality, but Duff Cooper was desperately keen to control all propaganda and he used it to frustrate the transfer of open propaganda to Dalton.

By November 1940 it was obvious that Duff Cooper had no intention of handing over open propaganda at any stage. In addition to basing his case on the parliamentary question problem he argued that overt and covert propaganda should be handled separately. This of course was a negation of SOE's charter, and reduced to despair those propagandists who wanted a unified department of propaganda.

Leeper summed up their exasperation in a long minute: 'It is fantastic for the Ministry of Information to interpret subversive propaganda as merely covert or underground propaganda. The most formidable instrument for propaganda today is broadcasting and the facilities offered by the BBC are far and away our most potent method of employing that instrument. It was obvious that MOI's propaganda to Germany and Italy was subversive and that they were encroaching on the province of the Minister of Economic Warfare, who had been charged by the War Cabinet to undertake this work. 'I do not feel that the Cabinet has fully grasped what has happened and I feel sure that if it were explained to them they could not justify the existing arrangement, as it largely defeats the purpose of the Minister of Economic Warfare's charter'. He concluded by pointing out that the only justification MOI could put forward for holding on to open propaganda was the difficulty about answering parliamentary questions. This was nonsense since SOE were already handling leaflet propaganda, to which the same technical objection applied, without difficulty. If necessary members of parliament could be told that the activities of the fourth fighting arm were just as secret as those of the other services.[38]

By December 1940 Dalton was satisfied that the secret side of SOE was in good running order and that the time was ripe to declare war on MOI. He asked Duff Cooper to hand over open propaganda broadcasting, and backed his demand with reasoned argument. Subversion was a single subject. All broadcasts to the enemy – open and secret – had the same objective: to destroy his power and at the appropriate moment to raise revolt among his slaves in the occupied countries. He suggested that the technicality about answering parliamentary questions was unimportant, since members were too busy these days to ask many questions. In any case, the Political Intelligence Department of the Foreign Office, which was the cover for SOE, already reported to the Ministry of Economic Warfare. PID was part of the published establishment of the Foreign Office, so it would be easy to arrange for the

[38] FO 898/9, pp. 57-8.

Foreign Secretary to take any parliamentary questions. Dalton concluded by saying that he would be happy to discuss 'these reflections' *à deux*, or if Duff Cooper preferred it, with their War Cabinet colleagues.[39]

Duff Cooper promptly replied that the existing position was perfectly satisfactory; and he circulated a paper to Ministers supporting this view. He agreed that ideally propaganda should be directed by one Department of State so that policy might be consistent; and that there was no real distinction between subversive and non-subversive propaganda, in spite of his earlier claim that they should be dealt with separately. He deplored the division which had developed. MEW had been given responsibility for special operations simply because the Secret Service was impossibly stretched; and it had been agreed that all Secret Service projects in enemy countries should be handled by one Ministry. If MEW took over open broadcasts it 'would break down the system – namely the division between overt and secret – and leave us with no system at all'. This, given the admission that there was no real distinction between subversive and non-subversive propaganda, did not make sense. He was on stronger ground in claiming that it would be more difficult for a secret unit to liaise with the allied governments now sitting in London; and once foreign governments knew what SOE was up to the House of Commons could hardly be kept in ignorance. Again, a whole chain of radio stations round the Mediterranean was controlled by press attachés who received their instructions from the Minister of Information. What would happen to them?

Finally, he repeated that all propaganda should be under one Department – either MOI or MEW. If MEW won, so much would be transferred from MOI that it would not be worth while carrying it on as a separate Department of State. This, of course, was petulant nonsense. MOI was floundering because its responsibilities were too great, and because it had never had a strong Minister.[40]

Dalton graciously thanked Duff Cooper for his memorandum and fired back his own with the comment: 'I think these two papers make quite a pretty debate!' The Prime Minister had entrusted him with the Chairmanship of SOE to co-ordinate 'all action by way of subversion and sabotage against the enemy overseas'; but MOI was still responsible for overt propaganda. This was anomalous and unsatisfactory. 'I have been told to arrange subversion against the enemy. In this task one of my most powerful instruments of propaganda is the BBC broadcasts. These, however, are not at my disposal, but remain in the control of another Ministry'. BBC broadcasts to enemy and enemy-occupied countries must be transferred to MEW.[41]

Churchill, who according to Duff Cooper was not interested in

[39] PREM 3/365/7, ff. 790-2; INF 1/893 (6.12.40).
[40] PREM 3/365/7, ff. 787-8; INF 1/893 (13.12.40).
[41] INF 1/893 (15.12.40).

propaganda 'because he knew it would not win the war, had no intention of taking the chair at Dalton's 'pretty debate'. Instead he ordered the Lord President, Sir John Anderson,[43] to knock together the heads of the two warring Ministers.[44] Anderson, who may have felt that the Labour man (Dalton) had a better case than his fellow Conservative, was reluctant to take sides and came up with a proposed arrangement that virtually maintained the status quo. Duff Cooper was delighted, but Dalton hastily proposed an alternative which the Minister of Information saw as 'most unsatisfactory'. He would have nothing to do with it.[45]

Anderson, who had rather botched his role of Solomon, confessed that they were no nearer a solution. Then with a flash of inspiration of which Solomon would have been proud, he enunciated three principles:

(a) the Minister of Information could not be responsible for secret propaganda;
(b) the Minister of Economic Warfare could not be responsible for overt propaganda; and
(c) all propaganda should have a common policy.

Officials should now use these principles to steer themselves towards a mutually satisfactory division of responsibility. He coyly told the Prime Minister about his three principles – although he wisely did not reveal what they were – and left the impression that all problems were now solved.[46]

They were not. Duff Cooper complained: 'This doesn't get us much further. He was asked by the Prime Minister to settle our differences with MEW and after some weeks of delay he tells us we had better settle them ourselves'. More important, he did *not* accept that MOI could not handle secret propaganda. Predictably Dalton did *not* accept that MEW could not handle overt propaganda.[47]

Officials from the two Departments were about to sit down with somebody from the Foreign Office to do the job which the Prime Minister had assigned to the Lord President when Dalton suddenly threw in the towel. He telephoned Walter Monckton, Director General of the Ministry of Information, suggesting a compromise which added up to no more than closer liaison between MOI and MEW. Lord Hood, Duff Cooper's private secretary, noted on the file: 'I am suspicious of this sudden desire of Dr Dalton to settle this matter, so to speak, out of court. I can only attribute it to his realization that at a meeting of

---

[42] *Old Men Forget* (London, 1953) p. 288.
[43] Later Viscount Waverley.
[44] PREM 3/365/7, f. 786.
[45] *Ibid* f. 785; INF 1/893 (1.1.41).
[46] PREM 3/365/7, f. 783; INF 1/893 (10.1.41).
[47] INF 1/893 (11, 14.1.41).

officials he would find himself in a minority of one.⁴⁸ A few days later Hood added: 'I do not think we should remain satisfied with Dr Dalton's present desire to leave things as they are'. It was still essential in his opinion to have a single propaganda department.⁴⁹

However, neither Minister was big enough willingly to give up any part of his empire in the national interest; and the feud might have gone on indefinitely had not Churchill scribbled a note on 2 March 'What has happened about this in the meantime? It seems to have settled itself'. He was wrong. Anthony Bevir,⁵⁰ one of his private secretaries, wrote to Norman Brook, Sir John Anderson's private secretary, saying that he did not want to stir anything up, but had the row between Dalton and Duff Cooper ended happily? On 19 March Brook said he thought it had: but he too was wrong.⁵¹

Sooner or later there had to be a showdown. It came on 16 May when Eden, Dalton and Duff Cooper met Anderson to arrive at a final solution. Or so they thought. Dalton would be responsible for secret propaganda; and Duff Cooper for overt. Together with Eden they would form a Ministerial Committee to ensure that they kept in step. The three Ministers would each appoint a senior official to provide co-operation at the working level.⁵²

These decisions attempted to sanctify the unholy division of responsibility in the fields of subversive warfare and propaganda which had bedevilled this part of the British war effort; but the main result, apart from preserving the *amour propre* of two Ministers of the Crown, was to perpetuate much of the inefficiency and frustration from which British propaganda had suffered.

The shooting war, to September 1941

The control of propaganda might seem to have been settled by the 'Anderson Award'; but no. Moreover, the Ministry of Information continued on other grounds to be a thorn in the government's side. It was new, misunderstood by everybody, especially the gentlemen of the press accustomed to gather their news live and not at second hand from moribund civil servants. It is doubtful if even the strongest Minister could have made much of the Department in the early days, but it was first commanded by two not very able men each with a short tenure of office, and its reputation went from bad to worse. The first Minister, Lord MacMillan, was replaced by Sir John Reith after four months. Reith was replaced by Duff Cooper four months later. He survived for over a year, but the task was too much for him.

In spite of having accepted the Anderson Award, Duff Cooper told

---

⁴⁸ INF 1/893 (22.1.41).
⁴⁹ *Ibid* (29.1.41).
⁵⁰ Later Sir Anthony.
⁵¹ PREM 3/365/7, ff. 777, 779-8
⁵² FO 898/9, p. 46.

Churchill at the beginning of June 1941 that he disliked it. He said that after a year's experience as Minister of Information he was convinced that the whole of foreign propaganda should be under the control of one Department. Unity of command was as important in this sphere as in any other. He had always recognized that propaganda must be consonant with foreign policy and that the Minister of Propaganda must carry out the policy of the Foreign Office; but this applied equally to the Service Departments. Neither the Admiralty nor the War Office would dream of opening hostilities in a new theatre of war without the consent of the Foreign Office; but that consent having been obtained the conduct of operations would be left to them. He added that the division of propaganda into overt and secret had not worked well.[53]

This attempt to reopen the whole question led the Prime Minister to call in Beaverbrook, then his trouble-shooting Minister of State ('pray see this file') who at once endorsed the proposal that there should be a Ministerial Committee of three;[54] and it was formally approved by Churchill on 13 June.[55] Nevertheless a week later Duff Cooper tackled the Prime Minister again saying, not for the first time, that if his Ministry was not to control all propaganda it might as well cease to exist.[56]

Churchill saw that this time-consuming squabble must be brought to an end. In a minute of 21 June to Beaverbrook he made it clear that there was to be no nonsense about shutting down the Ministry of Information. It was the settled policy of the government that it should continue, headed by a Minister of Cabinet rank. 'All arrangements must be conformable and compatible with this'. Would Beaverbrook immediately put proposals to the War Cabinet, carrying Eden and Dalton with him as far as possible. He did not mention Duff Cooper, which suggests that he had already decided to replace him.[57]

Beaverbrook's recommendations covered the whole of the Ministry's range of activities; but he had little to say about overseas propaganda. Simply that the Foreign Secretary should have absolute control of foreign policy on propaganda. His general directives must be accepted by the Minister of Information, who would be responsible for the execution of propaganda policy. He concluded with the proposition that the Ministry of Information must 'root-hog or die.[58] His paper had an unenthusiastic reception from the War Cabinet (principally because it proposed that all contact between the press and the government

[53] PREM 3/365/7, f. 771.
[54] Ibid f. 759.
[55] Ibid f. 755.
[56] Ibid ff, 746-7.
[57] Ibid ff. 741-2.
[58] CAB 66/17, ff. 74-5.

should be through MOI) and Churchill adjourned the discussion for a week to give himself time to think.[59]

Next day Duff Cooper sent round another paper in a last despairing effort to have propaganda played his way. The War Cabinet must decide whether MOI was to be run by 'a very important Minister' handling in addition to his other duties all political warfare, including secret, overt, cultural and political propaganda, or merely by an official at the beck and call of other Departments. If MOI did not have all these responsibilities it was difficult to justify its existence as a separate Department of State. It should be allowed to disintegrate into its component parts. He ended with a *cri de coeur* which was surely enough to settle his fate as Minister of Information. 'Owing to initial mistakes, many of them prenatal, the Ministry has never enjoyed the full confidence of the public. Once a Department has incurred ridicule it has great difficulty in regaining its status . . . unless it is given the authority it demands there is the danger of its ceasing to be an object of ridicule in order to become one only of pity.'[60]

Churchill probably considered by now that *any* firm line was better than the existing state of uncertainty. He drafted his own paper setting out points 'which, I think, may be taken as settled'. His main concern was to reorganize MOI in such a way that it would be accepted by the press and the public; but he also laid down the law about Ministerial speeches. Senior Ministers could use their discretion but 'Ministers not of Cabinet rank . . . ought not to discuss the general policy of the war, apart from exhortations to zeal and the happy restatement of accepted commonplaces, without reference to the Minister of Information'. He said nothing about overseas propaganda, perhaps to avoid further ventilating the row between Duff Cooper and Dalton, but acceptance of the Ministerial triumvirate was implicit in his silence.[61]

Beaverbrook was upset by the rejection of his proposals, and put in a paper pulling Churchill's blueprint to pieces. The Ministry was being stripped of power when in fact it needed more authority. He supported Duff Cooper. 'I advise enlarging the powers of the Ministry of Information, or abolishing it. The Ministry cannot go on in its present form'.[62]

The War Cabinet took these papers on 30 June. Duff Cooper elaborated his case. What was wanted was a strong Central Propaganda Ministry, but the Prime Minister's proposals would leave MOI much weaker. Beaverbrook (who had been appointed Minister of Supply the day before) agreed. He wanted an authoritative body to direct propaganda in its various forms, and to co-ordinate a propaganda

[59] CAB 65/18, f. 196; PREM 3/365/7, ff. 732-5.
[60] CAB 66/17, ff. 79-80.
[61] CAB 65/18, f. 204.
[62] CAB 66/17, f. 107.

campaign. The Dominions' Secretary (Viscount Cranborne) also thought that the Prime Minister left MOI with too little power. However, Churchill had made his mind up, and he had his way. He brought in Brendan Bracken to run the reshaped Ministry. Duff Cooper was sent off to report on the situation in the Far East.[63]

The three Ministers concerned with propaganda took some time to implement the arrangements they had agreed on 16 May. It was not until 8 August that they evolved a charter for the new organization, which was duly approved by the Prime Minister. They would act as a Standing Ministerial Committee to deal with major questions of propaganda policy; and they would be supported by an official committee of three, on which the Foreign Office would be represented by Robert Bruce Lockhart, who at that time was accredited to the provisional Czech government in London, MOI by Leeper, and MEW by Major General Dallas Brooks, a key man in SO 1, the propaganda wing of Dalton's Special Operations Executive.[64]

Dalton suggested that 'these three blameless officials' should be christened as a 'General Staff', adding 'I think this is the sort of phrase which Members of Parliament will greedily eat'. They would not head a Department of Political Warfare, but would merely 'co-ordinate and direct, in accordance with the policy of His Majesty's Government, all propaganda to Enemy and Enemy-Occupied Territories'. The other two Ministers accepted this suggestion and the charter laid down that the official committee would act 'as a General Staff for the conduct of political warfare'.[65]

The three officials, anxious to get on with the job, at once met and formulated proposals which included the amalgamation of certain sections of MOI, the BBC and SO 1 into an organization to be known as the Political Warfare Executive.[66] Leeper had guessed that in calling them a 'General Staff' Dalton was trying to restrict their powers so that he might retain effective control of SO 1.[67] So it proved.

When the officials submitted their plans Dalton immediately objected on the ground that they undermined his empire. They implied that SO 1 would be abolished: 'but I could not possibly agree to the complete disappearance of one half of the Special Operations Executive created under my charter from the Prime Minister and the War Cabinet, placing upon me the responsibility for co-ordinating all action by way of subversion and sabotage against the enemy overseas'. He suggested that the officials had misunderstood the position. It had been intended that

---

[63] In *Old Men Forget* (p. 288) Duff Cooper says he had already decided to throw his hand in.
[64] FO 898/11 (8.8.41).
[65] FO 898/9 pp. 38-9.
[66] FO 898/11 (14.8.41).
[67] FO 898/12 (7.8.41).

the Ministerial Committee should discuss only major questions of propaganda policy. On other matters the Ministers would have individual responsibility. The alternatives were that the various propaganda bodies should be completely fused – in which case there would be no need for joint Ministerial control; or that the Ministerial Committee should remain in permanent session – a three-headed monster that nobody wanted.[68]

Bruce Lockhart told Eden on 11 August that Dalton, who had been on the defensive from the beginning, was interpreting 'joint Ministerial control' to suit himself. 'The scientific definition of daltonism is inability to distinguish between green and red, and I doubt very much if he has ever seen any danger signal to himself. He still relies on his charter from the Prime Minister and this may have to be amended'. Always careful to say the right thing at the right time, he added: 'To you, Sir, who have achieved final agreement, both Ministers are grateful, and your role as mediator must have been admirably played for both Ministers claim you as an ally ... The Irishman and the Englishman both believe they have won a victory.'[69]

If the sycophantic Scot had hoped that his witticism would help to undermine Dalton he was disappointed. Eden did not follow up the hint that SOE's charter might be amended, but told Bruce Lockhart that the three Ministers had decided that it was inappropriate at that moment to work out a detailed plan for political warfare. Instead, 'the working machinery of your Executive Committee should be developed gradually from practical experience.'[70] This seemed ludicrous to the three long-suffering officials; and on 1 September they fired an angry joint reply at their masters. First, the plan they had prepared had failed to win approval simply because of an irrelevant difference of opinion between the Ministers. Second, on 27 August their secretary had been sent for by the Minister of Economic Warfare and handed a document initialled by two of the Ministers (Dalton and Bracken) instructing them to submit plans for 'the complete fusion' of the various elements in the propaganda department.

They suggested that this departure from the arrangements which had been blessed by the Prime Minister was not good enough. 'In view of the circumstances, and bearing in mind the inter-Departmental strife which has impeded the British propaganda effort for more than twelve months, we trust that the Joint Ministerial Committee will realize the difficulties of the task with which they have been confronted'. Their plan was the only possible basis for an efficient organization. 'For twelve months the energy of our whole propaganda effort, which should have been directed against the enemy, has been largely dissipated in

[68] FO 898/12 (20.8.41).
[69] FO 898/9, p. 171.
[70] FO 898 (22.8.41).

inter-Departmental intrigues and strife'. The angry trio concluded by pointing out that the importance of propaganda had been recognized by the War Cabinet, and that it was imperative that the deplorable state of affairs in which they found themselves should be ended immediately.[71]

Bruce Lockhart separately attacked Dalton in a minute to Bracken in which he wrote: 'The Executive Committee can only function efficiently if it has a minimum of interference by individual Ministers. Moreover, there is the particular danger of an intolerable situation being created if Dr Dalton makes a practice of sending for and questioning subordinates of the Executive Committee and of paying constant visits to Woburn and the BBC . . . He seems to have more time at his disposal than either yourself or the Foreign Secretary.'[72]

Dalton had one more shot in his locker, however. He proposed that all the Political Warfare Executive's activities outside Britain should be conducted through the Special Operations Executive 'to prevent the confusion and overlapping arising from the existence abroad of two organizations with separate communications, both carrying on subversive operations against the enemy, whether by propaganda or other means'. This would have made him sole commander of subversion, and Bracken was no more willing that that should happen than Duff Cooper had been. Fortified by his special relationship with Churchill he flatly refused that SOE should be the sole medium through which political warfare outside Britain would be conducted. He claimed that Dalton's point had already been taken care of by an undertaking that PWE agents would not be appointed in places where there were already SOE agents, and by agreement that PWE would use SOE agents as 'disseminators' wherever possible. Eden agreed; but as a sop to Dalton it was reaffirmed that PWE should seek Ministerial authority before appointing anyone in an area where SOE was already working.[73]

From now on the Executive Committee was allowed to manage its affairs more or less as it saw fit, subject to occasional guidance from the Ministerial Committee. Dalton took his defeat very hard. Leeper wrote to Bruce Lockhart: 'when Bowes-Lyon saw Dalton last night the latter was in a foul temper and not only attacked each of us three [ie Bruce Lockhart, Dallas Brooks, and Leeper] but was very sarcastic at our expense'.[74] But after two years and one week of war the British propaganda organization was free to get on with its job without worrying about Ministerial wrangling.

Ideally Ministers would have arranged a happy marriage between SOE and PWE, thus creating a single Department of Subversion; but

[71] FO 898/11 (1.9.41).
[72] FO 898/286 (8.9.41).
[73] FO 898/12 (28.8.41).
[74] *Ibid* (28.8.41).

although they saw the logic of this step they could not bring themselves to take it. For the rest of the war the two bodies were forced to live together, suffering all the discomforts of a close union, and enjoying none of the blessings.

2
Organization and Management

The Ministerial jockeying for the control of propaganda described in the preceding chapter made it difficult for the staff to get on with the job they were supposed to be doing. No organization can be fully efficient if the management is at war with itself and is constantly changing.

In the early days, however, there were no real problems. Campbell Stuart, the sole survivor of the 1918 propaganda organization, had no difficulty in managing his small department. His staff, whatever their native abilities, had no experience of wartime propaganda and were prepared to accept that Stuart knew more about the game than they did. It may be that this happy situation would not have obtained for long. Stuart naturally tackled the job with the eye of 1918, and sooner or later younger minds faced with new problems would have found themselves in revolt. He resigned in August 1940 – why it is not clear from the papers; but it may be that he, or someone else, became aware that what had done very well for the Kaiser's war would not do for the Führer's.

It was intended that there should be close co-operation between the British and French propaganda organizations as soon as hostilities began; and as part of the preparation for this an Anglo-French Propaganda Council was set up in Paris early in 1939. Campbell Stuart records that he found his French colleagues 'suspicious and superior', although he believed that the fact that he had been brought up in Montreal, the world's second largest French-speaking city, helped him to get on with them; but it proved impossible to co-ordinate the plans of the two countries, simply because the French had no plan.[1]

Nevertheless some progress was made. Matters considered by the Council included the arrangements for the preparation and distribution of leaflets, which were to be printed at Grenoble and Rheims; the storage of leaflet-carrying balloons; the location of the units which would release them – Nancy being selected as the most suitable place; the effective scatter of leaflets dropped from various heights; and the regions in Germany where it was believed that leaflets would have the greatest impact. The part which radio would play in the new war was

---

[1] Sir Campbell Stuart, *Opportunity Knocks Twice*, ch. 15.

examined, but its potential importance was not yet fully understood. The techniques of 1918, especially the ingenious leaflet balloon, loomed much larger in the mind of the Council.

On the outbreak of war it became apparent that the relationship between the two halves of the Council was not going to be easy. The French members were critical of the early British performance. Their leaflets were full of grammatical mistakes and words wrongly used; and it was said, not in the most tactful way, that they would amuse rather than impress the enemy. The British side could not fault the language of the French leaflets, so they attacked their poor layout. The officer in charge of the distribution of the French leaflets ('an oldish gentleman') did not hesitate to voice his cynicism about the success claimed by the British. When the war really got going they would find things much more difficult and their system would collapse. No doubt constructive criticism would have been welcomed by both sides, but the records of the Council support Campbell Stuart's implication that it was not a striking example of the success of international co-operation.[2]

The Council had to tackle one serious problem on the broadcasting front. The French and British authorities were agreed that if radio was to continue during the war, without allowing the enemy to use the transmitters as direction finders, all stations must use the same wavelength. However, a commercial radio station at Fécamp in Normandy (run by a company of which a British MP was chairman) refused to co-operate. This odd-man-out was of great value to German aircraft raiding the south coast of England. The French, despite the pleas of their armed forces, failed to get the station off the air; and the Council asked its British members to prevail on the War Cabinet to protest to the French government, and insist that the offending station should conform to the rules, or be closed down. If this is typical of the way the French managed their affairs during the phoney war it is hardly surprising that the Germans disposed of them as they did in June 1940.[3]

The maximum exchange of information between the two propaganda authorities was clearly desirable. EH was further from the scene of action than their French opposite numbers and considered that for the time being they would have to rely heavily on them for help – including reports on the examination of prisoners of war, on the effect of leaflets, and on conditions and events in Germany. In return, they were anxious to supply similar information to the French, in so far as they had access to it. A note of November 1939, however, suggests that the French were none too eager to play their part, and that it would take time to get them to agree to a general exchange of information.[4] The EH representatives tried to get across to the French the fact that British

[2] FO 898/194 and 195 (18.9.39).
[3] FO 898/195 (5.11.39).
[4] *Ibid* (20.11.39).

propaganda was in full swing and not the hand-to-mouth affair they considered French propaganda to be. 'All our policy directives, however many people have had a hand in drafting them, are only given to the BBC and leaflet writers etc. when they have had the full official imprimatur of the enemy propaganda unit'. It was felt that only when the French realized how much the British propaganda effort was based on 'expert and official thought' would they get round to setting up an organization comparable to Department EH.[5]

The Foreign Secretary did his best to nudge them in the right direction by writing to M. Paul Reynaud, their Foreign Minister. Reynaud, now Prime Minister, told Halifax on 15 May 1940 that he fully agreed about the importance of liaison between the propagandists of the two countries. He had appointed a former Under Secretary of State to take over the French organization (which was attached to the Ministry of Information) and instructed him to keep in close touch with the British. He added, however, that the French propaganda department would have to be further developed before full-scale co-operation was possible.[6] A month later the Germans effectively put a stop to further collaboration; and Department EH found itself working on its own again.

Shortly after Campbell Stuart left the propaganda department civil war, seemingly inevitable in this sector of government, broke out. Of the two branches of the Special Operations Executive, SO 1 planned and created secret propaganda. SO 2 disseminated it in addition to carrying out their more militant duties in the field. SO 1 supplied leaflets, or copy from which SO 2 had leaflets printed secretly in the country where they were operating overseas. Under a third alternative SO 1 provided their opposite numbers with a general directive, leaving it to them to draft the leaflet on the lines of the directive and to arrange for printing and distribution in the country concerned.

This was the theory; but in 1940 SO 2 did not yet have an adequate field force. In some areas, the Balkans, for example, they were well enough staffed to get on with their primary task – the organization of sabotage – but could do no more. They accepted that SO 1 might therefore want to send specially-trained propaganda officers to these areas, but insisted that they must be attached to SO 2. Even if SO 1 sent their own agents to countries where SO 2 were not operating, they must join SO 2 and communicate with SO 1 only through SO 2 channels.[7]

This might seem to be common sense. If the agents of the two branches worked independently, say in Bulgaria, it would not be long before they crossed wires in some way, even if they did not actually

[5] FO 898/195 (22.2.40).
[6] *Ibid* (15.5.40).
[7] FO 898/9, pp. 59-62.

start sabotaging each other. SO 1, however, saw in the arrangements proposed by SO 2 a threat to their empire. They argued that SO 2's claim to control all activities overseas was made by a virtually non-existent organization with no adequate means of communication. To give SO 2 sole rights abroad denied that SOE was a single entity with two branches – one concerned with the provision and dissemination of ideas, and the other with sabotage. The specialized nature of SO 1's function called for specialized representation overseas, but that did not mean that there were two rival organizations. So did SO 1 make their case for having their own overseas staff. In fact, the two branches behaved exactly as if they *were* rival organizations and the skill and enthusiasm with which they conducted their demarcation battle would have delighted many latter-day trade unionists. It would certainly have delighted their common enemy, had he known what they were up to.[8]

The appointment of the Ministerial Committee and the establishment of the Political Warfare Executive in August 1941 brought to an end the in-fighting among Ministers and senior officials. Dalton had given up his beloved SO 1. Bracken had less unwillingly transferred part of the Foreign Publicity Division of MOI. The relevant European sections of the BBC had also gone to PWE. The Executive's operational area had been formally defined as all enemy and enemy-occupied territory, Vichy France and French North Africa; and it was made responsible for all propaganda within or addressed to that area.[9] It was now up to the Executive Committee to weld these elements into an efficient machine.

Bruce Lockhart was given responsibility for the whole of the work of the Executive and for keeping in touch with the Foreign Office, the final arbiter on foreign policy aspects of propaganda. Leeper had charge of 'country headquarters' the code name for the secret activities at Woburn Abbey. Dallas Brooks was in command of the military wing and responsible for liaison with the Chiefs of Staff, the Joint Intelligence Committee and the Services generally – an important job since propaganda and strategy interacted upon each other.

Joint Ministerial leadership denied PWE the single-minded guidance which every Department is entitled to. It also could have given the senior officials a bigger hand in running the Executive than they would normally have had; but Bruce Lockhart regarded himself as no more than a link between Ministers and his lieutenants Dallas Brooks and Leeper – and Ritchie Calder[10] who played an important part in propaganda planning. The subordinate staff were a motley crew, many of them new to government service, and unfamiliar with the curious gyrations of the Whitehall machine, which consists of a large

[8] FO 898/9, p. 53.
[9] INF 1/895 (15, 20.9.41).
[10] Later Lord Ritchie Calder.

number of cogs at the lower levels enmeshing with a progressively smaller number of cogs enjoying greater seniority, experience, innate ability, and remuneration. That, at least, is the theory. The humble clerk does not question the wisdom of the Permanent Secretary, whatever his private opinion. The creative branches of PWE, however, were staffed almost exclusively with Permanent Secretaries who did not hesitate to question the judgement of the Executive when they felt so inclined.

This sometimes led to conflict which seriously affected the performance of the Executive's task. For example, in 1941 Mr. F. A. Voigt, the German adviser, made a violent attack on the German Section, which was in fact an attack on the head of the Section, Richard Crossman. 'With one exception, every talk, every directive and every report criticised in detail in the memorandum are those of Mr Crossman's.' The points to which the German Section took particular exception included that PWE's propaganda was being pursued in an atmosphere of ever-increasing make-believe; it was cheap, trivial, sneering and disingenuous, amateurish and misguided. The Section did admit, however, that much of its work could be improved, and that they were trying to do many of the things Voigt said they should be doing.[11]

Bruce Lockhart, commenting on this episode, said that every good propagandist is like a prima donna and must be given a reasonable amount of latitude. This is no doubt true but it did not mean that every good propagandist should have his say in running the propaganda department. That would have been carrying worker participation too far. Bruce Lockhart accepted that Voigt knew more about Germany but that Crossman was the better propagandist. One had to go, and it was Voigt.[12] The real significance of the row is that it illustrates the difficulty of managing the Executive. The able but ill-disciplined propagandists wanted often to become involved in matters that were not their business, and it would have taken a superman, which Bruce Lockhart was not, to keep them in order.

Seven Regional Directorates were the backbone of the Executive. They covered Germany and Austria (this Directorate developed out of the original German Section, and was by far the most important. Richard Crossman was in charge until he transferred to Allied Force Headquarters in Algiers in 1943), France, Italy, Scandinavia (Norway and Denmark), the Low Countries (Holland and Belgium), the Balkans, and Poland/Czechoslovakia. At first the Directorates relied on the Foreign Office for intelligence about their target countries (except for Germany and Austria which had their own service right from the start) but as time went on the other Regional Directorates became responsible

[11] FO 898/181 (14.4.41).
[12] *Giants cast long shadows*, p. 92.

for their own intelligence. Eventually a Central Intelligence Directorate was set up.

Small sections of the Executive were responsible for liaison with MOI, MEW, MI 5 (the counter-espionage branch) and the Secret Service. The principal addition to the organization was a Central Planning Section to carry out forward planning and to analyse the quality of propaganda put out week by week.

Open propaganda was handled by the BBC, largely according to directives provided by the propaganda department. The appointment of Ivone Kirkpatrick, the BBC's Foreign Adviser, to the Political Warfare Executive provided an essential link between the two organizations. The Executive's Regional Directors submitted their weekly directives to him for approval before they went on to the Executive Committee and the BBC Regional Editors. The latter were free to make their own selection and presentation of news items, so long as they kept within the general framework laid down; and since the BBC Editor-in-Chief was also responsible to Kirkpatrick it meant that the directives and the programmes based on them were supervised by the same individual. Conformity was further ensured by an instruction that the PWE Regional Directors should keep in close touch with the BBC Editors and satisfy themselves that transmissions were within the agreed policy. Kirkpatrick was empowered to resolve disputes between the Regional Directors and the BBC Editors, who had a right of appeal to the Executive Committee.[13]

Immediately after the Executive was formed a committee was appointed to streamline the propaganda department with particular reference to any overlapping between its intelligence services and those of the BBC. There had been a rapid increase in staff both in London and at Woburn and the ever-watchful Treasury had to be convinced that all were making a worthwhile contribution to the war effort. Between October 1940 and August 1941 the propaganda department's London staff, including the military wing and liaison officers, had increased from 57 to 74; and the staff at Woburn from 152 to 458.[14]

The fact that the department was located in two places did not make for efficiency. It meant that common services had to be duplicated and that senior staff had to waste time travelling to meetings at the other place. The investigating committee had no doubt that ideally the whole organization would be under one roof – something like 'the complete fusion' – which Dalton had spoken about and which officials had not been prepared to accept – but they realized that this was not possible. It was necessary that the work concerned with black propaganda should be carried on away from London, particularly since it involved the

[13] FO 898/11 and 12 (1, 20 September 1941); INF 1/474 (15.9.41); INF 1/895 (20.9.40).
[14] FO 898/35 (7.11.41).

B

employment of aliens whose connection with it had to be kept secret. In any case, there was no suitable building available in London. An establishment in the depths of the country was therefore essential; and the staff and the work had to be organized to get the best results in spite of the geographical handicap.

PWE began to implement the committee's recommendations including some which proposed that they should take over the BBC's intelligence services, before the BBC had had a chance to study the report properly. This sparked off a row, but eventually, after an acrimonious debate some BBC staff were transferred to PWE. The BBC's own intelligence services continued to function, but on a reduced scale.[15]

In February 1942 Hugh Dalton went from MEW to the Board of Trade – a promotion which he accepted with some reluctance. His successor, Viscount Wolmer (later Earl of Selborne) felt less passionately about special operations and propaganda and opted out of the Ministerial Committee. At this point Eden confessed to the Prime Minister that the Committee had not been a success. He recommended that he himself should look after only the foreign policy aspects of propaganda and that the whole of the administrative control should belong to the Minister of Information. His advice was accepted and this arrangement held good for the rest of the war.

The Executive Committee also disappeared from the scene. Bruce Lockhart became Director General of Political Warfare, reporting to the Foreign Secretary on foreign policy and to the Minister of Information on operational matters. He was assisted by a Propaganda Committee comprising Dallas Brooks, who became his deputy, Leeper, still in charge of black propaganda at Woburn, and Kirkpatrick, PWE's link with the BBC. Eden assured Churchill that now for the first time all propaganda would be effectively under one Minister (he meant Bracken, with himself acting as a long stop on foreign policy) and that as a result speed of decision and action would increase – which meant of course that hitherto speed of action and decision had been slower than they need have been.[16]

The Regional Directorates continued to be the backbone of the organization. Such structural changes as there were were designed to facilitate their work. They included the appointment of a Director of Production 'to close the gap between those who provide propaganda and those who print it,'[17] who was put in charge of the printing of PWE's mass-produced white propaganda – millions of leaflets, miniature periodicals and newspapers, for which the British government could openly accept responsibility. In September 1939 there had been

[15] FO 898/12 (7.1.42).
[16] INF 1/895 (13, 20.3.42).
[17] FO 898/12 (3.3.42).

established at Woburn Abbey a small printing unit which included two compositors from Oxford University Press. The early leaflets were set by hand in old-fashioned German *Fraktur* types and printed by rotary letterpress at the Stationery Office at Harrow – undistinguished examples of the printer's art.

The German occupation of most of Western Europe and the entry of Italy into the war greatly increased the demand for white propaganda. The printing unit was transferred to Marylands, a large house near Woburn where Monotype equipment was installed in a hut in the grounds. The composing room staff was augmented to enable the unit to work round the clock. Expert typographers and graphic artists were recruited, and the quality of the unit's output was much improved – an important point, since the impact of a leaflet depends perhaps as much on its technical excellence as on its content. Printing was now carried out by the Sun Engraving Company at Watford and Waterlow's at Dunstable – specialists in photogravure. This made it possible to reproduce photographs successfully and to use colour.

The design and printing of the much smaller volume of highly-specialized black or covert material (that is, printed matter whose British origin had to be concealed) was carried out from November 1941 under the supervision of Ellic Howe, whose experience and talents fitted him singularly well for the production of black printed material. He had been trained as a printer, had expert knowledge of continental typographical styles and conventions, had made a study of forgery techniques, and was fluent in German, French and Italian. In the summer of 1941 he found that as a sergeant-major at Anti-Aircraft Command Headquarters he was unable to make the best use of his particular skills and submitted to the intelligence authorities a paper on the use of forgery in the war effort, which led to his transfer to PWE. He was employed by the propaganda department as a civilian until the end of the war, with a miniscule staff including a German lady who was an expert type designer and graphic artist.

Whereas the white unit produced a more or less standard product in terms of format and typeface (Times Roman), 'Mr Howe's Unit', as it was known, which operated from Bush House, manufactured anything from a small quantity of forged German postage stamps (for postal operations contrived by SOE inside Germany) to forged passes and ration cards, and highly-subversive booklets which had to appear as if they had been printed in Germany, and often bore the imprint of a German printing firm. The unit's main production centre was a small but highly-efficient letterpress firm in St Martin's Lane. Later it monopolised the services of a larger firm off Fleet Street, and had its own process engraving plant close by. The forged stamps and ration cards were produced by specialist security printers. Except for the ration cards, which were dropped by the RAF, the great bulk of the unit's output was delivered to its ultimate destination through SOE's underground channels.

Other organizational changes were the consolidation and concentration in London of the Woburn intelligence sections into a highly-sophisticated Political Warfare Intelligence Directorate; the central planning organization was further developed under Ritchie Calder; and two Directors of Political Warfare were appointed, one to take charge of propaganda to enemy and satellite countries, and the other of propaganda to the occupied countries. The last change reflected an upgrading of the work of PWE as a whole, and it also recognized that the line to be taken with the occupied countries on the one hand and enemy and satellite countries on the other had to be very different.[18]

As the war progressed the propaganda department established outposts overseas to carry out its functions nearer to the territories aimed at, but which were closely-controlled by directives from London. Some of these outposts were developed from SOE missions already acting as PWE's agents on the spot.

At the end of 1940 a three-man mission went to West Africa.[19] In addition to its other activities it prepared and disseminated leaflets in the neighbouring French territories, so that when French West Africa and Madagascar were brought into PWE's operational area there was in existence an embryo propaganda organization.[20] Political warfare was specifically mentioned in the instructions to the Minister Resident, West Africa, in June 1942. He was to ensure that those concerned with propaganda, subversion, and economic warfare kept in line with government policy. PWE were formally in charge of operations in West Africa, but SOE controlled all agents in the field, and expanded their staff to help in the production of propaganda material. The mission were authorized to disseminate their own locally-produced rumours but they were warned against the manufacture of 'strategic deceit' rumours. This was of supreme importance since those who practised the art of influencing enemy strategy by means of false rumours could not afford to have outsiders butting into their subtle game. When the Americans proposed a joint propaganda organization in West Africa PWE were unenthusiastic; but an offer of 40,000 dollars and a hint that if they were not allowed to operate from British territory they would establish themselves in Liberia won the day.[21]

In September 1941 a mission went to India to visit Italian prisoner of war camps, ostensibly to distribute comforts provided by Italians in the United States, but in fact to assess the possibility of forming a free

[18] FO 898/35 (23.12.42). 31.1.43, 29.4.43).
[19] FO 898/124.
[20] *Ibid* (5.11.41).
[21] *Ibid* (8.6.42, 6.7.42).

ORGANIZATION AND MANAGEMENT

Italian force, and to advise the Commander-in-Chief on the nature of the propaganda to be fed to the Italian prisoners.[22]

The most important of PWE's overseas missions was in the Middle East. It was started towards the end of 1942 to direct propaganda to Italy and the Balkans.[23] SOE was already well-established in the Middle East, both on its own account and as PWE's agent; but the Executive was unhappy with the service from its sister organization. There were signs of friction and Ministers decided to define the duties of the two bodies in such a way that there would be no room for argument. SOE would hand over to PWE its radio stations in Cairo and Jerusalem together with 400 propaganda staff, leaving it to PWE to provide the broadcasting facilities needed by SOE. PWE would send no agents into the field. The dissemination of written propaganda and rumours, the influencing of opinion, and the gleaning of information would all be left to SOE.[24]

Paul Vellacott, Master of Peterhouse, was appointed on 10 September 1942 to direct the new mission. His appointment was strongly resented by Lord Glenconner, in charge of SOE in the Middle East. He set out his objections in a violent letter to the office of the Resident Minister in Cairo, a copy of which was in Vellacott's intray when he arrived.

The newcomer dealt with SOE's intemperate assault in unhurried periods, as befitted the Master of a Cambridge College. The Ministerial reallocation of function did not stress the difference between their work but rather aimed at enabling the two organizations to make a united contribution to the defeat of the common enemy. Whereas

> the implied answer to the question put by Lord Glenconner in the penultimate paragraph of his letter must be, by the preceding terms of the letter, that Mr Vellacott should now return to England, I, on my side begin with a full recognition of what has been and is being achieved by SOE ... Nevertheless, these sentiments do not preclude me from thinking that a measure of relief given to SOE from the burden of control in one activity will not necessarily detract from the cogency of their effort in another, and as I understand, their chief activity.

Translated, this masterpiece of English prose said: 'I shall gladly co-operate in spite of SOE's bloody-minded attitude; and if they stick to their own job – sabotage – they'll do it rather better.'

Vellacott told Bruce Lockhart that the plain truth was that SOE had built up an elaborate organization, and that they had no intention of giving up any part of it. It was quite shocking that the energies of PWE and SOE 'should be consumed to a large extent in a fight with each

[22] FO 898/12 (12.9.41).
[23] FO 898/63 (6.9.42).
[24] FO 898/118 (2.9.42).

other'. It would be intolerable if the fight was prolonged.²⁵ It was not. Common sense, and Vellacott's firmness prevailed.

In the early days of the war Campbell Stuart had explored the use of radio transmitters in the United States and Canada for British propaganda to the enemy but he got no encouragement from Ministers. In the months before the United States entered the war the SOE mission in New York kept in touch with the American secret agencies; and in November 1941 to the considerable astonishment of PWE, SOE reported that the Office of Strategic Services (which corresponded – very roughly – to SO 2) wanted the RAF to drop United States propaganda pamphlets on enemy and enemy-occupied countries. This remarkable proposal naturally had to go before British Ministers; but before they could decide on the propriety of helping even a friendly neutral in this way the problem was simplified by the Japanese attack on Pearl Harbour. The first United States leaflets were dropped by the RAF on the night of 6/7 January 1942.²⁶

With the United States entry into the war it became more necessary for PWE to keep in touch with their American colleagues. In July 1942 they opened an office in New York to collect information and to distribute material from the United Kingdom.²⁷ There were many listening posts in the United States, diplomats and businessmen who were willing targets for information. Before long the inevitable conflict with SOE developed. In August 1942 the heads of the two British organizations in the United States had to be instructed to get together to resolve difficulties arising between them in areas where their responsibilities were not clearly defined.²⁸

In the middle of 1942 representatives of the American Office of War Information (which corresponded broadly to PWE) began to meet weekly in London with representatives of PWE to discuss matters of common interest. At this time the Americans explained that General Eisenhower found it impossible to draw a clear line between subversive propaganda and subversive activities, and had accordingly ruled that when OWI (the propagandists) or OSS (the saboteurs) wanted to discuss any project with the military authorities they must be accompanied by a member of the other organization²⁹ – further evidence, if more be needed, of the logic of keeping propaganda and sabotage under the same management, which the British had failed to achieve. In August 1942 members of OWI's staff went to Woburn to study PWE's methods of leaflet production.³⁰

In 1943 an Anglo-American Psychological Warfare Branch (PWB)

---

[25] FO 898/118.
[26] FO 898/104 (31.1.42).
[27] *Ibid* (6, 20.7.42).
[28] *Ibid* (25.8.42).
[29] *Ibid* (31.7.42).

was set up in Algiers and attached to Eisenhower's headquarters under Brigadier General Robert McClure, an American. Its purpose was to handle all propaganda in the Mediterranean theatre, and it included representatives of PWE, MOI, OSS, and OWI.[31] Neither side, British or American, was superior to the other – the function of the new organization was simply to co-ordinate the propaganda directives of the two countries, and generally to ensure that a common line was followed.

The Americans took the view, however, that the main impetus in propaganda should arise as near to the military action as possible, whereas PWE considered that their outposts should do what they were told by London. PWE New York said that so many senior American propagandists were being sent to Algiers that the PWE team there would become 'even more inconspicuous'. (There were only 60 United Kingdom staff compared with 360 Americans). Worse, there was the danger that 'local and short-term propaganda would override the basic conception of long-term propaganda of a much wider nature'. *That* meant that PWE thought that propaganda should be used to help to win the peace as well as the war, whereas the Americans put first things first. PWE decided that they could not possibly match the numbers which OWI proposed for Algiers and consoled themselves with the belief that if they sent 'three or four top-notchers' it would go a long way to balancing the battalions which OWI were sending.[32]

The French were now beginning to reassert themselves in the propaganda field, in which they had not scored much success in the early days of the war, and they soon came into conflict with PWB. Their Secretariat of Information and Propaganda, based in Algiers, prepared, printed and distributed over France a leaflet about which they gave PWB no advance information. It gave the impression, in direct contravention of instructions from the Combined Chiefs of Staff, that allied forces would land in France in the near future. The French were told that while there was no objection to their disseminating their own propaganda, it must be in line with PWB directives.[33] This sort of administrative confusion worked the other way round. When PWB disseminated 'a message of the United Nations to the railroad workers of France' without discussing it with the French the latter were incensed.

At the end of 1943 when the Allies were beginning to look forward to their assault on Europe, a Publicity and Psychological Division was set up under the control of Headquarters, Chief of Staff, Supreme

[30] FO 898/63 (8.8.42).
[31] RG 208/OWI/Box 836 (1.7.43).
[32] FO 898/137 (3, 4, 8.8.43).
[33] RG 208/OWI/Box 836 (1.7.43). An American post-war inquest decided that PWB had been badly organized. The radio side had been satisfactory but its output of leaflets had never been properly controlled (*Ibid*, 13.6.45).

Allied Commander (COSSAC). This organization, which was designed to ensure the maximum collaboration between the British and American propagandists, who this time had equal representation, grew out of PWB Algiers, via G 6 Division of SHAEF, and was also commanded by General McClure. It was to be responsible for combat, strategic and consolidation propaganda – the latest classification of the developing art, reflecting the change of emphasis caused by the changing military situation. Combat propaganda was defined as tactical propaganda against enemy forces in the forward areas and the population immediately behind the enemy lines; strategic, to further strategic aims; and consolidation, to win the co-operation of the people of the invaded country.[34] In practice propaganda could not be pigeon-holed so precisely. A report on the first three months of the invasion of Europe by the allies says: 'As the campaign progressed it became increasingly difficult to draw a sharp line between Combat and so-called Consolidation propaganda . . . one flowed into the other to the same degree that military mopping-up operations follow upon initial break-throughs.'[35]

The Executive Committee never became deeply involved in propaganda to the Far East. Ministers decided in 1943 that there should be a Japanese Regional Directorate but it proved impossible to find satisfactory staff. Instead, the Foreign Office formed a Political Warfare (Japan) Committee with Dallas Brooks as chairman and with representatives of the Foreign Office, MOI and MEW. Later it was expanded to include the Colonial, India, Burma, and Dominions Offices, and the Services. The conduct of political warfare against the Japanese was entrusted to MOI's Far Eastern Bureau in New Delhi and by an expansion of the PWE mission in the United States.

One other piece of machinery must be mentioned. In August 1943 Eisenhower, conforming to the American line that the armed forces should have a big say in propaganda, suggested that the co-ordination and dissemination of propaganda directives in respect of major military and political objectives should be carried out by the combined British and American Chiefs of Staff. Eden did not like the idea but agreed that it should be tried for the immediately pending operations (*Baytown* against Salerno and Naples, and *Avalanche* against Calabria) since there was little time to discuss the proposal. He pointed out that the Americans had had no difficulty in accepting joint PWE/OWI directives worked out in London for routine matters, and proposed as an alternative to Eisenhower's suggestion that when directives involving high policy were required they should be drafted by PWE/OWI and then approved by the Defence Committee of the War Cabinet with

---

[34] INF 1/898 (1.1.44). There is an account of the joint organizations in *United States Army in World War II, The European Theatre of Operations: the supreme command* (Washington DC, 1954), pp. 84-8.
[35] WO 219/4751 (10.10.44).

representatives of the United States Embassy in London and the United States Chief of Staff sitting in.[36]

At the beginning of September 1943 the Combined Chiefs of Staff, following up Eisenhower's idea, claimed that the existing Anglo-American propaganda machinery 'neither functions with sufficient speed nor avoids contradiction when operating under conditions of emergency'; and proposed that joint committees should be set up in London, Washington and New Delhi to issue special propaganda directives when the ordinary arrangements proved inadequate.[37] Elmer Davis and Robert Sherwood of OWI supported them, except that they wanted only one committee, in Washington.[38] This impelled Churchill, who was in Washington at the time, to make one of his rare incursions into the propaganda field. He wrote on 5 September:

> Mr Davis seems to be under some illusion that the British are willing that propaganda should be conducted by Generals. Nothing could be more absurd. In Britain there is a well-co-ordinated propaganda machine under civilian control, and long may it remain thus. There are satisfactory arrangements for the co-ordination of long-term policy with the Chiefs of Staff and the United States authorities. All the great propaganda gaffes have been made as a result of soldiers interfering in publicity matters . . .[39]

In the event it was agreed to set up three new committees – the London Political Warfare Co-ordinating Committee for the European theatre, and parallel committees with equally high-sounding names in Washington for the Pacific and in New Delhi for the Far East – with power to decide propaganda policy when there was no time to use the normal machinery. Churchill deprecated the formation of more committees but he may have considered it a reasonable price to pay for keeping the ultimate control of propaganda out of the hands of the military. He said as much to Roosevelt and reminded him that the guidance which he (Churchill) and the President might want to give singly or jointly would be in no way affected. Whatever the generals wanted, the statesmen would have the last word.[40]

Before the New Delhi committee could be formed the Americans had second thoughts. It would be bad for their image in Asia to be associated too closely with British propaganda. The United States' objective was purely military – the defeat of Japan; but Britain was also interested in the recovery of her territories in the Far East. OWI decided that British propaganda would be so political that United States' membership of

[36] PREM 3/365/9, ff. 844, 846.
[37] RG 208/Memorandum to President and Prime Minister (3.9.43).
[38] *Ibid* Memorandum to President (3.9.43).
[39] PREM 3/365/9, f. 281.
[40] *Ibid* ff. 803-4.

B*

the New Delhi committee would imply support for Britain in opposing the aspirations of the peoples of Asia. Its functions were therefore transferred to the London committee, but the Americans need not have worried about the tarnishing of their image. The minutes of both the London and Washington committees reveal little more than the superhuman efforts of highly-paid officials struggling to find something useful to talk about – not for the first time in the history of administration.[41]

People were appointed to the propaganda department on the strength of their qualifications, and thrown in at the deep end. Wartime propaganda was a new art to all of them – Campbell Stuart excepted – and training had to be done on the job. This was not too difficult since most of the recruits were accustomed to the use of words and ideas. It may not have been the ideal way of staffing the department; but there was no time to evolve any other method. Had a Propaganda Ministry been established at the time when war was seen to be inevitable more thought could have been given to the selection and training of staff.

According to one psychologist who interested himself in the affairs of the propaganda department:

> If propaganda for the enemy is to be conducted on psychological lines, this implies a rare gift, that which enables one on demand to think like someone else ... The best novelists have it but practise it, in all probability, intuitively rather than in a reasoned conscious way. Anthropologists and sociologists ought to cultivate it, and some of them do. Successful diplomats and foreign salesmen and foreign newspaper correspondents must have it, but only those would be successful propagandists who can reconstruct the foreign viewpoint when at home: a certain number of them are probably successful abroad because they have the gift of sympathetic understanding in personal encounter.

This expert then went on to consider who would make the worst propagandist:

> He will be the salesman, advertiser, or politician who has an uncanny gift for knowing what the public wants. In other words, the man whose success in a career of publicity is most outstanding is just the one to pander to the prejudices of his countrymen when that is wanted. But he is certain merely to amuse the enemy or convince him that he is right in being an enemy...[42]

There may be some truth in this, although it is perhaps a little bit too cut and dried; but recruitment to PWE was certainly not guided by these principles.

[41] RG 208/OWI Memorandum (5.11.43).
[42] FO 898/191 (9.3.39).

ORGANIZATION AND MANAGEMENT

Although the propagandists as a whole were given no formal instruction, specialized training was provided for some exponents of political warfare. Agents suitable for work in the field were selected jointly by PWE and SOE and then sent to a training school near Woburn where they were instructed by PWE and SOE officers. The training course covered intelligence, broadcasting, leaflet-writing, printing and the assessment of public opinion.

The agents, who were trained to be either organizers or active propagandists, were smuggled into the occupied countries or dropped by parachute at points where 'reception committees' were waiting for them. Their principal assignments were to feed the clandestine press with material from Britain which was dropped to them in containers, to carry out oral propaganda, and to write leaflets which were printed locally; but with the approach of D-day they had many other duties. SOE were responsible for getting them to their posts, for communicating with them, and for transporting the material prepared for them by PWE.[43]

In 1943 and 1944 large numbers of 'political survey officers'[44] (according to one member of the Executive 'patriots, idealists, out-of-work journalists, schoolmasters whose main object is to avoid the asperities of warfare . . . and one or two intellectually honest men')[45] were trained for service in the liberated countries and Germany. Just before D-Day there were courses for a small number of British and American officers who were due to be dropped behind the enemy lines to associate with the local resistance movements in driving out the enemy, and to prepare the people to receive the allied forces. These men were given very strenuous training which included field-craft, weapon training, intelligence, communications, rounded off with two weeks of instruction in the theory of political warfare.[46]

[43] FO 898/61 (17.12.42).
[44] Later known as 'propaganda intelligence officers' (WO 219/4722).
[45] FO 898/98 (19.11.43).
[46] FO 898/358 (4.5.44).

3
Articles of association: Propaganda policy

In April 1939 Sir Campbell Stuart set down three principles for British propaganda. It must be related to a clearly defined policy. It must be rigorously truthful. It must never be self-contradictory – which might perhaps seem to follow from the second principle.

The first task would be to sow doubt in the mind of the German people about the Nazi regime's wisdom in embarking on war. In a second stage it would be necessary to counter enemy falsehoods and thus establish British propaganda's reputation for trustworthiness. Thirdly, when fissures began to appear in the fabric of German society, they must be exploited to the full. Only then would propaganda become fully effective.[1] The rules of the game as defined by Stuart were pleasantly simple. They made no provision for black propaganda, which he perhaps deemed to be unsporting. In five years of war the rules became more elaborate.

On 3 September 1939, the day on which Britain declared war, the War Cabinet found itself debating whether or not the RAF should drop propaganda leaflets on Germany. It may seem strange that such a matter should engage their attention at this momentous hour in the history of Britain. The explanation no doubt is that they felt the need to do something positive, so long as it was not too dramatic with unpredictable consequences. Leaflet dropping – *faute de mieux* – was the answer. The fact that British aircraft could fly over Germany with impunity would have an important effect, or so it was believed. The risk to air crews was not great. Leaflets would have their maximum impact in the first few hours of war – Horace Wilson's earlier point that the Germans would be much too excited to pay any attention to leaflets was conveniently forgotten. It was therefore agreed that a leaflet dropping operation should be carried out that night, the targets being Hamburg, Bremen and the Ruhr. Whitleys and Wellingtons set off with the first load of leaflets – 'A warning to the German people' and a message from Chamberlain. One aircraft was lost. The operation was repeated the following night, and again on the night of 7/8 September.

[1] FO 898/3.

By this time the War Cabinet had become aware that there was strong criticism both at home and abroad of the policy of dropping scraps of paper on Germany at a time when the Germans were dropping large quantities of high explosive on Poland. Nevertheless it was concluded that leaflet-dropping was a valuable exercise which should be repeated from time to time 'as and when opportunity offered'.[2] The last phrase was to become the keynote of leaflet-dropping policy. For the whole war the propaganda department was at the mercy of the RAF. Bomber Command would gladly drop their leaflets – but only where and when it suited Bomber Command.

The War Cabinet's curious interest in propaganda policy persisted during the first weeks of the war. They took account of the view of Sir Nevile Henderson (lately ambassador to Germany, who had had to apologise to Hitler for the fact that the British government dared even to think about propaganda)[3] that leaflets had little value, and that what was wanted was straight news broadcasts. They considered that leaflets should have more factual information; and they asked the Lord Privy Seal (Sir Samuel Hoare) to look into the matter. When he had done so he reaffirmed the earlier doubts about the wisdom of dropping leaflets while Warsaw was being bombed. Some members of the War Cabinet who thought the leaflets were not pithy enough were reminded that the German mentality differed from the British. Germans would read on to the bitter end but the British would lose interest after a sentence or two. The Foreign Secretary (Lord Halifax) referred to a report from two German businessmen, well disposed towards the allies, that leaflets were not having a good effect, and that the Press and BBC made too much of them. (They could hardly be blamed – there was little else to make anything of.) At the end of September it was agreed that the leaflet campaign had not been successful.[4]

In December Lord MacMillan, the first Minister of Information, put forward his ideas about propaganda policy. He had no positive proposals, but merely set out principles to direct and inspire British propaganda in the war – which were less simple than Stuart's. 'We can only hope to defeat the machinations of Dr Goebbels and to make the fullest use of propaganda as an essential arm of defence, if the Ministry of Information is able to relate the whole of its activities to a single coherent and planned policy'. If periods of inactivity became strategically necessary (how prescient!) these very periods should be represented as being fraught with particular and purposeful significance.[5] Just how this rabbit was to be produced from the hat for the benefit of Dr Goebbels and the Nazi regime was left to the imagination of the War

[2] CAB 65/1, ff. 16, 22, 27, 50, 56, 98.
[3] See above p. 10.
[4] CAB 65/1, ff. 99, 143, 151, 177, 185, 234, 241.
[5] CAB 67/3, ff. 361-4 (22.12.39).

Cabinet. Alas, MacMillan was denied the chance of actually performing his conjuring trick since he was removed from office two weeks later.

His successor, Sir John Reith, agreed with MacMillan's line but he was doubtful whether it laid enough emphasis on 'defeat and destroy'. The document should contain something more positive against the Nazi system. He put a revised paper to the War Cabinet on 30 January 1940. In their discussion they favoured a hard line. A compromise peace with an unbeaten Germany would be tantamount to defeat; and the whole German people must be held responsible for the war.[6]

Duff Cooper, appointed Minister of Information in May 1940 in succession to Reith, tried to get the War Cabinet to apply its mind to propaganda and to lay down policy guidelines; but it was no easy task, for propaganda was a subject on which all Ministers believed that they were expert. Duff Cooper was particularly anxious to get agreement about Britain's post-war aims, for he saw that the propagandists would be in a stronger position if they could tell the peoples of Germany and the satellite countries that an allied victory would not lead to their utter destruction. This would have been *his* rabbit out of the hat, had he been allowed to produce it.

He had a remarkable vision of 'a Europe united by goodwill and friendship, not by force and in terror, but a Europe based on some federal system details of which will be worked out after the war with the glad co-operation of all nations . . . it is not necessary here to elaborate the scheme but it would be the duty of those engaged in propaganda to elaborate it'. This led to the appointment of a committee of Ministers 'to make suggestions in regard to a post-war European and world system, with particular regard to the economic needs of the various nations and to the problem of adjusting the free life of small countries in a durable international order'. Not only had Duff Cooper pointed the way to a convincing propaganda campaign, he had sketched out in a few sentences, almost before the war had begun, a formula for a united post-war Europe of which Britain would be the proud and honoured leader.

The importance of finding a carrot for the home front was not overlooked. The Ministerial committee was required also to consider means of perpetuating the national unity achieved during the war 'through a social and economic structure designed to secure equality of opportunity and service among all classes of the community'.[7]

A joint paper from the Ministers of Information and Economic Warfare, critical of the propaganda performance so far, was put to the War Cabinet in November 1940. The machinery had been unable to react quickly enough, for example, to the German invasion of France

---

[6] CAB 65/5, f. 133; WP(G)(40)20.
[7] CAB 66/10, f. 24.

and Norway. Otherwise it might have been possible to use propaganda to save something from the wreckage of these events. The government should have been clear from the outset what line it would take when faced with this sort of disaster. The paper then philosophised about the place of propaganda in the strategy of total warfare. The purpose of psychological warfare was to destroy the moral force of the enemy's cause, and to enforce conviction in the righteousness of the allies' cause; and by co-operating with the other arms to prepare the way for, and to exploit the effects of, the military and economic offensives. It was essential for the *government* to tackle the problem of propaganda policy and to see that it was soundly based.

The principles on which propaganda should be planned were now seen to be much more complex. The strategical situation must always be taken into account, and there must be the closest liaison between the Ministries of Information and Economic Warfare and the Chiefs of Staff. News published in open propaganda must be true and accurate. Unpleasant facts should not be covered up. Britain's ability to match terror with terror and to mete out retribution to her enemies in her own good time should be stressed; but this did not mean that she was committed to reprisals. She must hold out the hope of a fair deal in a British peace. Duff Cooper's earlier advice was repeated. Post-war aims should be formulated in broad terms, partly to sustain the British people, and partly to provide a counter to the German conception of a new order in Europe.[8]

The War Cabinet would not commit itself to a detailed statement of post-war aims at this stage on the ground that it would either be too specific, and therefore dangerous, or too vague, and therefore pointless. It was, however, prepared to see an alternative to Hitler's scheme for a new Europe to be sketched out, not because it shared Duff Cooper's vision but simply because of reports from Berne that European business circles were becoming convinced that they would have to accept German financial and economic domination for the future; and it was agreed that Maynard Keynes[9] should be asked to provide ammunition to rebut this proposition. Doubt was expressed as to whether the arrangements for co-ordinating propaganda policy, in which the Foreign Office, the Ministries of Information and Economic Warfare and the three Service Departments were interested, were adequate; but it was decided that there should be no change for the time being.[10]

Thus was lost a great opportunity of providing a basis for much more effective propaganda in the earlier years of the war, and of staking a claim to the leadership of post-war Europe. This was virtually the last occasion on which the War Cabinet applied its collective mind to the

[8] CAB 66/13, f. 129 (15.11.40).
[9] Later Lord Keynes.
[10] CAB 65/10, f. 85 (20.11.40).

problem of propaganda policy, from which it might be deduced that Duff Cooper was right when he said that the Prime Minister did not rate the war of words very high in the total war effort. In fact, Churchill did take an interest in propaganda, especially when it related to military operations; but it was left first to the committee of three Ministers – Foreign Secretary, Minister of Economic Warfare, and Minister of Information – and later to the Foreign Secretary and Minister of Information, to take the lead in settling the broad lines of policy of the propaganda department.

The fact that the propagandists had to look to more than one Minister for guidance was something of a handicap. At first the Foreign Secretary did not provide dynamic guidance – a fact which was noted by the American propagandists working in London.[11] So long as the proposals put forward by the Executive did not cut across foreign policy he was as a rule content to endorse them. Much the same was true of the Minister of Information whose portfolio contained a great deal more than overseas propaganda. Of the original triumvirate the Minister of Economic Warfare, who logically should have been in sole charge of the propaganda department, had the strongest professional interest in its activities.

He also had a strong political interest, and the guidance which he regularly provided for his officials usually had a strong socialist flavour which may have made some of the working propagandists less eager to follow his lead. In December 1941 he prepared a lengthy paper suggesting that in the long run Britain's best allies in the occupied countries would be the working classes, and that propaganda therefore should be directed to them. He believed that in the occupied countries the left was more patriotic than the right, and that in neutral countries the left was more favourable to the allied cause. The keystone of British propaganda policy must be the Atlantic Charter – especially the articles dealing with freedom to govern, access to trade and raw materials, social security and improved labour standards, and freedom from fear and want. Suitably presented and interpreted, the Charter would bring new hope to the desperate millions of Hitler's European slaves. While it was not PWE's business to plan this brave new world, those engaged in post-war planning must be made aware of the opportunities it offered. Britain must provide Europe with an alternative to communism.[12]

When this paper was examined by the conservative-led Ministry of Information it was roughly handled. Lord Hood observed: 'Apart from passages where Dr Dalton's political prejudices run away with him there is nothing particularly objectionable or original in this paper.'[13] Nevertheless the Minister was at least trying to give the propagandists a lead.

[11] RG 208/OWI/Box 74: Outposts, London (8.6.42).
[12] INF 1/895 (6.12.41).
[13] *Ibid* (9.12.41).

On the whole, however, for most of the war the Executive had to make its own policy objectives. At first this was not easy. In the absence of any military success, and of a satisfactory definition of allied peace aims, there was nothing to beat the drum about. All that the propagandists could do was to seek to undermine the morale of the enemy – which meant announcing that the Nazis faced certain defeat because of the strength, solidarity and resolution of the allies. If they were misguided enough to carry on the war, they would bring upon themselves economic collapse, social disintegration, and violent revolution. Secondly, the unpleasant features of the Nazi regime, and its undoubted responsibility for the war, must be emphasized. Thirdly, the news-hungry censor-ridden German people should be fed the truth through all available channels.[14] This was the best the propagandists could offer at a time when the German war machine was on the crest of an enormous wave, within a month or two of sweeping the allies out of Europe.

One of the policy-makers' more difficult tasks was to determine the balance between 'preparatory' and 'operational' propaganda. The former meant the psychological preparation of peoples so that they would be conditioned to do what PWE asked of them at a later date: the latter had immediate sabotage as its objective.

As early as July 1940, when the Germans were carrying all before them, and the allied propagandists were no less frustrated than the armed forces, a Department EH memorandum said that the blockade would not by itself lead to revolt in Germany. It should therefore be supplemented by propaganda fomenting disaffection, for example, in the German north coast ports, the Ruhr, and the industrial areas of Silesia.[15] Nothing was done, however, and nine months later one of the theorists in whom the propaganda department abounded pointed out that the Executive was still failing to distinguish between preparatory and operational propaganda, and to make the best use of each.

He claimed that virtually all the propaganda aimed at France was preparatory, whereas there was abundant evidence that the French were now ready to receive and be influenced by operational propaganda. They could be educated in the art of sabotage – the loosening of railway lines, the manufacture of home-made bombs, the extraction of poison from hedgerow plants.[16] The black propagandists were simply doing the same job that the Ministry of Information were doing through the BBC, whereas they should be using the secret radio stations to recruit 200 million allies who would turn Europe into a seething cauldron.[17] Since these secret radio stations were supposed to be inside Europe

[14] FO 898/3, ff. 224-8 (April 1940).
[15] FO 898/297 (20.7.40).
[16] *Ibid* (25.4.41).
[17] See Chapter 6, 'The Spoken Word'.

their use would not generate complaints that the British were asking people to take risks which they themselves did not face.[18]

In June 1941 senior men in the propaganda department at last accepted that operational propaganda must be given greater prominence, and set up a special section to collect intelligence for the purpose;[19] but little more was done largely because the BBC's V campaign – which came very near to operational propaganda through open broadcasting – was engaging all the attention of the department's policy-makers.[20] There were new efforts to define operational propaganda – 'that type of propaganda in which we attempt to persuade our listeners to *do* something rather than to *feel* something'.[21] Ritchie Calder lucubrated on the subject and demonstrated that there was still confusion in the mind of the department. Operational propaganda had to be part of a wider strategy bound up first with economic disruption, and ultimately with military operations. That statement fitted all right with the current theory, but curiously he then went on to say 'Short of these objectives operational propaganda should be confined to morale making [ie in the occupied countries] and morale breaking [ie in enemy countries] which is precisely the purpose of preparatory propaganda.[22]

The poor co-ordination – more accurately, the enmity – between the propagandists of SO 1 and the saboteurs of SO2 had an important bearing on the use of operational propaganda in the earlier part of the war. SO 2's working men in the field ran infinitely greater risks than their chairborne SO 1 colleagues in Britain, and they wanted as far as possible to be a self-contained unit. This may have arisen partly from a feeling of superiority – the sabotaging of a power station seems to pay a greater dividend than broadcasting obscene tales about high-ranking German officers – but it was primarily based on the need for security. At first SO 2 firmly opposed broadcasts urging major sabotage operations or suggesting specific targets to the people of the occupied countries. Their own agents might already have an operation in hand, and if a local resistance group was encouraged to undertake a similar operation it could land both groups in trouble. Whatever the propagandists might think, sabotage could succeed only with the most careful planning and accurate timing; and it had to be carried out by trained operators with special qualifications and using special devices.[23]

In February 1942 six months after SO 1 had been transferred to PWE Ritchie Calder was appointed chairman of a committee to consider

[18] FO 898/297 (2.5.41).
[19] *Ibid* (24.6.41).
[20] See Chapter 7, 'V'.
[21] FO 898/297 (28.7.41).
[22] *Ibid* (7.8.41).
[23] *Ibid* (16.8.41).

the use of operational propaganda in open broadcasting, with special reference to sabotage. SOE continued to argue that operational propaganda should be limited to agents in the field. It was practical work – not a matter of vague talk and loose ideas (this might seem to be a swipe at the pure propagandists). The agent was a wholesaler who enabled the retailers in his territory to achieve 'paying results', for example by raising money to enable workers to dodge transfers to Germany, by the establishment of patriotic black markets to upset German manipulation of rations, and by the management of 'go-slow' campaigns. The SOE agent was not concerned with the dissemination of 'indefinite pro-British or anti-German sentiment' (another swipe) but achieved his objectives by reviving trade union activities, reconciling differences in religion and party politics, and indoctrinating youth movements.[24]

Nevertheless the committee concluded that there was a case for operational propaganda on a large scale. Instruction in subversive activity by means of open broadcasting would increase militant action in occupied countries, and would help the allies – provided that it was properly controlled and directed. It therefore recommended that the BBC should use open broadcasting to give instruction in subversive activity including sabotage. In spite of the misgivings they had expressed SOE agreed that incitement to sabotage in some countries was desirable, even if it led to reprisals and the shooting of hostages. Their only proviso was that separate broadcasts should be arranged country by country so that local conditions could be fully taken into account. This conclusion was welcomed by the working propagandists, who believed that the foreign press was becoming hostile to the United Kingdom cause, that radio audiences were shrinking as sets wore out and repression became more severe, and that the effect of leaflets was steadily diminishing.[25]

In submitting his report Ritchie Calder was at pains to remind Bruce Lockhart that one of the objections to the V broadcasts was the danger that audiences would resent incitement to sabotage broadcast by United Kingdom citizens living in perfect safety. He added that there was also the danger that instructions about undetectable sabotage might be picked up by listeners in Britain and acted on by them.[26] Nevertheless, the propaganda department had virtually committed itself to all-out operational propaganda, when on 17 March a sudden 'divergence of view on policy' emerged. The Regional Directors had expressed reservations about the recommendation committing them to encourage sabotage, and had asked that this should not be mandatory. A meeting which had been arranged, presumably to rubber stamp the recommendation,

[24] FO 898/297 (24.2, 2.3.42).
[25] *Ibid* (24.2.42).
[26] See Chapter 7, 'V'.

was cancelled at short notice. Dallas Brooks went off to talk with General Ismay. Bruce Lockhart had an interview with the Foreign Secretary.[27]

There is on file a draft memorandum dated 25 March which sets out the case for a vigorous campaign of operational propaganda. Both PWE and the BBC were agreed that not enough was being done by way of giving instructions to the occupied countries to encourage them to slow German production; but by special broadcasts to those sections of the populations which looked to London for guidance breakdowns in factories working for the Germans could be engineered. The fullest co-ordination between PWE's open and clandestine activities, SOE, and the fighting services was essential – and that co-ordination had been assured. The Foreign Office and the Chiefs of Staff also supported the proposals. They agreed that the time had come to make a forward move. Separate plans would be worked out for each occupied country, since industry and the temper of the peoples varied.

All this would give effect to the sort of operation Colonel Britton had proposed in his V broadcasts, but in a more acceptable form.[28]

PWE seemed set for a major breakthrough; but at a meeting on 24 March, the day before the above memorandum summarized the position as it had been generally understood, Bruce Lockhart effectively killed the proposals. In spite of the fact that his own parent Department – the Foreign Office – and the Chiefs of Staff had favoured a militant propaganda line, in the belief that it would materially help the allied war effort Bruce Lockhart spoke against the proposals with all the vigour at his command. He said it would be difficult to give detailed instructions in sabotage since it would mean instructing the oppressed peoples of Europe in an art about which they knew much more than the British did; and that there would be no response until Britain herself was playing a more active role in the general conflict. Further, it would warn the Germans what to look for in the way of subversive activity. These points had of course been taken into account by the committee and had carried little weight with them; but when restated by the Director General they won the day. The meeting had no option but to abandon the plans which had been unanimously agreed, and to fall back on the mixture as before – broadcasting news of sabotage, drawing listeners' attention to the things on which the Germans most relied, oil and transport, for example, and leaving it to them to take the initiative. Positive encouragement was ruled out.[29]

SOE, who had overcome their earlier scruples and supported the proposed operational propaganda campaign were astonished that a proposal which had such a wide backing should be thrown out by the

---

[27] FO 898/297 (24.3.42).
[28] Ibid (25.3.42).
[29] Ibid (24.3.42).

head of PWE apparently off his own bat. Their representative who had already agreed to join a new committee to plan the operational propaganda programme refused to join the committee which was set up merely to carry on the gentle propaganda which had been the order of the day since the foundation of the propaganda department.[30]

There is, alas, no way of telling what the effect of an all-out operational propaganda campaign would have been. It is possible that like the V campaign it would have produced quite unforeseen results and created serious problems for the Germans: or it might have done more harm than good to the allied cause. But when the success of the 'Intruder' operations in 1945[31] is borne in mind it suggests that PWE were quite wrong to reject operational propaganda out of hand. It could have been tried experimentally in one country, and abandoned or extended to others in the light of experience.

The propaganda department's relationship with the allied governments in exile in Britain posed particularly difficult policy questions. On the one hand, these governments were allies, deemed to be the true governments of the German-occupied countries, and therefore deserving of every consideration from Britain. On the other hand, PWE's propaganda to their countries had to be consonant with British foreign policy; and while most of the time the allies were content with the line taken by PWE, there were occasions when it upset them. The position was complicated by the fact that although Hitler was the common enemy, the domestic political position of the expatriate governments varied greatly and did not necessarily coincide with that of the British government. There was therefore no question of giving them all a free hand to broadcast whatever they chose to their own people. Not only had their transmissions to be reconciled with the British, they had to be reconciled with each other; and this was possible only if the British authorities controlled the total output.

PWE's Regional Directors kept in close touch with the appropriate Ministry in each allied government and as far as possible consulted it in advance on the open propaganda to be used towards its home country; and from their nationals in Britain the governments provided editors and broadcasters for the BBC regional sections. These people were almost invariably paid by the BBC and it was assumed that their first loyalty was to Britain.

In February 1941 the Prime Minister had to give a ruling on this subject. There had been trouble with the Belgians as to which government was the ultimate authority in what was said to Belgium. The formula provided by Churchill said that in all questions of propaganda in Belgium, whether by broadcasts or the dropping of leaflets, the view

[30] FO 898/297 (27.3.42).
[31] See Chapter 8.

of the recognized Belgian government should normally prevail. Only when there was a clash between the policy of the British War Cabinet and that of the Belgian government should any question of restraint arise. Then the decision would rest with the Foreign Secretary. This principle should apply to all the countries which had recognized governments resident in Britain. Thus the British authorities still had the last word.[32]

Most of the time it was left to the Regional Directors to fight their own battles with the government with which they were concerned, but occasionally there was an attempt to encourage all the governments to follow the same policy. In November 1941, when the question of inciting the peoples of occupied Europe to violence was under consideration, Eden wrote to the allied governments to ensure that as far as possible all followed the same line. He set out the British position: the government did not want to arouse Europe, but equally they would not discourage acts of violence; and they did not presume to determine what advice the allied governments should give their people over the BBC. Nevertheless, the British government would like to know in advance what line any particular government intended to take. The governments consulted – French, Polish, Czechoslovakian, Norwegian, Belgian, Yugoslavian, Greek, and Dutch – all dutifully replied that their policy was much the same as Britain's.[33]

The policy on open propaganda vis-à-vis the allied governments was difficult enough; but black propaganda presented almost insuperable problems. It was laid down at first that the allied governments were in no circumstances to be told even of the existence of the freedom stations through which PWE broadcast to their countries, much less about the content of their programmes. Thus when PWE were recruiting staff to man the Dutch freedom station in May 1941 it was made a condition that no one, not even the Dutch Prime Minister, should be told the nature of the work for which the men were required.[34] The same rule was laid down for the first Belgian station; and in July 1941 Dalton made a point of issuing special instructions that on no account should the Yugoslav government be told about the activity of the Yugoslav freedom radio.[35]

PWE's dealings with the Norwegian government illustrate the problems in this area. Relations were perfectly amicable before the middle of 1941; but on 6 June Mr Trygve Lie,[36] the Norwegian Foreign Minister, became 'increasingly restive' about the arrangements for the production of propaganda leaflets destined for Norway. Leeper considered that he

---

[32] FO 898/9 (11.2.41).
[33] FO 898/12 (12.11.41; FO 898/11 (19.1.42).
[34] FO 898/1 (15.5.41).
[35] *Ibid* (7.7.41).
[36] Later Secretary General of the United Nations.

was being unreasonable since every leaflet sent to Norway had been agreed with the Norwegian Government Press Bureau. He wrote: 'It is to be feared that Mr Lie is thinking more of bolstering up the prestige of his government in Norway after the war than of the quality of propaganda.'[37]

Matters came to a head in September 1941 when Lie met the Regional Director for Scandinavia (T. G. Barman) and showed him a telegram from the Norwegian Legation in Stockholm summarizing two recent transmissions by PWE's Norwegian freedom station in which the staff of the Legation were violently attacked. The telegram claimed that the broadcasts originated in Britain, and Lie said that he believed that Barman was responsible for them. At first Barman hedged, but eventually (having earlier got Bruce Lockhart's permission to come clean about the freedom station if he was cornered by Lie) admitted the truth.[38]

This was the first shot in a battle which rumbled on for a year. Now that the British had admitted the existence of the freedom station the Norwegians asked to be allowed to control it as a matter of principle. PWE were prepared to work hand in glove with them, but drew the line at complete surrender. All broadcasting to Norway through the BBC was already in the hands of Norwegians paid by the Norwegian government so that if they took over the freedom station as well Britain would lose virtually all control of radio propaganda to Norway – and it was essential on policy and security grounds to know what the Norwegian government was saying to its people.[39]

PWE's resistance to the Norwegian demands was fortified by the fact that although the Norwegian government was trying to stop Britain from sending propaganda to Norway, they themselves were busily disseminating their own propaganda in Britain, using very scarce paper made available by the British authorities. Further, some of the Norwegian propaganda destined for Norway and produced for the Norwegian government by PWE was considered to be positively harmful – for example, an article in a Christmas annual describing how units of the Norwegian army in Scotland were rolling in money which they spent on drinks and fur coats for their girl friends, and how the frequent marriages between Norwegian soldiers and Scots girls had often to be followed by immediate christenings. It was wrong that this sort of thing should be fed to people living on the verge of starvation, and suffering from the German occupation.[40]

PWE failed to make the Norwegians see reason, and in June 1942 the Foreign Office stepped in to take a stronger line. They pointed out that

[37] FO 898/241 (6.6.41).
[38] *Ibid* (23.9.41).
[39] *Ibid* (6.11.41).
[40] FO 898/241 (4.12.41).

the British government had gladly agreed to give the Norwegian broadcasting authority time on the BBC, but that it was PWE's responsibility to co-ordinate all forms of propaganda to enemy and enemy-occupied countries; and concluded with a very firm request 'that your government will instruct the Norwegian State Broadcasting to keep in closest touch with PWE and adhere closely to the directives laid down by that body for BBC broadcasts'.[41] This did the trick. It is recorded a month later that 'the Norwegian government has now realized that co-operation with His Majesty's Government is essential for the carrying out of propaganda to Norway'; and that satisfactory liaison arrangements had been agreed between the two governments. Bruce Lockhart wrote to Lie on 11 September 1942 setting out the terms which had been agreed and they were formally accepted by the Norwegians on 28 September.[42]

While he was still Minister of Economic Warfare Dalton cautioned PWE against 'boosting too hard' the various exiled allied governments, on the ground that it might turn out that they would not have much following 'when the storm breaks in their homelands'. He thought that the old politicians would find themselves replaced by men who had stayed and faced out the occupation, and would have bolder and more revolutionary ideas than those who had lived not very dangerously abroad. The longer the period of exile the more would the expatriate government lose touch with the facts of life in their country; and some, the Belgian, for example, had never been very representative at the best of times. In some cases crowned heads might remain, simply as a symbol of unity and independence but there was no certainty even of that. Dalton then echoed the point made earlier by Duff Cooper when he looked forward to a Europe 'united by goodwill and friendship'[43]. PWE should do nothing to discourage the formation of European blocs, lest the British government be accused of fighting to prevent the unification of Germany under the German leadership, without offering any alternative.[44]

This passion to win the peace even before the war had properly started was no doubt meritorious; but it is possible that the propaganda department's performance would have been improved if Ministers had seen to it that they had concentrated all their energies on the current struggle and taken a chance on post-war developments, the nature of which no-one could foretell.

The Chiefs of Staff inevitably had a considerable interest in the policies of the propaganda department. They were given an opportunity of working closely with Department EH when Campbell Stuart set up a Services Consultative Committee, which had its first meeting in

[41] FO 898/241 (25.6.42).
[42] *Ibid* 6.7.42, 11, 28.9.42.
[43] Above, pp. 46-7.
[44] FO 898/12; INF 1/895 (6.12.41).

November 1939. High ranking officers had to listen to Stuart reading an interminable speech explaining that his department was the fourth arm of offensive warfare, and asking to be provided with the fullest possible information from the three Services to help in Department EH's attack on enemy civilian morale. This committee, which might have played a useful part in tailoring propaganda policy to suit the needs of the Services, ceased to meet early in 1940, perhaps because the Service members found Stuart an intolerable bore. Contacts were still maintained with the Services, but at a lower level.[45]

It may be that at this stage the Chiefs of Staff had little faith in the ability of a new and untried civilian organization to facilitate their tasks; but at least one senior commander took a different view. In spite of his pre-occupation with the German advance in North Africa and the Eastern Mediterranean General Wavell, who had made use of leaflet and loud hailer attacks on enemy morale, found time to make far-reaching proposals in the field of political warfare. He believed that the Axis powers enjoyed a great advantage over the allies in that they had recognized that diplomacy, foreign propaganda, and economic warfare formed a fourth arm (Campbell Stuart's favourite expression) in modern warfare; and that the sooner the allies caught up with them the better. He suggested that a single Minister should be appointed to take charge of these three subjects; and that he should be represented on the Chiefs of Staff Committee by a Civilian Chief of Staff. This was a remarkable proposal to come from a professional soldier; and it was much too revolutionary to be welcomed by his colleagues in London.[46]

The propaganda department kept in touch with the Services, through its military wing. Its senior members were invited from time to time to attend meetings of the Chiefs of Staff Committee but these meetings were concerned more with *ad hoc* matters than with the exploitation of propaganda for the purposes of strategy. For example, at the beginning of 1942 when it was reported by the Governor of Burma that rumours were damaging the allied cause in the Far East, the Chiefs of Staff invited PWE to comment on the possibility of jamming the radio stations in Tokyo and Bangkok. They were told that this was the responsibility of the Director of Publicity in Singapore; and that in PWE's opinion it was better to avoid jamming enemy radio as far as possible. It implied fear of the information the enemy was broadcasting, and it would lead to reprisals.[47]

From early in 1942 the Chiefs of Staff came more into the policy-making picture. PWE occasionally put papers to the Chiefs of Staff Committee to get their blessing for new proposals – for example, the encouragement of undetectable sabotage which in March 1942 was

[45] FO 898/6 (13.11.39).
[46] PREM 3/365/11, f. 922 (18.4.41).
[47] CAB 79/15, f. 123 (23.10.41); FO 898/23 (2, 6.1.42).

considered to be necessary because the effect of PWE's go-slow campaign among the workers of Europe was beginning to wear off. The proposed campaign would increase the number of minor breakdowns in factories, it would mean more supervisors, and it would encourage the fainthearted to go slow. The Chiefs of Staff approved this programme on 23 March.[48] In the following month they invited PWE to join in the planning of Operation *Ironclad* (the allied invasion of Madagascar).[49] In May, the Chiefs of Staff said they would welcome the attendance of a senior man from PWE say three times a month, thus finally recognizing that the policies of the propaganda department were relevant to strategical planning.[50]

From the time of Operation *Torch* onwards[51] the propagandists were deeply involved in every major operation, particularly because the Americans rated the contribution of psychological warfare very high. The British Chiefs of Staff seem to have been less thoroughly convinced of its importance. When in July 1944 the Chief of the Imperial General Staff (Sir Alan Brooke)[52] asked why PWE's monthly summary of their activities was no longer made available to the Chiefs of Staff the Secretary of the Chiefs of Staff Committee told PWE that he had the impression that the Chiefs of Staff had completely lost touch with what was going on in the propaganda field, which was an unhappy state of affairs. One member of the Committee did not even know that PWE existed.[53]

[48] FO 898/23 (20, 23.3.42).
[49] *Ibid* (29.4.42).
[50] *Ibid* (4.5.42).
[51] See Chapter 8, 'Operation Torch'.
[52] Later Lord Alanbrooke.
[53] FO 898/23 (18.7.44).

4
Market Research: Intelligence

Without intelligence there could be no propaganda: or at least no effective propaganda. The propagandist had to know intimately the country and the people whom he was addressing – so intimately that when he spoke to them or drafted a leaflet for them not a single false note would creep in. He had to be familiar with their state of mind week by week – 'what the housewife says waiting in a food queue; what workmen talk about in a factory; what the farmer feels about the government; what a street in the capital looks like; what shopkeepers and tradesmen think about the business outlook; what the ordinary man is saying about air raids'.[1]

A radio broadcast which revealed less than complete mastery of the subject under discussion, or a leaflet that got some fact wrong, could do more harm than good. It would show up the propagandist for what he was – a propagandist – and would boost rather than undermine the morale of the enemy. When the German radio proudly announced the sinking with all hands of HMS *Ganges* or some other shore station in Britain it not only amused the British listener, but it led him to distrust other German news items, perhaps including some that were perfectly true.

Therefore, if propaganda in all its forms was to have the maximum impact, indeed if it was to succeed at all, the propagandists had to keep abreast of developments in Germany, and in the satellite and occupied countries. They must have at their fingertips the latest, fullest, and most accurate information about their target, whether it was a whole population, or a particular section, say the industrial workers, so that whatever they were saying to them it would be said with authority.

It is easy for commercial advertisers to gather information on which they can base a national campaign to induce people to buy their product; and they can measure their success in terms of increased sales. The propagandist was less happily placed. He was like a general who must know the strength and dispositions of the enemy before he can begin to plan an operation; but the military commander needs intelligence only for planning. The propagandist needs to know the state of mind and

[1] FO 898/30 (11.8.40).

general circumstances of the people he is aiming at first to decide where and when to attack, and second to shape the ammunition he uses – his propaganda messages. For example, the information that the German farmers were rioting in protest about the requisition of their crops would suggest that it might be worth while mounting a separate campaign to encourage further rioting; and the same information would be essential for the preparation of material for the campaign.

Not only was it necessary to find out what was going on in enemy and enemy-occupied countries, the information had to reach the propaganda department as soon as possible after the events, if it was to be of any real use; and in the early days of Department EH it was sometimes necessary to fall back on guesswork and deduction, perhaps helped sometimes by an element of wishful thinking.

Before the German military successes in the middle of 1940 the propaganda department found itself in much the same position, as far as the supply of intelligence was concerned, as the Department of Enemy Propaganda had done in 1918. It was able to organize the supply of a large number of German daily newspapers through agents in neutral countries. By the spring of 1940 EH was receiving 90 German newspapers, periodicals, trade and labour journals; more than 100 allied and neutral newspapers from 16 different countries; and a large number of the publications of refugee groups in the United Kingdom. Its Intelligence Division had five linguists studying this mountain of paper, and quarrying from it everything that seemed likely to help the propagandists. EH also subscribed through cover organizations in neutral countries to neutral and enemy news agencies. All this material reached London reasonably soon after publication, but if something merited immediate consideration it was telegraphed by the British missions in the European capitals.

The Press attachés appointed as a result of Vansittart's efforts in 1938 should have contributed to the flow of information, but most of them were too busy dealing with the local press – feeding information about Britain – to have much time for the business of the propaganda department. In Holland, for example, when it was proposed that the press attaché should send a daily cable summarizing the principal items in the German press he claimed that he was too occupied with other matters to tackle the job. Instead, the *Daily Herald* Dutch correspondent was asked to help out; but he failed to produce what the propagandists wanted. This was a succinct telegram setting out German stories that should be replied to immediately, important world news items that had not been allowed to appear in the German press, distortions of fact which the BBC should correct, and the trend of German policy as reflected in the press. All these matters should have been covered in 'a short crisp cable' – so the propaganda department said when assessing the shortcomings of the *Daily Herald* man; but it is unlikely that the most brilliant of correspondents could have met the specification.²

The BBC was the other main source of information at this time. The Corporation monitored every significant word broadcast in Europe, and transcriptions were provided for the propagandists within a matter of hours. This service enabled them to know what was happening in Germany, and later in the occupied countries – or at least to know the enemy's version of what was happening. Here the propagandist's sixth sense was brought into play. If he detected that something had been omitted from a particular news bulletin, or something unduly emphasized, he had to find an explanation for the aberration from the strict truth. What was the enemy trying to cover up? And having answered this question he then had to consider how the point should be dealt with in the propaganda department's next transmissions – which the German propagandists would be waiting for with interest. It was all rather like a game of tennis in which the ball became visible only when it reached the player's racket, and there was very little time to make an effective stroke in reply.

There were of course many sources of information other than press and radio. The Ministry of Information, which covered the whole world; the intelligence branches of the three Service Departments, with which Electra House had been in touch ever since it was a shadow organization; the Political Intelligence Department of the Foreign Office, which received a great volume of information from diplomatic, military and other sources, and which had the benefit of considerable experience of the countries to which the information related (and which was also the cover for the propaganda department); the Ministry of Economic Warfare, which proved to be particularly useful; private individuals who still had contacts in Germany; refugees, whose contributions had to be most carefully vetted; the War Cabinet secretariat, which had a special interest in information required for 'strategic deception'; the Secret Service, of which the propagandists did not think very highly – 'the fatuous snippets sent in by the Secret Service were of no value whatsoever'. Another assessment was only slightly kinder: 'While the Secret Service reports are useful as far as they go, they are of no great value as sources of information for a propaganda departmen';³ prisoners of war – not too numerous in the early days – to whom Electra House had access through their own agent; and finally, through its Paris office it received, or was supposed to receive, intelligence from the French army and Secret Service.⁴

An assessment of the state of affairs in Germany made by the propaganda department in February 1940 was based on material drawn

² FO 898/30 (30.12.39).
³ *Ibid* (11.8.40).
⁴ *Ibid* (18.2.40).

from these various sources. Tension had been increasing since the beginning of the war, and there was now little enthusiasm for the struggle. One section of German opinion believed that if the country could survive a long siege allied morale would collapse. Another considered that an all-out attack on Britain would force a German victory but it was feared that this could be achieved only at enormous cost in German lives. The man in the street was beginning to say 'we shall never surrender' rather than 'we shall win'. There was no sign that the régime was about to be upset by a political revolution, although in some quarters the glimmering of a critical attitude could be detected. That the Germans were regarded as pariahs throughout the civilized world was appreciated only by a small intellectual class in the Reich. No one was starving, although most people could eat more than they were getting; but the shortage of clothing, leather, and soap was beginning to hit people, especially in the middle classes. There was growing discontent among the industrial workers at their long hours, and the theoretical payment of overtime, which they never received. There was some over-organization and bureaucratic interference and muddle. Shopkeepers and artisans had been badly affected. Hitler was still a mystical personification of German power. It was accepted that he had made mistakes, but most people thought he would get away with them. Reports from Poland confirmed that German officials there were open to bribery. In Germany fear of Bolshevism was off-set by the belief that the association with Russia would bring benefits, including the supply of raw materials, and security in the east.[5]

This was the picture of the enemy's situation as presented to the working propagandists after all the available material had been sifted and evaluated – the picture which they had to study for chinks in his armour which might be widened by propaganda. There were precious few; but almost before the *Daily Herald* man in The Hague could be made to understand what the propagandists really wanted from him, the Germans had begun their lightning move westwards, and many of Electra House's main sources of intelligence were either cut off or seriously impaired. The whole French contribution was swept away – but perhaps that was no great loss.

Electra House was now faced with the complete re-organization of its sources of information. Sweden, Switzerland, Spain and Portugal were the only neutral countries left to which the propaganda department could look for help, and communication with them was none too easy. The British Legation in Stockholm was instructed to buy every newspaper from the occupied countries they could lay their hands on and fly them to Britain once a week in an RAF plane, which would carry British newspapers back to Sweden – in itself a useful piece of propaganda.

---

[5] FO 898/9, p. 203 (10.2.40).

People were escaping by sea fairly regularly from occupied Norway, and some agreed to return there to instruct others as to the sort of material the propaganda department wanted, so that future escapers could come well equipped. The Germans had banned the sending of newspapers out of Holland and Belgium so that it was now difficult to get them even in the neutral countries, although German, French and Italian papers could still be bought freely in Spain and Portugal. It was arranged to bring them to London by air, but even so they were often many days out of date, and their value for propaganda purposes was much diminished.

A concerted effort to provide information was made in September 1940 when a press reading bureau was established in the Legation in Stockholm. It took over the comprehensive reading of the German press which had hitherto been done in Switzerland; and arranged for the reading of all the newspapers that could be got from neutral and occupied countries. Material which might be useful for propaganda was sent to London by bag or cable. A year later there was a staff of over 30 engaged in this work, although the Minister[6] was sceptical about the use made of the material supplied by the Legation. He said it was very difficult to know just what PWE wanted. When they were asked specific questions on this subject they usually failed to reply. 'Moreover the initiative as regards tapping new sources of press information has usually been taken here rather than in London'. (That was hardly a matter to complain about since it was easier for the Legation to know about new sources than it was for PWE, and there is no reason why the staff of a Legation should not occasionally show initiative.) The Minister also said that he had reason to believe that the information provided was not being circulated to the interested Departments – no doubt, he added kindly, owing to pressure of other business in PWE.[7]

The propaganda department's intelligence services were re-organized periodically in an attempt to meet the growing sophistication of the propagandists' requirements. The first major change was introduced early in 1942, partly because the Treasury suspected that there was some overlapping between PWE's services and those of the BBC. The bodies concerned with propaganda intelligence at this time included the BBC Central News Room, the BBC European Records Unit (catering for the European Intelligence Service which prepared Surveys of European Audiences and a Monthly Intelligence Report intended to be used for propaganda); the BBC Overseas Research Unit, which analysed foreign propaganda; the PWE Propaganda Research Station at Woburn, concerned with target research (that is, the study of conditions in the country at which propaganda was to be

---

[6] Mr Victor (later Sir Victor) Mallet.
[7] FO 898/252 (16.10.41).

aimed) and the analysis of propaganda output; the PWE press cutting and filing Library, also at Woburn; and the BBC News Information Bureau in Bush House. These BBC and PWE bodies had developed independently of each other; and the three-man committee which investigated them (a representative from each of the BBC and PWE under the chairmanship of Sir Leonard Browett) decided that there was scope for rationalization.

They were impressed by the argument that target research, analysis of propaganda output, propaganda policy and its execution should be closely associated with each other. They therefore decided in favour of 'regionalization' of these activities, by which they meant that as far as possible they should all be concentrated under a director who would be responsible for all the propaganda work related to a single country, or group of countries – rather than that information should be collected and analysed by a central organization and parcelled out to the working propagandists. One of the practical objections to the centralization of the information service was that it would lead to the duplication of staff, since linguists would be needed both to handle information centrally, and to use it to prepare propaganda in the Regional Directorate. This would cause no real problem so far as French or German were concerned but it would be difficult to find enough experts in the more obscure languages.

The committee accordingly recommended that the BBC European Intelligence Section, including the European Records Unit, and the Overseas Research Unit, should be disbanded and that suitable people in these sections should be transferred to PWE. An argument in favour of transferring staff to PWE rather than the other way round was that the BBC was not a government Department, and therefore could not be given access to all the secret information available to PWE. It was also recommended that a Director of Intelligence should be appointed to ensure co-ordination between the intelligence officers to be appointed to the Regional Directorates and the other sections of the Executive concerned with information.[8]

The Ministerial Committee approved virtually all the committee's recommendations and instructed Bruce Lockhart to have them implemented. He in turn wrote to Sir Allan Powell, Chairman of Governors of the BBC, saying how grateful PWE were for the Corporation's help in the past, and that he was most eager that relations should continue to be close and friendly.[9] He was to be disappointed. The BBC were upset at losing out to PWE, and more so by the high-handed speed with which the Executive proceeded to take over BBC staff without proper consultation. Although the Corporation was not a government Depart-

[8] FO 898/35 (7.11.41).
[9] *Ibid* (4.12.41).

ment it could not very well resist the decisions of the Ministerial triumvirate, especially as the Corporation had been represented on the Browett committee. It could, however, be awkward. When PWE looked for the BBC staff due to come to them they found that some of them had been transferred to other work within the BBC, and that they were therefore not available for transfer. Much high level argument ensued, and it was finally decided that while the principle of 'regionalization' (which some people in the BBC did not like) would stand, a Central PWE Intelligence Unit would be formed in London primarily to cater for the needs of the BBC.[10] The staff for this unit would be supplied mainly from the BBC.[11]

Perhaps because of this the unit came in for a great deal of criticism. An early appraisal of its performance began: 'The time now seems come when we can cease to dismiss the eccentricities of this unit as the natural flounderings of beginners, intent on proving the necessity of their existence at the expense of their own and other people's time, and of the nation's limited paper supply'; and went on to list its main crimes. It was doing things badly which other people or organizations were already doing better; it was circulating material that already enjoyed a wide circulation; and much of what it was doing had no value at all.[12]

The general dissatisfaction with the arrangements led to yet another inquiry into the intelligence services. This was carried out by Brigadier Eric Sachs, who recommended numerous changes including the strengthening of the intelligence staff attached to the Regional Directors, and also the strengthening of the central directorate. It was also decided at this time that the majority of the intelligence staff should work in London.[13] This remained the pattern of the intelligence work for the rest of the war. Sachs was appointed Director of Intelligence, and the efficiency of the new arrangements was largely due to his strict control.

The information which poured into PWE had to be carefully classified and indexed. It might have to be used right away but much of it might not be needed for months or even years. It had to be possible for the staff of the Regional Directorates to lay their hands on any given item at short notice. In 1944 more than half a million documents were received and filed for future use. The classification employed was designed to simplify the propagandist's task in assessing the state and fluctuations of public opinion in all its aspects. Thus German material was located in eight main groups, four dealing with attitudes of representative cross-sections of the population, attitudes to the war, air raids, and the Russian campaign. Three groups covered the opinions

---

[10] FO 898/35 (27.1.42).
[11] *Ibid* (7.3.42).
[12] *Ibid* (17.6.42).
[13] *Ibid* (19.1.43).

and attitudes of the army, navy and Luftwaffe. The eighth group was a rag-bag containing everything else.

These main groups were further broken down: 'Attitudes of representative cross-sections' had five sub-groups: geographical units (twelve regions, supplemented with separate files for the principal towns); occupational and social units (ranging from workers to landed gentry, students to pensioners and Party officials); physiological units (age groups, and sex groups); political units (active Party, neutral, opposition, and underground movements); and finally, religious units (Catholic, Protestant, Neo-Pagan, Sect, and General).

The second main group ('attitudes to the war') had ten subdivisions, including duration and outcome of the war (how long will war last, victory doubtful, defeat certain, etc); peace (compromise peace, fear in case of defeat, etc); character of war (self-defence, aggression, inevitable to obtain *lebensraum*, etc); economic factors (clothing, housing, food and drink, black market, etc); internal politics (faith in Hitler, attitude to Gestapo, loyalty to régime, etc); and propaganda (British news trusted/mistrusted, German reports trusted/mistrusted, all propaganda mistrusted); and finally morale (determination and resolve, indifference, resignation, discontent, depression and gloom, defiance and revolt).

The miscellaneous rag-bag had 34 widely-varied sub-divisions which included grumbles, fears, rumours, sabotage, spies, civilian suicides, atrocities, health and epidemics, mercy killing, anecdotes and jokes.

It was possible for the propagandist to use a selection of these files (which had been built up over the years) to determine how morale was changing in quite small sectors of the community – always provided that the information filed was accurate, or detectably inaccurate, which was just as valuable for the purposes of propaganda. The longer the war went on the easier it was to deduce the state of morale and to detect the influence of British propaganda on the German people as a whole.[14]

In the early days of the war the main weight of propaganda was directed at the civilians of enemy and enemy-occupied countries; but as time went on the German soldier became a more and more important target. If propaganda aimed at the armed forces was to have the maximum effect it was necessary to have the fullest possible intelligence about the attitude to the war of the Wehrmacht; and in this the interrogation of prisoners of war played an important part. A review based on prisoner of war opinion made at the end of 1943 concluded that in 1940 and 1941 virtually every German soldier believed that victory was just round the corner. After the failure of the German armies before Moscow and the entry of the United States into the war most of them still believed that it would be possible to crush Russia before Britain and

[14] FO 898/35 (September 1942).

the United States had fully mobilized their resources; but the Germans' defeat at Stalingrad completely changed their attitude. It was estimated that at the beginning of 1943 30 per cent of the German armed forces still had complete confidence in a German victory. By the end of the year it had dropped to 8 per cent.

The men's attitude to Hitler was also studied. Many Germans who disliked the SS, the Gestapo, the concentration camps, the Hitler Youth, the corruption in the Nazi Party, still retained great faith in Hitler. Indeed, the more difficult it became not to criticize some aspects of the régime the more did some German troops cling to the belief that the Führer was above human error. In the first four years of the war more than half the prisoners of war put Hitler above criticism, some on almost religious grounds, others because they felt that they must owe unquestioning loyalty to the head of state.

These studies of the mental attitudes of prisoners of war paid particular attention to the men's attitude to propaganda, so that themes could be modified in the light of experience. The concensus was that so far as their own propaganda was concerned, it was necessary in wartime, and Dr Goebbels did it rather well. The numbers listening to British propaganda increased as the war went on, and eventually it was listened to quite openly in barrack-rooms. Different people had different motives for listening. Airmen and U-boat crews hoped to hear news of missing comrades. Others enjoyed the dance music. The greatest attraction, however, was news, to which they listened with close attention as a cross-check on the communiqués of their High Command. The BBC's objectivity and candid admission of allied losses and setbacks much impressed the men. They also listened eagerly to factual talks about the war situation so long as they did not adopt a patronizing or sneering tone, and which did not obviously try to put across propaganda.[15]

Prisoners of war were sometimes used to test the efficacy of aspects of propaganda. In a study in May 1944, for example, six were cross-examined on their reactions to a set of propaganda leaflets. Four of them were professed anti-Nazis, one was not firmly convinced one way or the other, and the sixth was a true Nazi – 'very recalcitrant and inclined to be violent', a native of Kiel who had served in U-boats. All were other ranks and were presumed to be intelligent.

The Nazi was prepared to comment only on three or four of the leaflets which they were shown. Of one illustrating the comfortable life in British, American and Canadian prisoner of war camps, he said 'Surely you don't expect me to believe that?' When shown a leaflet dealing with U-boat losses, he admitted that Germany was losing many U-boats, but consoled himself with the thought that every U-boat that was sunk took with it to the bottom a destroyer, corvette or tanker. He

[15] FO 898/99, pp. 468-75.

grudgingly admitted that one or two of the leaflets were good propaganda.

The anti-Nazis did their best to provide a balanced judgement, and their comments were as a rule unanimous. They felt that the prisoner of war camp pictures, which the Nazi had dismissed as fiction, were almost too good to be true. They would be more convincing if the captions explained that the reason for the sumptuous accommodation was that many hotels which the war had deprived of their customers were being used to house prisoners of war. Three leaflets showing where allied aircraft were being manufactured, that the United States were producing a new plane every five minutes, and that German production had fallen from its peak by a quarter, on which the Nazi said 'Impressive – if it were true', led the anti-Nazis to express astonishment. The output figures were most impressive.

The moderate Nazi's reactions were equally predictable. He was quite prepared to answer all the questions he was asked, and appeared to give honest replies. Of the allied prisoner of war camps he said 'We have nothing like this in Germany. I can hardly believe such camp conditions to be a reality'. As to the leaflet which the anti-Nazis thought the best of all ('A German soldier's questions and our answers') he agreed that it looked convincing but said that he would have to study it in detail before he committed himself. Of the others he admitted that there was probably some truth in what they said.[16]

It was difficult to assess the value of this sort of intelligence, so many assumptions had to be made. There was no guarantee that the guinea pigs' view of the Nazi régime was what they professed it to be. There was no certainty that the men chosen for these special exercises were typical of the mass of the German armed forces. They may often have thought that it would be in their own interest to give the sort of answer they thought their inquisitors would want to hear. And there was always the over-riding difficulty that when people are promoted to the status of guinea-pig they cease to be typical.

[16] FO 898/466 (25.5.44).

5
The product: Propaganda themes

The Political Warfare Executive intended that the propaganda themes they pumped into Europe during the five years of war should have one thing in common. They would hasten an allied victory by weakening the enemy's appetite for war, by hindering his ability to fight, or by sustaining the occupied countries' will to resist.

Although open broadcasting was confined to the truth, on the ground that honesty is the best policy, it did not necessarily have to be the whole truth. While the white broadcasters were required to promote the current approved propaganda themes no less than were their black brethren, some truths would support them better than others, and some were best left untold. For the black propagandist, however, no holds were barred. A well-thought-out lie might be worth more than the most shining of truths. In a total war of propaganda (if the shade of William Blake will permit)

> A lie that's told with good intent
> Beats all the truth you can present.[1]

The line taken at the beginning of the war, as expounded by Sir Campbell Stuart in a memorandum for the War Cabinet, was unsophisticated, and tended to favour white propaganda. He believed that it was necessary to address the German people as a whole. There should be no attempt to cultivate sectional interests – for example, the peasants or the industrial workers – until a clear case had been established for such special treatment. Nor should Hitler be attacked personally. Every German soldier had taken an oath of loyalty to him, so that an anti-Hitler theme might prove to be counter-productive. The Nazi Party, however, was fair game. Themes should be as simple as possible, both in conception and expression, since the vast majority of listeners and readers were working class. Stuart defensively reminded the War Cabinet that it was the German version of propaganda leaflets that mattered. There had been a good deal of criticism of the department's

---

[1] Blake preferred:
> A truth that's told with bad intent
> Beats all the lies you can invent
> (*Auguries of Innocence*)

performance in this field, but he claimed that it was directed against the English version of the text, which was unfair.²

The flexibility of mind of those charged with the task of evolving propaganda is illustrated by a proposal in the autumn of 1940, when one of the established themes was that Britain was solidly behind the occupied countries in their opposition to the Germans. It was suggested that Britain should now throw the occupied countries overboard. The new line would be that Britain, having shown that she could successfully defend herself against invasion, had no further interest in the fate of occupied Europe, and planned to achieve a satisfactory peace – from her own point of view – through a series of bargains with Hitler. The idea was that this would have such an impact in the occupied countries that instead of waiting patiently to be rescued by an allied invasion they would be impelled to fight their own more active battle against the occupying power. It might be disastrous for them in the short run, because of German reprisals, but might work to Britain's advantage in the long run by weakening the power of the Wehrmacht.³ In fact this theme was not adopted, but that it was even considered shows how far the black propagandists were prepared to go in manipulating the truth if it seemed to suit their interests.

The propaganda themes adopted month by month and year by year were the product of the combined wisdom of the propagandists. They ate, slept and dreamed propaganda; and living closely together as they did, especially in the academic atmosphere of Woburn (a college which might have taken as its motto 'Nation shall speak lies unto nation' – a minor variation of the BBC's own motto)⁴ had ample opportunity to try ideas out on each other. The implementation and development of the themes currently in use was discussed at the weekly meetings of the Regional Directors. This was important, since there was always the danger that individual Directors, steeped in the particular problems of their own country or group of countries, which were not necessarily common to the rest of Europe, would adopt a theme which might embarrass their colleagues.

Radio transmissions did not recognize national boundaries. Quite early in the war PWE received convincing evidence of 'cross-listening' – people in one country listening to programmes aimed at another – which meant that the programmes directed to the seven regions (Germany/Austria, France, Italy, the Low Countries, Scandinavia, the Balkans, and Poland/Czechoslovakia) had to have a lowest common denominator so that all could be heard in the other regions without cutting across the programmes directed to them. Equally, themes aimed at individual sectors of the population of Europe (in spite of Campbell

² CAB 68/1, ff. 182-8 (29.9.39).
³ FO 898/9, p. 237 (12.10.40).
⁴ 'Nation shall speak peace unto nation'.

Stuart's early caution the propaganda department soon began to aim at particular groups) had to be reconciled with the general themes and with each other. All this limited the choice open to the propagandists. An ingenious line might have to be rejected simply because the target countries were not self-contained pigeon-holes. This restriction applied primarily to radio transmissions, but it could also affect leaflets, especially before they were accurately disseminated by leaflet bomb.[5] In the early days it was quite possible for leaflets scattered from a great height to drift into the wrong country.

The 'common denominator' was more important for the white propagandist than for the black. The great strength of the BBC lay in the trust which its straight news, talks and features enjoyed throughout the whole of Europe. This trust would have been weakened if listeners (who, it must never be forgotten, ran a serious risk every time they tuned in to the BBC) had detected discrepancies either in programmes intended for them, or in programmes they picked up by cross-listening.

The black radio stations had less need to reconcile their outputs since they were by definition not British, and were supposed to have no connection with each other. Each had *carte blanche* to follow themes of its own invention. There remained the danger, however, that the transmissions of the 'Research Units', to use their code name,[6] might sometimes cancel each other out, or potentially more troublesome, so directly echo the BBC's white line that it would suggest that they were under the same management, and thus cast doubt on the honesty of the BBC transmissions. It was therefore essential that those concerned with black propaganda should keep in close touch with their white colleagues.

The nature of the themes favoured by the propagandists varied according to the state of the war. During the defensive period, when Britain stood alone, the propaganda department had to rely on defensive propaganda, and the BBC had to set about attracting an audience in Europe by providing a reliable news service. Although the communiqués of the German High Command were much more truthful than later on in the war (there is less need to tell lies when you are winning easily) many Germans wanted to hear what someone other than their Propaganda Ministry had to say about the progress of the war. They became more interested when the German communiqués played down the Luftwaffe's defeat in the Battle of Britain; and there was no doubt that 'the persistent accuracy' of the BBC news service did much to restore Britain's standing in German eyes.[7]

While the BBC was dispassionately reporting facts – usually unpleasant from Britain's point of view – the ingenuity of the propaganda department was taxed to the utmost in its attempts to make bricks

[5] See Chapter 6.
[6] See Chapter 6.
[7] FO 898/101, ff. 151-8.

without straw. There was virtually nothing to boast about. The best themes it could evolve for Germany were 'the long war'; 'Germany has lost the war'; 'Hitler's war guilt'; and 'the new European order' – not a very impressive collection with which to influence the thinking of a powerful and all-conquering enemy.

The theme of 'the long war' was not yet likely to make much impression. Whatever privations the Germans were suffering as a result of the war they had reason to believe they would soon be a thing of the past – when the Führer had finally defeated Britain. However, the propaganda department did their best with 'the long war'. Now that Germany had failed to win in the summer of 1940 the struggle was bound to be prolonged. Britain had access to all the raw materials she needed, and could fight on for ever. She could rely on ever-increasing help from the Dominions and the United States. On the other hand, thanks to the blockade, Germany must become steadily weaker. Care should be taken, however, to avoid saying anything that would foster the German propaganda legend that a socialist Germany was at war with a plutocratic Britain; and in putting across the idea that Britain could get all the raw materials she needed Germany's comparative poverty in this respect must not be unduly stressed.

The Germans must be told, not only that they faced a long war, but that the Nazi system was one of war without end. Even if Germany won the present struggle, another would follow. Without war the Nazi machine had no meaning. Germany might have made great conquests, but the conquered peoples were her enemies, and sooner or later would rise against her. It was only because of Hitler and the Nazis that the war continued.

The propaganda department believed that the war at sea and in the air were now likely to be of supreme importance for the purposes of political warfare. The efficacy of the British blockade and the weakness of the German counter-blockade must be emphasized; but the Royal Navy must not be shown as the agent of the British plutocrats who planned to starve Europe. There should be no attempt to jeer at German or Italian sailors, though their brutality and in particular the brutality of German attacks on merchant shipping should be high-lighted. The line on the war in the air was simple. The most must be made of the Battle of Britain, in which Germany suffered her first defeat. It should be described as an 'aerial Marne'. When it had been sufficiently drummed home to the German people that the Luftwaffe had in fact lost a vital battle, the RAF's success should be made an assumption of propaganda rather than a theme that needed advertising. Further, the RAF's bombing raids on Germany should be played up as an indication of a big coming British offensive.[8]

[8] FO 898/3, ff. 76-80 (2.9.40).

The danger in which the people stood was also stressed although it was difficult to make much of this when the Nazis still seemed to be winning the war. Sir Edward Spears[9] sent a memorandum to Dalton and Duff Cooper urging that the fear theme should be given pride of place. He claimed that next to hunger it was perhaps the strongest of human motives. 'We have been slow to realize the power of propaganda, so lacking in imagination when explaining the possibilities of this terrible weapon which is capable of turning a part of every enemy into an ally by preying on his imagination and destroying his will to fight . . .' Dalton approved of this line – he was as a rule prepared to give uncritical approval to a new idea – but the working men of the propaganda department were less impressed. The Germans were still too strong to be moved by threats. Richard Crossman cynically observed: 'Good – but I read it all in the *Evening Standard* last week.'[10]

Nevertheless, Crossman was stung by Spears's criticism into writing a massive essay 'On the use of the motifs of fear, guilt and hate in our propaganda to Germany'. Fear was already being exploited through reports of British bombing raids, warnings of the fate awaiting any German force that tried to invade Britain, reports of increasing American aid, news items supporting the theme that it would be a long war, and that Germany would lose it; but was it wise to intensify the propaganda assault and direct it at the whole German people? Crossman thought not. 'In order to create a frame of mind in Germany by which, when the time is ripe, we can profit in terms of internal opposition, our propaganda must be such as to enable opponents (a) to feel they share a common enemy with Britain and (b) through this feeling to concentrate their hatred upon that enemy, and not upon the British people. Propaganda cannot achieve ambitious objectives, but can only keep alive and intensify such differences as already exist. These differences cannot become politically significant until we have proved by military action that Germany cannot win the war'. If, however, there could be created in Germany a body of opinion which looked forward to a British victory 'we may be able to spare ourselves a long period of war'.

He thought it was nonsense to think that the German people could be terrified at that point of time. At best they might be made to feel rather uncomfortable. To emphasize the guilt of the Germans as a whole would be tantamount to introducing into British propaganda the hate motif which dominated German propaganda; it would destroy any hope of an alternative régime acceptable to moderate Germans; and it would drive resistance groups into alliance with either the Nazis or the communists. Above all, it would be premature, since such

---

[9] At this time head of the British Mission to General de Gaulle.
[10] FO 898/178 (19.12.40).
[11] *Ibid* (3.2.41).

propaganda was effective only when accompanied by physical force.[11]

Perhaps the propaganda department's greatest handicap was the failure of the allies to agree on a statement of war aims which the propagandists could use to support the 'divide and conquer' theme which Crossman thought could shorten the war. The essential point was, were the Nazis to blame for the war, or the whole German people? Whatever the facts, and there was no satisfactory way of apportioning the guilt, by far the most profitable theme, or so the propagandists believed, was that the Nazi Party had dragged an unwilling German people to war. However false the premise on which this was based, most of the propagandists, who were concerned with the exploitation of words and ideas rather than with the dissemination of the truth, would have made much of it in the hope that many would oppose the Nazis, encouraged by the belief that they would have their reward when peace came.

The advantages of appealing to good Germans were recognized in the early days of Electra House. Propaganda was addressed 'to those German circles from whom a new and peaceful government is most likely to be formed'; but Campbell Stuart admitted that no one really knew who 'those German circles' were. The early leaflets, and Chamberlain's speeches, were addressed 'to the German people' with whom Britain had no quarrel; but the totalitarian organization of the Nazi Party went deep into the German people. Stuart saw no real distinction between the régime and the people. 'We absolve the German people of responsibility both for their government and for this war, and at the same time to incite them against the régime which we say *is* responsible for the war. We try, in other words, to infuse into them a responsibility for their future, when we admit that they have no responsibility for the present or past'. The French in their propaganda made no distinction between the German people and the régime. Stuart now had it in mind that the divergent themes of the two countries should be reconciled. The French would have to accept that the Germans might be offered the chance of redemption; and the British would have to accept that the German people was as yet unredeemed. If it became clear that the German nation was at one with its war-mongering régime it could expect little mercy; but if some Germans were ready to live peaceably with their neighbours they would be told that they would be dealt with justly and generously.[12]

A neutral who left Germany in November 1939 had no doubt about the line that British propaganda should take. He considered that the tone of British leaflets showed that the propagandists had failed to understand the German mind. The one argument they should never use was that there was a distinction between the German people and its

---

[12] FO 898/195 (20.12.39).

leaders. For twenty years the implications of the Treaty of Versailles had been hammered into every German child. In the first war too the allies had been against the régime, and not the people – and look what had happened. In short, 'the confetti war is not going to break a single position'.[13] Next month an Italian said that no one would believe Britain's claim that she was not fighting the German people when she said in the same breath that the blockade would soon force them to submit.[14] A member of the Foreign Service who was interned in Germany in the early part of the war and who later joined PWE was convinced that it would be impossible to drive a wedge between the people and the Nazi Party. He wrote in November 1941, after his return to Britain: '. . . there are certainly many Germans both free and in prison who object to Nazi methods, and these people may have been more vocal in time of peace; but on the showing of sixteen months' internment in Germany at war, I can only express the conviction that Nazism is the quintessence of Germanism, the deification of Force for Force's sake. Until the German soldier's faith in his leaders has been shattered by defeat in the field, and until the German civilian's faith in the soldier has been shattered by the same defeat I for one will dare make no distinction between the Nazi Party and the rest'.[15]

In the absence of a clear line from the War Cabinet on this key issue the propagandists had to make their own minds up; and while the majority favoured a soft line with Germans hostile to the régime, there was no unanimity. In February 1940 it was argued that all Germans knew quite well what their leaders were up to, and by their silence acquiesced in their crimes. Propaganda themes for Germany should include the threat of the dismemberment of the Reich and the confiscation of the private possessions of the individual.[16] Again, 'in every tone and manner we should insist relentlessly upon the war guilt of Germany. This also implies the war guilt of the Nazi Party, and thus of each individual German who did not vote against the Nazi régime. Thus the present European disaster is in no small measure the responsibility of each individual German . . . When the political German isn't bullying he is often whining. After the last war he went round Europe whining that "he had not known" and that "he had been misled". Let it be made clear that no whining will avail after this war'.[17]

Dallas Brooks, however, took the opposite view. In April 1940 he said that failing an outstanding military success (of which there was no sign) 'the best propaganda material for the present time' would be a concrete statement of allied war aims, the purpose of which would be

[13] FO 898/462 (11.39).
[14] *Ibid* (6.12.39).
[15] FO 898/37 (7.11.41).
[16] FO 898/1 (4.2.40).
[17] *Ibid* (August 1940).

to assure the German people that Britain's objective was not to crush them.[18] No such statement was forthcoming, however, and the lack of it continued to be a handicap. In May 1941 a PWE directive for the BBC said that the theme of war aims was all right for Empire programmes, but it must be used with the greatest caution to enemy countries. In the absence of a policy declaration by the government broadcasters could say no more than that the primary British war aim was the defence of freedom in Europe and the Commonwealth.

In July 1941 Crossman tried again to get a clear ruling on the line to be taken with the German people. Should they be expressly excluded from the list of peoples whom an allied victory would liberate? And could the sentence in a recent speech by the Prime Minister 'Any man or state who fights against Nazism will have our aid: any man or state who marches with Hitler is our foe' be used in propaganda to Germany to apply to Germans who fought against the régime? Crossman had no doubt about the right answer. The German people should be given the benefit of this dispensation; and he went so far as to suggest that the Prime Minister or Foreign Secretary should develop the point in a public statement.[19] Four months later when PWE came under fire for the quality of its propaganda to Germany Crossman told Bruce Lockhart that the government was to blame for failing to define its post-war policy for Germany. Worse, the attitude of Ministers varied. Some viewed the German people as potential allies. Others warned that a long period of discipline would be needed after the war to cure them of National Socialism. It was therefore quite impossible to evolve a satisfactory theme on this vital subject. Should PWE broadcast messages of hope, or retribution?[20]

The Minister of Economic Warfare was not prepared to decide one way or the other. He said: 'I hope and believe that when the time comes, even though we may not kill, we shall not strive officiously to keep alive, a German unity'. In any case, he thought it unlikely that Britain would be able to preserve the Germans from the fury of those nations whom they had brutally oppressed and tortured. Propaganda themes should therefore avoid both definite threats of dismemberment and definite undertakings that this process would not occur. There was no objection to hints that the longer they went on fighting the more frightful would be their collapse, and the more difficult it would be for the Western democracies to organize their economic salvation. 'We should therefore appeal to their instinctive feelings of "doom" or ineluctable fate, culminating in a "Gotterdämmerung". This is a familiar idea to the Germans. We should harp incessantly on the theme that the

[18] FO 898/4 (3.4.40).
[19] FO 898/9 (7.7.41).
[20] FO 898/183 (3.11.41).

greater Germany's conquests the more certain her ultimate downfall and the more appalling her ultimate crash'.[21]

On the whole, the statesmen – perhaps one should say the politicians – were to be of no help to the propagandists. They had to have their pound of flesh, perhaps because many of the electorate, especially in the United States, would have been outraged by something that would have been seen as kowtowing to the enemy. When Eisenhower, with the support of the British Chiefs of Staff, suggested in 1943 that the theme of peace with honour might be put across to the Italians to facilitate the first allied landings in Italy, Roosevelt and Churchill were very quick to throw the idea out. They knew better than the soldiers – and the propagandists.[22] It seems conceivable that even if it had been conclusively demonstrated to the British and later to the American leaders that a soft line with Germany would shorten the war, the desire to punish would have prevailed – regardless of the extra cost in allied lives.

The only positive theme that PWE could offer to Germany was hope for a new European order; but so long as the objective was unconditional surrender, and the subsequent treatment of a conquered Germany in the way which the Nazis would have treated a conquered Britain there was no chance of persuading Germans to help to create a liberal new Europe. PWE had to concentrate on attacking the Nazi new order, and to wait hopefully – but in vain – for the government to spell out long-term intentions which would support the theme they favoured.[23]

Themes for the occupied countries had, of course, to be quite different from those provided for Germany and the satellites; and they were tailored as far as possible to cater for the particular needs of the country as assessed by PWE. At the beginning of May 1941, for example, it was known that even those Frenchmen who were well-disposed to Britain (a minority) were beginning to lose faith in her chances of victory because of the reverses she had suffered in mainland Greece, Crete and North Africa. Propaganda to France began to stress that time was on Britain's side. The Germans' success, which could not be denied, was due to the mechanization of their forces, but thanks to the vast industrial resources of the British Empire and the United States Britain would soon be able to match the Germans' armour. All the time the power of the RAF was growing steadily.

Subordinate themes were designed to encourage French hatred of Germany. They included references to the diversion to Germany of food and raw materials from the French colonies, which showed that the British blockade was fully justified; the Germans' design on the French colonial empire; their manipulation of France's finances, which was likely to lead to inflation; their efforts to force French workers to

[21] INF 1/895 (6.12.41).
[22] See Chapter 8, 'Operation Husky'.
[23] FO 898/3, ff. 76-80 (2.9.40).

go to Germany, which revealed how serious their labour position was. To counter the theme of 'the gentle German' which the Nazis were putting over in occupied France, much was made of German brutality. Prominence was given to statements by General de Gaulle, and to topics which it was believed would reduce collaboration. Britain's military reverses were reported with complete frankness and no effort was made to hide the gravity of her situation. This honesty in adversity much impressed the BBC's French audience, and went some way to restore French confidence in Britain – which had been seriously shaken by Vichy and German propaganda that the British troops had left the French in the lurch at the time of Dunkirk.[24]

White propaganda themes were constructed by the PWE regional staff within the broad guidance provided by the Executive, and having regard to their own ideas as to how their listeners would react to them. Black themes were arrived at by an entirely different process. They had of course the same ultimate objective of all propaganda – facilitating the defeat of the enemy – but they did not necessarily derive from white propaganda themes. They might include themes which would have served no useful purpose, or might even have been positively damaging had they been used in open broadcasts. They were developed simply from the propagandists' assessments of the probable reaction in Germany or elsewhere in Europe to a particular type of black programme.

The clandestine radio stations were the artistic creations of some of the more lively minds of the propaganda department, who, Pygmalion-like, gave personalities to the products of their imaginations in the hope that they would mould the thought of their listening audience. That at least was the theory. When two new German freedom stations were proposed in September 1940, one was to rely principally on patriotic themes which would reveal it as being loyal to 'the true Germany', which was not the Germany of the Nazis. The other was to appear to be run by socialists using a 'revolutionary Europe' theme aimed at German industrial workers. The blueprint provided that the latter must not be communist, social democratic, or trade unionist, but should give a lead to groups of industrial and black-coated workers who had lost faith in the older political parties, and were disappointed by the National Socialist régime. It would adopt a European rather than an international outlook, and while its designers hoped that its transmissions would eventually conform to those of stations broadcasting black propaganda in other languages; to start off it would be self-contained. Both the new stations would of course pretend to be located in Germany, an illusion which the medium of radio made possible.[25]

When the personality of a secret radio station had been finally built

---

[24] FO 898/9, pp. 2-3 (7.5.41).
[25] *Ibid* p. 218 (6.9.40).

up and approved by PWE, it was left to the regional directorate concerned to develop or modify its themes in the light of their own knowledge of conditions in the country where the station was supposedly located, advice from the country's nationals attached to the station, and such listener reaction as they were able to pick up through SOE, the Secret Service, or other sources.

A monitoring report on F 4 (Radio Gaulle) – PWE monitored all the freedom stations to ensure that their output, however outrageous, was keeping step with agreed policy – reveals some of the topics put across to France by one freedom station in 1941–42. Half the station's transmission time was devoted to hatred of the German people – rather than of the Nazi régime. News items were used to illustrate how France was being exploited by the occupying power, but in the course of 1942 these were overshadowed by atrocity stories dealing with the brutality of the Germans throughout occupied Europe. The Vichy régime was constantly attacked, and it was hinted that if only the French fleet and colonial empire had remained on the side of the allies the Germans might already have been defeated. Listeners were encouraged to continue the struggle against the Nazis, but not to resist actively – to kill Germans would merely lead to unpleasant reprisals. There was no reason, however, why German morale should not be attacked. Examples were given of how this was being done in other countries. Collaborators should be demonstrated against – 'T' for 'Traitor' might be painted on their front doors. Occasional violence against them would not come amiss, but there should be no attempt at concerted action just yet. When the station had attracted a large audience 'alors nous nous mettrons vraiment au travail'.[26]

The performance of this secret station illustrates the point made above that a theme that was right for one medium might be wrong for another. The propaganda department would not have tolerated an identifiable British theme for Germany which blamed the whole German people for the war; but there was no objection to the use of that theme by an ostensibly French station to arouse hatred of all Germans by reviving memories of 1870 and 1914 – for which the Nazis could hardly be held responsible.

Another secret station (LF) broadcast news items to Germany which were chosen to induce listeners to do something which might have unpleasant consequences. For example, it announced that details of air raid casualties could be obtained from the local police stations, in the hope that the overburdened staff there would be inundated with enquiries from anxious relatives. This ploy had a secondary benefit. It seemed likely that the police would soon tumble to the fact that the enquirers must all have been listening illegally to an enemy radio station, which

[26] FO 898/60 (25.8–11.10.41; 5.1–23.2.42).

would mean more trouble all round. It was also described how the SS regularly took certain named sleeping pills, in the hope that listeners would start using the same pills to help them to sleep through air raids. The pills were habit-forming, and with luck many would become addicted to them. A dramatic account was broadcast of the disaster which had befallen the young family of a woman who had been fire-watching in the factory where she worked – to encourage others to shirk their fire-watching duties. These items illustrate one aspect of the art of black radio. There was no direct attempt to order listeners to do anything. It was left to them to ponder the news story they had just heard, and then of their own volition to do whatever the propagandists had planned they should do.[27]

Station LF occasionally introduced pornographic themes to catch the attention of listeners. It might describe in breath-taking detail the eccentricities of a Hitler Youth Leader. The greatest exponent of the pornographic theme, however, was 'Gustav Siegfried Eins' (GS 1). This was a purely subversive station, its purpose being to stimulate distrust of the Nazis, the SS, and the administration in general. It also sought by rumour and insinuation to stir up friction between the Nazi Party and the Wehrmacht.[28]

The speaker, and brains behind GS 1, was Mr Sefton Delmer. He was *Der Chef*, purporting to be a tough patriotic Prussian who was disgusted by the corruption and depravity flourishing under the Nazi régime. 'With fiery indignation he denounces the abuses of those in authority and by so doing gives the impression to his listeners that under their present régime the country is going to the dogs'. *Der Chef's* patriotism and pornography drew a very large listening audience. American diplomats in Berlin – while Germany and the United States were still at peace – had no doubt that it was the pornographic element in the transmissions that attracted the listeners.

An unsolicited tribute from an SOE colleague in Sweden (who believed that GS 1 was operating in Germany) shows how successful the station was. He claimed that more people listened to it than to any other station in the Third Reich. It ensured a regular audience by providing more or less open pornography, which attracted people already coarsened by the Nazi way of life. At first the political standpoint of the station had been uncertain, but it was now clear that it was against the SS and the Nazi Party. It demanded that the Wehrmacht should be allowed to run the war on its own, which strengthened the

---

[27] FO 898/60 (17.6.41).
[28] GS1 attracted the attention of the German High Command quite early on. A report of 22 October 1941 referred to its 'quite unusually wicked hate propaganda'. It was following the line of British propagandists in the first war. Then they tried to set the army against the Kaiser: now it was the army against the Party. (FO 898/532, 22.10.41).

belief that it must be financed by the Wehrmacht. GS 1 was destroying faith in the Nazis, awakening a critical sense among the German people, and affording them the necessary material to judge their leaders – 'scandal, corruption, tyranny of the Nazi bigwigs, crying injustices'. So far, however, a real rallying point was lacking. The political credo of *Der Chef* was too vague; and if the army was behind the station it showed up their political ineptitude. GS 1 might begin to have political significance one day; and if it did come to a split between the Nazi Party and the Wehrmacht, the station would have an important part to play.

The SOE agent concluded his report with a survey of recent transmissions. *Der Chef* had been accusing the Party of refusing to bomb London, so that Berlin might be left unmolested. The present attacks on England were useless. One must aim at the heart, which meant London. So far the bombings had not so much as tickled Churchill under the armpits. German propaganda was killing the spirit of attack by propagating the war of defence. It had created terror of a British invasion. In the west the Wehrmacht trained only for defence, so much so that the officers went to the brothels complete with loaded revolvers, and the soldiers to the latrines with loaded rifles. London must be bombed – reduced to a heap of ashes! The Reich owed it to the dead and the living in Cologne, Lübeck, and Rostock.[29]

One of GS 1's broadcasts was the subject of a curious ministerial fuss. A Russian drew the attention of Sir Stafford Cripps, then British Ambassador in Moscow, to one of *Der Chef's* more lurid performances in which the star had been a depraved German admiral who had been spared nothing. Cripps, being Cripps, was naturally very upset. He passed the complaint on to the Foreign Office, expressing his own disgust. Eden was equally shocked. Bruce Lockhart, who seldom disagreed with his political masters, agreed that the broadcast went too far.

It was left to Leeper to defend *Der Chef*. He told Delmer that a complaint had been received about his German admiral's orgy, without revealing the source; and then he penned an odd minute to Bruce Lockhart:

> I am not pornographic myself. It bores me and for that reason disgusts me perhaps less than it would otherwise, provided I can see a purpose behind it in the fight against 'evil things'. If in the Secret Service we were to be too squeamish, the Secret Service could not operate. We all know that women are used by them for purposes which we would not like our women to be used, but we say nothing. Has any protest ever been made? This is war with the gloves off, and when I was asked to deal with black propaganda I did not try to

[29] FO 898/60 (18.6.42).
[30] Head of the Secret Service.

restrain my people more than 'C'[30] would restrain his, because if you are told to fight you must fight all out. I am not conscious that it has depraved me. I dislike the baser sides of human life as much as Sir Stafford Cripps does, but in this case moral indignation does not seem to be called for.

Delmer is a rare artist and a good fellow. I want to back him in the work he is doing . . .

Leeper went on to justify the pornographic and sadistic themes which were common form in the transmission from GS 1. They were not intended to win the Germans to the allied side, but to set German against German, and thereby to weaken the German war machine:

There is a sadism in the German nature quite alien to the British nature, and German listeners are very far from being revolted by the sadistic content of some of these broadcasts. The official in charge of the station has an intimate understanding of German psychology and has only introduced coarse realism into the broadcasts in so far as it is likely to assist the subversive purpose of the station.

He claimed that there was evidence to prove that the station was succeeding in its purpose; and also that if the nature of its themes had to be changed there would be no point in carrying it on. No secret subversive organization could operate successfully if it had to work to the moral standards to which the British government worked in its public business.[31]

GS 1 was allowed to carry on. Its themes were toned down a little. Even so, it is unlikely that they would have won the unqualified approval of Austerity Cripps.

Freedom stations were occasionally used for long-term political purposes, rather than for propaganda to win the war. At the beginning of 1942 it was mooted that a Greek station should be set up to counteract the performance of a genuine freedom station in Greece which was attacking the exiled government. It would have no connection with that government, and would (as was usual with the freedom stations) be kept secret from it. Its political stand would start with an agitation by an association of Greeks critical of the government for its failure to say anything explicit about the constitutional position – an important issue in Greece. It would support SOE's considerable interests in the country.[32] The British Foreign Office would seek to extract helpful statements on the constitutional position from the Greek government and the King, which PWE would use to increase the prestige of the station, and help it to contribute to 'the weary task of "selling" the Greek government to the Greek people'.

The provision of staff to man the station was a problem. They had to

[31] FO 898/60 (16.6.42).
[32] FO 898/54 (6.1.42).

be drawn from the Greek community in Britain – fewer than 4,000 – with a minimum of five years' residence in the country. Other conditions were that candidates must come from mainland Greece – Islanders need not apply – and they must be neither violent militarists nor members of the Greek shipping fraternity in Britain.[33]

The effect of this station on the military position of the Germans can only have been marginal. No doubt every little helped – every German committed in Greece meant one fewer to oppose the allied invasion of western Europe; but in percentage terms the effect was negligible. A secret radio station was being established to exert an influence on Greece for Britain's post-war purposes, on the assumption that after the war Britain would continue to be a world power, a forgiveable error of judgement on the part of the propaganda department.

After Hitler became embroiled with Russia in June 1941 it was possible for the propaganda department to be less on the defensive. The earlier themes were still used, but the tone became more aggressive. Instead of suggesting that Britain could not lose the war, the line became more that Germany had not the slightest chance of winning. The attack on Hitler's leadership was intensified. He had foolishly become involved in a major war against Russia; his assumption of command of the forces in December 1941 was evidence of trouble between him and his military advisers; and his new judicial powers – taken in April 1942 – implied a tightening of Nazi domestic tyranny. The propagandists felt that it was almost enough at this stage of the war to let events speak for themselves; and the credibility which the BBC now enjoyed meant that for many Germans and the vast majority of the people in the occupied countries the British version of the news was accepted as the truth.

It was at this period more than any other that PWE felt the handicap of the government's unforthcoming attitude about the post-war position of Germany. In a review made at the beginning of 1944 PWE complained that instead of saying what might be done for good Germans, they had to concentrate on the fate of the bad – the Nazi leaders, the SS, and the war criminals generally. But they suffered from the lack of definition of a war criminal, and felt that they should have had some help from the government on this. 'What was required was the authority of Mr Eden or Mr Churchill, and on points of detail it was not always there'. The Executive went as far as they dared with the theme that there would be room for a reconstituted Germany in a peaceful and prosperous Europe, realizing that they were skating on very thin ice. They believed that they had discovered two golden rules. First, Britain's short-term aims – the punishment of war criminals and the disarmament of Germany – should in propaganda be clearly differentiated from the long-term objective of the establishment of a peaceful Europe; and

[33] FO 898/54 (12.1.42).

second, the long-term objective should be presented in terms of Britain's self-interest, and not of her benevolence towards a defeated enemy.[34]

Religion presented the propagandists with some difficulty. It was believed that the use of religious themes could be effective; but it was also felt that to exploit religion was not playing the game. The Religious Broadcasting Department of the BBC proposed in January 1940 that religious services should be broadcast to Germany, on religious and not political grounds; but it was pointed out that to start broadcasting religious services in the middle of a war must inevitably seem to be using religion for political purposes. In any case, transmission time was limited and the propagandists considered that it would be impossible to accommodate all the eligible denominations. The Corporation, with Department's EH's full approval, turned down the proposal on the ground that it would be politically unwise.[35]

It was impossible, however, to avoid all deference to religion, and the propagandists drew up their own guidelines. Hitler must not be referred to as 'anti-Christ' since the term was too wide to be applied exclusively to one man. Nor should National Socialism be called a pagan faith. The greatest minds of classical antiquity had been pagan. Goethe, in no derogatory sense, could be called a pagan. To show that National Socialism was a false religion the term normally applied to it should be *'Ersatzreligion'*.[36]

Many were prepared to put forward themes which used religion. Even the Joint Intelligence Committee produced a paper in November 1940 claiming that Germany was ripe for a religious revival. There was a good chance that her new god Hitler, who had promised peace by Christmas, would shortly be discredited. 'A human god can only last while his reputation for wisdom and infallibility is unspoiled. Mahomet lasted, but Napoleon fell'. Younger people should be encouraged to doubt the truth of the Nazi creed; the older should be reminded of the peace and happiness of the true faith; and all should be given hope of better things if they returned to the belief of their forefathers.[37]

The different approach of the churchmen and propagandists continued for the greater part of the war. The former argued that leaflets should occasionally contain a religious motif, but PWE would not have it. They did, however, accept that the Christian German, who had been able to fight for his country in 1914–1918 with a clear conscience, was no longer in that happy position; and both the professional churchmen and propagandists agreed that this disability could properly be referred to in broadcasts.[38]

---

[34] FO 898/101 (23.2.44).
[35] FO 898/177 (31.1, 12.2, 28.3.40).
[36] *Ibid* (30.7.40).
[37] *Ibid* (18.11.40).

There was more heart-searching in 1941. A BBC memorandum sought to analyse the Executive's performance in the sphere of religious propaganda, and concluded that the whole question had been approached in the wrong way 'as if there can be a clear distinction between our religion and our politics'. Those who objected to the exploitation of religion for political propaganda, and those who protested that there was no question of exploiting religion, were equally wrong. The author of this paper went on to ask: 'Presuming that we really do believe that our cause is that of civilization, and that this is not just a war of rival imperialisms, how can we speak of purely religious propaganda?' If British propaganda was to have any force at all, and be more than a hobby for pseudo-intellectuals, it would have to include a convincing projection of the part played by Christianity in British history, in national life at the present, and the part it would play in the future. Those who objected to the inclusion of a religious motif in propaganda merely revealed that they did not understand the problem. It was not a question of broadcasting religious services, although that might be desirable on important national occasions. 'If we wish to convey to fellow Christians in Europe that we are in communion with them we must allow religion to take its natural and fitting place as part of our everyday propaganda, and let it be read between the lines instead of ostentatiously presented as a phenomenon of wartime England.'[39]

Although the dislike of broadcasting religious services, except on very special occasions, persisted throughout the war, there were regular religious programmes, including a programme for Germany which dealt with religious and spiritual issues every Sunday. The main target was the catholic community which was reckoned to be the only organized body that had any chance of disturbing the régime.[40] There was also a black French radio station 'Radio Catholique' operated by a catholic priest. It aimed at the parish priests in France, and tried to put across the theme that if they were not themselves prepared actively to encourage resistance at least they should not stand in the way of any of their parishioners who *were* willing to have a go at the occupying forces.

The propaganda department continued to exploit its themes to the people of Germany and occupied Europe right up to VE-Day, but their relative importance diminished. Transmission time, and indeed PWE's capacity, were limited; and as D-Day approached there was ever-increasing need to communicate with the resistance movements in Europe about the contribution they would be expected to make when the invasion was launched. This work, which was more of a military operation than political warfare (although it did include the despatch of propaganda material) began in 1942 and intensified year by year. In

---

[38] FO 898/177 (21.12.40, 20.1.41).
[39] *Ibid* (5.5.44).
[40] *Ibid* (24.6, 26.7.41).

Belgium alone there were nearly twenty agents at the receiving end of these arrangements, each with his or her elaborate network of cells and radio transmitters. In June 1944, for example, the agent Samoyede III had nine contacts: Nelly, Tybalt, Gaby, Socrates, Cesar II, Otello II, Mandrill III, the *armée secrète*, and the *Mouvement National Belge*.[41] PWE and SOE were closely associated in this work, and although relations between the two organizations had improved, there was once again some friction between them. SOE were accused of originating messages relating to PWE responsibilities without consulting the propagandists, and of altering messages to PWE agents before they were transmitted.[42]

The increasing part played by the Americans also had its effect on the allies' propaganda as a whole. British propaganda always had at least half an eye on post-war Europe, which did not much interest their American colleagues; but with the approach of D-Day it became more and more necessary to concentrate on propaganda designed to weaken the resistance of front-line troops, and propaganda, or rather instruction, to the civilian populations of Europe as to how they might facilitate the invasion and the eventual advance of the allied armies. A great deal of effort also went into the arrangements for dropping supplies and their collection at secret rendezvous. The day of the carefully-worked-out intellectual theme which PWE hoped would change the thinking of whole populations had gone. What mattered now was the unsubtle and unequivocal order to enemy troops and to civilians, reinforced by equally unsubtle and unequivocal high explosive.

[41] FO 898/84 (8.6.44).
[42] *Ibid* (13.1.44).

6
Delivering the goods: Propaganda techniques

The written word
From the very first day of the war the RAF was saddled with the chore of dropping propaganda leaflets. To begin with it was their sole operational effort – apart from reconnaissance – a great anti-climax to young men eagerly looking forward to doing the job for which they had been trained. For most of them a single bomb spoke louder than volumes of leaflets. Later on, leaflet dropping became an unpopular optional extra on bombing missions.

It was not only that the men had little faith in the postal service wished on them. The distribution of leaflets from the air was more dangerous than the layman might think. Bombers were designed to carry bombs in their bomb bay and heavy loads of paper stowed elsewhere affected the trim of the aircraft. At the most dangerous moments of the flight at least two men had to abandon their normal duties to throw out the leaflets. Air Chief Marshal Harris, head of Bomber Command, pointed out that when night fighters were in the vicinity the tail gunner could not safely be spared for ten seconds, let alone ten minutes.[1] Bundles caught in the slipstream might damage the aircraft by striking projecting parts of the tail unit, or by removing radio aerials. Loose leaflets blown about inside could foul the controls. Considerable physical effort was needed to dispose of a load, especially at the altitude from which leaflets were dropped; and the fact that they *were* dropped from a great height – 8,000 feet at night and 20,000 by day – meant that it was virtually impossible to land them anywhere near a given target.[2] It is not surprising that most of the early air crews had little enthusiasm for an activity which they deemed unprofitable.

Towards the end of 1941 there was an attempt to persuade them that leaflets were in fact a useful part of the war effort. PWE prepared a booklet – propaganda for propaganda – to show the RAF what had been achieved to date. It was warmly welcomed by the Secretary of State for Air (Sir Archibald Sinclair) but had a less enthusiastic

---

[1] FO 898/458 (30.4.42).
[2] *Ibid* (31.12.43).

welcome from air crews. Some agreed that it would bring about a more helpful attitude, others claimed that it was a waste of time, money and paper. PWE also conducted a campaign by letter and personal visits to convince RAF Commands, Groups, and the 62 Stations from which leaflets were carried of the importance of increasing dissemination. They concluded that as a result most airmen became more sympathetic towards this branch of political warfare.[3]

Soon afterwards the RAF suddenly found itself temporarily a willing partner in the dissemination of leaflets.[4] It was becoming more hazardous to carry out bombing missions because of the increased efficiency of enemy radar-assisted anti-aircraft fire. Radar, however, could be confused by relatively small quantities of metal foil sheets dropped by the raiding aircraft. To conceal the true purpose of these sheets as long as possible it was suggested that they should be disguised as leaflets. This may seem to reveal singular optimism, since the Germans were bound to tumble to the stratagem immediately; but PWE was gratified to find that the RAF was actually soliciting its services and willingly co-operated in the production of metal propaganda leaflets.

In some cases the message was printed direct on the metal foil (usually aluminium, about six inches by four) but when pictures were included the metal was laminated with paper. A typical example of the latter was a photograph of a badly-blitzed area of Coventry, balanced by one of equally heavy air-raid damage in Lübeck. Each was accompanied by a caption taken from a German newspaper: in the case of Coventry, from the *Völkischer Beobachter* of 25 December 1940 'Our bombers dropped more than 5 million kilos of high explosive bombs on Coventry . . . the town is in ruins'; and in the case of Lübeck from the *Hamburger Fremdenblatt* of 2 April 1942 'The British radio described on Wednesday evening the attack of the British airmen on Lübeck as "one of the most devastating attacks of the war". We can assure England that we shall not forget'. On the back of the leaflet, in bold scarlet lettering which stood out against the shining silver of the foil, was the sentence: 'Above all, I will see to it that the enemy will not be able to drop any bombs. Goering, 9.ix.39'.[5]

On the whole, however, the partnership between the propaganda department and the RAF was uneasy. There was a wide gulf between what PWE thought was necessary and the actual volume of propaganda disseminated from aircraft. In 1941 distribution in France was still limited to the Operational Training Units of the RAF based on five stations in Britain. As a rule there was no more than a single sortie nightly from each station, and each aircraft carried only 8,000 to 24,000 leaflets, depending on the weight of the paper – a fraction of what PWE

[3] FO 898/458 (27.12.41).
[4] FO 898/459 (3.1.42).
[5] *Ibid.*

would have liked. It was accepted that the crews – especially at the beginning of their period of training and because they had to fly at night – would find it difficult to identify their targets. When the propagandists suggested in May 1941 that the OTUs should cover Holland and Belgium the idea was rejected by the Air Ministry on the ground that the concentration of German fighters was much heavier in those countries than in France.[6]

The position was even less satisfactory in Germany. There leaflets were carried by the operational units of Bomber Command, but only when it suited them. There was no guarantee that PWE would want to aim at the same targets as the bombing aircraft, and even if they did Bomber Command's objectives might be changed at the eleventh hour. This made it impossible to launch a leaflet attack at short notice, say to profit from a sudden change in the political situation, and that for the most part leaflets carried by bombing aircraft had to be 'timeless' – that is to say, general statements of a standard propaganda theme rather than attempts to strike while some particular iron was hot.

Norway and Denmark were covered by Coastal Command, which found it much easier to meet PWE's requirements than did Bomber Command and the OTUs. Most of the time they were engaged in reconnaissance, and the scattering of leaflets did not interfere with more important bombing missions. It was however difficult for them to penetrate inland, especially in the short northern summer nights; but leaflets dropped high enough offshore could be driven far inland by favourable winds.[7]

The Air Ministry were willing enough to help, but there was always some rider attached to their promises. At the beginning of 1942 they agreed to 'a more active policy' in leaflet dropping. Bomber Command would carry the maximum number on every operation, the effort of the OTUs would be increased, freshman crews in operational squadrons would be told off to carry leaflets when conditions were unsuitable for bombing – but the last word about what would actually be done always rested with the RAF.[8]

It was mooted in April 1942 that a PWE squadron should be established to serve France, Holland, and Belgium, leaving Germany to Bomber Command and Scandinavia to Coastal Command.[9] The case was based partly on a comparison between the number of leaflets being dropped and the minimum considered essential. The disparity is striking.

In the occupied zone of France in the first four months of 1942 the average weekly dissemination of leaflets – mainly the newspaper *Le*

[6] FO 898/458 (May 1941).
[7] FO 898/450 (11.7.42).
[8] FO 898/12 (15.1.42).
[9] FO 898/458 (2, 14.4.42).

Courrier de l'Air – was just under 400,000, compared with the 2 million that PWE wanted. In the unoccupied zone the target was 2.5 million, but not a single leaflet had been dropped. The same order of disparity ruled in other countries: Belgium 76,000 against a target of 1 million; Holland 51,000 against 1 million; Norway 74,000 against 625,000; Denmark 3,500 against 250,000; and Italy, Poland and Czechoslovakia together 8,500 against 250,000. The overall target was 20 million a week, compared with the mere 2 million actually being dropped.[10]

Eden believed that PWE should have their own aircraft. It was important to keep Europe well-informed by means of newspapers dropped from the air; and he suggested that he might take the matter up with the Defence Committee.[11] The RAF, however, with the backing of the Air Ministry, resisted a proposal that PWE should have their own squadron, arguing that the propagandists would get better service from the whole of Bomber Command than from a single squadron of their own which because of weather and technical difficulties could not possibly operate every day of the week.

PWE accepted defeat, perhaps too easily, and advised the Foreign Secretary not to tackle the Defence Committee. They consoled themselves with the thought that the Air Staff and Bomber Command were now fully alive to their needs and that the continuing expansion of the RAF would automatically increase the capacity available for carrying leaflets.[12]

The propagandists became impossibly frustrated when the United States Air Force arrived in Britain and began to operate in the field of psychological warfare on a scale which threw into unhappy relief the inadequacy of the British attack. PWE's inability to plan ahead, because of the uncertainty of Bomber Command's programme, virtually ruled out topical 'tactical' leaflets prepared at short notice to take advantage of a particular event. It also meant holding very large stocks of timeless 'strategic' leaflets at all the many stations from which Bomber Command operated, to ensure that propaganda material was available whenever there was a chance to carry it. This tied up huge quantities of scarce paper. In any case, the preparation of copy, printing, approval by the Air Ministry, and transport to Bomber Command took so long that even if there had been unlimited paper for 'tactical' leaflets they would have lost much of their topicality before they could be dropped.

Whereas PWE were condemned to do everything wrong when it came to delivering leaflets, their American professional brothers were enabled to play this part of the game of psychological warfare exactly right, both from the political and military point of view. Their more efficient production and dissemination allowed them to operate effectively at a

[10] FO 898/458 (5, 21.5.42).
[11] *Ibid* (21.5.42).
[12] *Ibid* (9.6.42).

time when PWE knew that they were failing to play a full part in the joint allied war effort. Indeed, they felt that they were handicapping the Americans, who would have made better use of some of the paper devoted to British leaflets. It was the American practice to carry out special leaflet raids at special times against special targets. Their performance – largely thanks to the leaflet bomb with which they ensured accurate delivery – was vastly superior and ought to be copied. This was Dallas Brooks's assessment in the middle of 1944.[13]

A squadron of Flying Fortresses was devoted exclusively to disseminating leaflets where and when those responsible for propaganda directed. This meant, for example, that they could mount a propaganda attack on the occupied countries, whereas PWE could operate only where Bomber Command chose to go over enemy countries. In addition, two aircraft in each of the six operational squadrons of the 8th USAAF accompanied their comrades on bombing missions carrying nothing but leaflets, which unlike Bomber Command they would drop on nominated points en route to their main target.[14] The Americans' contribution far outweighed that of the RAF. Just after D-Day it was estimated that the total leaflet-carrying capacity of the allies was 300 million a month, of which the leaflet squadron of the USAAF accounted for 160 million. The balance of 140 million was shared between the bombing missions of the American Air Force and the RAF.[15] It is surprising that PWE did not press harder for their own aircraft; and indeed Eden may have sensed a feeling of defeatism. In April 1942 he wrote: 'I hope PWE will not hesitate to come to me if they are held up in their work. Its priority now ranks high, and I am sure that the War Cabinet would take that view. But those who don't ask can't get'.[16]

Although they were never allocated a squadron for their exclusive use PWE were occasionally allowed a few aircraft for special purposes. In April 1942 the Foreign Secretary asked the Prime Minister to agree to the use of half a dozen aircraft to drop leaflets on unoccupied France. Churchill replied: 'This is most important. Pray make proposals'. In the event, aircraft of the Special Operations Executive, which did have its own squadrons, and which could do their normal job – the landing of agents and supplies – only round about the full moon, were employed.[17] In July of the following year Eden asked for twelve aircraft to drop copies of the Prime Minister's latest speech over Northern Italy and this was also agreed.[18]

SOE were in the habit of carrying small quantities of leaflets on their

[13] FO 898/458 (16.7.44).
[14] *Ibid* (11.8.44).
[15] *Ibid* (23.6.42).
[16] *Ibid* (26.4.42).
[17] PREM 3/365/11 ff. 1049–50.
[18] *Ibid* f. 1028.

operational flights as a form of cover; but the Germans tumbled to this ruse and began to associate the dropping of leaflets with the delivery of arms. SOE then suggested that the leaflets carried in their planes ('any old leaflet is good enough') should be dropped at least a hundred miles from the place where a 'Reception Committee' was waiting to receive arms or to welcome an agent; but by this time (May 1944) there were so many points at which arms and agents were being dropped that it was feared that the 'camouflage' leaflets might accidentally lead the Germans to some other Reception Committee.[19]

It seems strange that the idea of a leaflet bomb did not occur to someone in PWE, in the crews of Bomber Command who had the unpopular task of shovelling leaflets into the hostile German night, or in the research establishments which were aware of the problems. In April 1942 Harris did promise to introduce an automatic leaflet release,[20] but when two months later PWE suggested that the RAF might adopt some form of container the idea did not appeal to him. He told Bracken that while the Ministry of Aircraft Production were experimenting with metal containers in the wings of aircraft he was sure that they would be too small to be of any use even if they were technically feasible, which he doubted. A possible alternative was to carry containers inside the aircraft, but that would reduce the bomb load, which he deprecated. He promised to do all he could to help, but made it clear that it would be precious little. His attitude was that of a kindly father telling his son to go away and play while he got on with the job that really mattered.[21]

It was left to the Americans to perfect an efficient device. Like Bomber Command they had found that the simplest method of dissemination was far from satisfactory. They started by carrying leaflets in boxes attached to the sides of Flying Fortresses – 300,000 leaflets per aircraft – but when they were released at 25,000 feet they landed anything from 50 to 100 miles from the target area. Next they tried dropping the leaflets in bundles which would be burst open at about 2,000 feet above the target by a device triggered off by the atmospheric pressure at that height. This was little better, since the bundles simply disintegrated in the slipstream of the aircraft. After four months' experience of these unsatisfactory methods it was decided that a foolproof leaflet bomb was essential.

The first version was a laminated paper cylinder, normally used to contain the 'Amiable Cluster Chemical Bomb', which was packed with leaflets and blown open by a fuse after it had dropped the requisite distance. In July 1944 the paper cylinder was replaced by one of metal,[22]

[19] FO 898/25 (15, 27.5.44).
[20] FO 898/458 (26.4.42).
[21] *Ibid* (26.4.42; 3, 9.6.42).
[22] FO 898/459 (17.10.42).

and in the same month PWE asked the RAF to start using it.[23] As usual Bomber Command dragged their heels. They claimed that thanks to their lower operational height their aircraft were achieving a satisfactory scatter of leaflets; and also that thanks to improved navigational equipment the Operational Training Units were now able to get much better results.[24] Once again PWE humbly accepted the RAF's answer; but Bruce Lockhart returned to the charge at the end of 1944, when Bomber Command agreed to drop 8 leaflet bombs a day – later increased to 400 a month.[25] These, however, would be dropped only in areas under bomb attack; and since at this time the whole of the strategic bombing offensive was concentrated on the Ruhr it meant that PWE's propaganda was not carried very deep into Germany. PWE deprecated the decision not to make trips to nominated targets, but sadly concluded that there was no point in fighting it at that stage in the war.[26]

The leaflet-carrying balloon – simple, ingenious, and cheap (it cost about £5), but not very effective – was developed from the smaller balloon used to scatter propaganda behind the German lines in 1918, when balloons were pressed into service because of German threats against leaflet-scattering British airmen.[27]

The initial trials of this curious weapon, designed by the Balloon Development Establishment, took place in the grounds of the National Physical Laboratory in March 1939. It carried a wooden framework on which the leaflets were hung, half in a single bundle in the middle, and the other half in eight smaller bundles round the sides. They were attached to the framework by a string threaded through holes punched in them, and then through a slow-burning wick which cut the strings at hourly intervals.

The smaller bundles doubled as ballast, and as each was released it compensated for the loss of hydrogen and returned the balloon to its operational height of 10,000 feet. When it had covered its maximum distance after a flight of eight to nine hours the central half-load was released at one fell swoop. The slow wick then ignited a fast-burning fuse which exploded the gas and destroyed the balloon.[28] That, at least, was the theory. It did not always work in practice.

An improved 'M' balloon was introduced in May 1940. It was eight feet in diameter, with a payload of 10 pounds, later increased to 12 (equivalent to 3,000 to 4,000 leaflets) and the fabric was now rubberized.[29] In April 1942 the Ministry of Aircraft Production was forced

[23] FO 898/458 (27.11.42).
[24] *Ibid*
[25] *Ibid* (3, 10.11.44).
[26] *Ibid* (7.11.44).
[27] Sir Campbell Stuart, *Secrets of Crewe House*, pp. 54–5.
[28] AIR 2/131.
[29] AIR 2/4189/40A.

by the British defeat in the Far East to scrutinize very carefully all uses of rubber. They decided that PWE's balloons, which took a ton a day, had a low priority.[30] PWE agreed to stop their service to Germany, Belgium and Holland; but they thought it essential to send balloons to unoccupied France, which could not be reached by any other means. They had 21,000 balloons in stock and in course of manufacture, enough to continue the service to unoccupied France until the Operational Training Units of the RAF could begin to deliver to this territory. Further manufacture was stopped[31] and was not resumed until the end of 1943 when the rubberized fabric was replaced with a fabric treated with nitro-cellulose.[32] This development came in the nick of time, for it had been virtually decided to close down No 1 (and only) 'M' Balloon Unit.[33]

The first operational release by the Balloon Unit was made on 30 September 1939 in the depths of the French countryside near Nancy. It was reckoned that Electra House leaflet No 156 was carried 100 miles into Germany somewhere between Frankfurt and Strasburg. The early 'M' balloons proved to be unsatisfactory, however. The wicks which released the leaflets disintegrated in wet weather, and the workmanship generally was poor.[34]

At the end of October the Unit (at this time 26-strong: it was later doubled in size) moved to a more congenial location at Sarrebourg about 70 miles from the German border, where it remained until May 1940 when the German advance forced it to destroy its stocks of leaflets (code-name nickels) and withdraw to England.[35] It was re-established at Manston by the middle of July, but on 24 August direct hits by two heavy German bombs destroyed all its equipment and it had to move again – to Birchington, and finally to Walmer. It returned to the continent – to Blankenburg – in January 1945, and was finally wound up in May.[36]

The Unit could launch up to 200 balloons a night. Daylight launching was ruled out since the stream of balloons would lead enemy reconnaissance planes to its source. They were always at the mercy of the weather. The wind had to blow strongly in the right direction, but not in gusts which would upset their equilibrium. A study of performance in the first half of 1941 shows just how unreliable they were. Only 65 per cent reached France, 60 per cent Germany, 25 per cent Belgium, and not a

---

[30] FO 898/458 (4.4.42).
[31] *Ibid* (2.5, 15.7.42).
[32] AIR 13/132 (27.9.44).
[33] AIR 2/4190/278A.
[34] AIR 2/4189 (1.10.39).
[35] *Ibid* 46A.
[36] AIR 2/4191.

single balloon reached Holland.³⁷ On average the wind was favourable on only seven nights in a month.³⁸

It was impossible to pinpoint a given objective. At the end of its journey the balloon might find itself over sparsely-populated territory and waste its sweetness on the desert air. Even if it finished up near a town the odds were heavily against the leaflets falling in the middle of it. A 30 mph wind – needed to carry the balloon a reasonable distance – would seize the released leaflets and carry them on a further twenty miles, finally scattering them over a circle eight miles in diameter. Freak weather could make nonsense of the most careful meteorological calculations. In April 1941 a number of balloons with part of a consignment of 50,000 copies of the weekly newspaper *Le Courrier de l'Air* destined for France actually got as far as Bilbao in Spain before they discharged their loads.³⁹ Others reached Sweden and Switzerland.⁴⁰

There was no limit to the puckish behaviour of the balloons. A flight found itself travelling the wrong way and landed in Henley-on-Thames and the RAF Station at Benson. The latter pointed out to the Air Ministry that they were the Royal, not the German Air Force. It was therefore unnecessary for the 'M' Balloon Unit to invite them to break away from the Nazi Party; but if there was any doubt about their loyalty they would be happy to give satisfaction. Let 'M' Balloon Unit choose their weapons. The Air Ministry said in reply that while there was little doubt about their loyalty – or that of the burgesses of Henley – further proof in the shape of a gift of eggs, butter and cream would not come amiss.⁴¹

An encounter with the Royal Navy was less light-hearted. At the end of June 1944 a stray flight occasioned alarm if not despondency among ships of the Royal Navy in the Phoenix anchorage at Littlestone in Kent. The balloons were presumed to be a new type of German parachute mine, and the naval vessels were ordered to weigh anchor and shoot them down. The Air Ministry answered the formal protest of the Lords Commissioners of the Admiralty by pointing out that these balloons had been regularly launched for the last four years – a fact which Their Lordships ought to have known; and they observed (privately) that on this occasion the Royal Navy must have been overcome by the excitements of D-Day and after.⁴²

The following tables show the number and destination of leaflets carried by RAF aircraft and balloons between 1939 and 1945. British aircraft took some American leaflets and vice versa, but broadly these

---

[37] AIR 2/4190/134A.
[38] AIR 2/4189/96A.
[39] *Ibid* 222A.
[40] *Ibid* 168A.
[41] *Ibid* 276A.
[42] AIR 2/4190/380A.

figures represent British leaflets disseminated by the British:

Year	Leaflets (nearest million)		
	Aircraft	Balloons	Total
1939	31	3	34
1940	70	6	76
1941	58	27	85
1942	291	23	314
1943	548	25	573
1944	346	10	356
1945	73	1	74
Total	1,417	95	1,512

Destination	Leaflets (nearest million)		
	Aircraft	Balloons	Total
Germany	709	48	757
France	644	32	676
Belgium	11	9	20
Italy	19	nil	19
Holland	10	6	16
Norway	11	nil	11
Denmark	6	nil	6
Czechoslovakia	4	nil	4
Poland	1	nil	1
Miscellaneous	2	nil	2
Total	1,417	95	1,512 [43]

Not every leaflet reached its destination. Of those that did perhaps one in ten was picked up.[44] Not every one that was picked up was read. Not every reader reacted in the way the propagandists had planned.

Leaflets were also delivered, in relatively small quantities, by SOE agents acting on behalf of PWE. For example, 5,000 copies of a leaflet commemorating the death of Lauro de Bosis in 1931, with the text of the anti-Mussolini message he dropped over Rome, were distributed by hand in Italy;[45] but the scope for this method of delivery in Italy was limited.[46] Elsewhere in Europe leaflets were disseminated by SOE agents, some of whom had been specially selected because of their aptitude for propaganda work, and had been trained at Woburn. These agents had their own ideas about the nature of the leaflets they handled, and it was accepted by PWE that successful distribution depended on the provision of material in which the agents had confidence. This was

[43] FO 898/457.
[44] FO 898/349 (6.5.43).
[45] FO 898/60 (18.9.42).
[46] Ibid (3.3.43).

particularly important in the case of material which had to be pushed through letter boxes, which was reckoned to be the most dangerous form of delivery. In the middle of 1942 SOE were prepared to carry out this postal service in North West, West and South West Germany, but only if they were satisfied that the game was worth the candle. At this time they had just lost an agent who had been caught on a postal delivery.[47]

Leaflets for hand distribution might be dropped in containers carried in SOE aircraft, or the copy of a leaflet approved in London could be provided for reproduction by means of a clandestine press in the country concerned. A message reproduced in this way and passed from hand to hand could reach many people.

When the enemy were within range of allied guns it was possible to fire bundles of leaflets at the front line troops – a method used in North Africa and Italy. The British used the 25 pounder gun and the Americans the 105 mm.[48] As a rule the messages suggested that the only sensible thing to do was to surrender. It was not an efficient means of distribution, but at least the messages were delivered to the people for whom they were intended. It was claimed that the firing of leaflets into the monastery at Monte Cassino demanding that the Germans should surrender rather than allow the monastery to be destroyed were of great value to the allied cause in that it created sympathy and understanding on the part of the Italians. But artillery leaflets were often partially burned when they arrived. The troops remained in their foxholes by day, and when darkness fell it was difficult to locate leaflets, and to read them.[49] For this reason it was considered better to drop them behind the enemy lines where they could be read in comfort by the supply troops 'who are teachers, bank clerks, and cooks' and who would deliver them to the front line troops. [50] Mobile printing presses were first used in Tunisia.[51]

Paper propaganda varied enormously – from messages printed on a single sheet to forty-eight-page miniature magazines photographically reduced to the smallest legible size, which the finder could slip in his pocket to read at leisure in the comparative safety of his home, from miniature novels (eg *Last Train from Berlin*) to ingenious trick folders which when opened showed an animated Hitler in unflattering situations.[52] In the first winter of the war only three or four leaflets (ie 'issues') a week were dropped, all of them in German; but by the middle of 1943 there were between 50 and 60 publications each month, printed on specially thin paper, some in full colour. In 1940 it was a noteworthy

---

[47] FO 898/62 (18.6.42).
[48] WO 219/4751 (10.10.44).
[49] FO 898/469 (8.3.44).
[50] *Ibid* (27.4.44).
[51] WO 219/4751 (10.10.44).
[52] FO 898/63 Pt. 1 (13.12.42).

event if a million leaflets were dropped in a single night. In November 1942 (at the time of the allied landings in North Africa) 23 million were dropped in two nights in selected areas of France.[53]

Ideally leaflets combined the function of a poster – to catch the eye and convey a simple message to the passer-by afraid to pick them up – and a news sheet packed with information and argument for the benefit of those who risked pocketing them. Leaflets dropped on the occupied territories had a better chance of being read. They varied according to PWE's assessment of the needs of the recipient country. A wide variety was prepared for France, for example, since it was a large country in which regional tastes differed; but in the smaller more densely populated Holland and Belgium the main attack was through a single magazine.[54]

A typical programme for France included *Le Courrier de l'Air*, an illustrated supplement, and *La Revue de la Presse Libre* (extracts from the world's press for more serious readers and for the use of clandestine newspapers) – all issued weekly. *Le Courrier Illustré*, full of striking photographs, and *La Revue du Monde Libre*, were monthlies. Straightforward leaflets included 'impact leaflets' dealing in a popular way with a single striking idea, 'timeless leaflets' about a major topic, for example the war at sea, which could be dropped whenever the opportunity offered, and 'operational leaflets', usually warnings about air raids prepared in conjunction with the Air Ministry.[55] There were also leaflets advertising the clandestine radio stations: *'Ecoutez tous les soirs Radio Patrie'*, for example, and *'Ecoutez les voix connues de la Radio Inconnue. Tous les jours (avec la permission de la Gestapo et de la Police).'*

One of the propaganda department's experts on German affairs claimed that leaflets played a much bigger part in German political life than in British, and that the Germans were the world's greatest masters of propaganda – as anyone who had observed a German election must admit. A central argument, idea, aim, or objective could be conveyed in a flash. 'The layout, the type, the quality of the paper are all important'. In his view none of the early British leaflets would have been passed by any German political party. They reflected the mentality of the advertising agent, whereas they should be animated by the spirit of combat, not salesmanship. Even the language was suspect in his opinion; and some of the leaflets were contemptible.[56] These strictures show how difficult it was.

Black leaflets included a whole range of ingenious forgeries: posters purporting to be of German origin, designed to mislead the occupying troops, which were distributed by SOE agents; currency notes; clothing coupons; ration cards; postage stamps, usually imitations of the real

[53] FO 898/63 (15.11.42).
[54] FO 898/3 pp. 224–8 (April 1940); 898/458 (31.3.43).
[55] FO 898/181 or 458 (31.3.43).
[56] *Ibid* (3.41).

thing, but including one issue with Himmler's head to support the rumour that he was angling to become Führer; official notices headed 'Heil Himmler!' for the same purpose; fake issues of the German army news sheet *Skorpion West* and *Nachrichten für die Truppe* (technically 'grey', most of their contents being truthful, to give credibility to a small proportion of ingenious falsehood); imitations of German health instruction booklets with subtle deviations from the original text to persuade the reader that negligible symptoms were deadly serious; a booklet entitled *The hundred best ways to cook fish* which was concerned not with *haute cuisine* but with high explosive; handbooks for the use of would-be malingering soldiers, which also had innocent titles on the outside cover, for example, *Pocket Guide to Oslo*, *The Soldier's Songbook*, *Ballistic Tables*. Some of these contained phonetic instructions in ten languages to enable the soldier to ask in every occupied country from Finland to Greece for the things needed to fake the malady of his choice. (The picture of monolingual German troops queueing up in chemists' shops to enunciate carefully in phonetic Dutch, Bulgarian or Greek 'I require a small quantity of oil of turpentine' is almost as unbelievable as that of British businessmen in Germany preaching the gospel according to Chamberlain as envisaged by the Foreign Secretary in 1938; but there is on record at least one success in this field).[57]

Other choice items in PWE's library of deception were: *Le Rôle des Vitamines dans la Lutte contre la Sous-Alimentation*, which contained instructions how to avoid conscription for war work in Germany; *Chansons de la BBC*, anti-German songs set to popular French airs, and illustrated in colour; and *Ce qu'une jeune fille bien élevée doit savoir*, which was an account of the first year of the German occupation of France. A 1944 German pocket diary had a quotation for each month of the year from speeches by Hitler and other German leaders: for example, Hitler's claim '1941 will see the greatest victory in our history'. Postal franking stamps were supplied with the names of many French towns, the date being replaced with the words, 'Vive la RAF'. There was also a plain red circle stamp for surreptitious use on letters and documents to hint at the existence of a non-existent underground organization. Cigarette paper packets contained instead beautifully-printed well-illustrated sabotage instructions. One of the more telling stickers produced by PWE, which was black in origin rather than in content, simply bore the date '1918' in bold figures. The letter headings of German government departments, leading business firms and banks were imitated so that agents might be provided with correspondence to help to establish their bona fides. The great bulk of this material was produced by 'Mr Howe's unit'.[58]

An issue of *Skorpion West* included the announcement 'Troops are

[57] See page 172 below.
[58] See p. 35 above.

authorized to liquidate commanders who order them to retreat: but the privilege must not be abused'. This sort of thing not only put dangerous ideas into the minds of the rank and file, but undermined confidence in the genuine news sheet, so good was the forgery. Troops were ordered to ignore copies of the paper which they found lying on the ground, and to read only those which were handed out by their units. The same technique was used for *Nachrichten für die Truppe,* which included items favourable to the Nazi cause, and unfavourable to the allies' in such exaggerated terms that they were hardly credible and led the reader to question the honesty of the paper as a whole.[59]

PWE went to great lengths to produce exact imitations of the German documents that were to be dropped. It would be a waste of effort if ration cards, for example, were so obviously false that the finder would spot them as forgeries. Paper, ink, type face, layout – all had to be as near the real thing as possible. The ultimate goal was to produce something that would deceive the authorities, which was not easy. When it was suspected that quantities of black documents were circulating in a particular district, Gauleiters would be provided with detailed scientific comparisons of the forgery and the item it imitated. For example in September 1943 the minute differences between false travel and meal coupons ('*Reise und Gaststattenmarken*') dropped by the RAF and the real thing were set out in a police circular. Whereas the paper of the genuine article was pure white, the forgery had a yellowish tinge, the perforations were more accurate, and the sheets were 2 mm narrower.[60] The purpose of these forgeries was of course to enable those who found them to acquire rationed goods above their entitlement, and thus to distort the rationing system and cause dissension.[61] It was, however, possible to be too clever. A proposal in 1944 that PWE should drop forged leave passes – in which the finder would have to do no more than fill in his name – was objected to by SOE whose agents were at this time relying heavily on such forgeries. It was feared that if they were dropped indiscriminately the Germans would be forced to take counter measures which might accidentally affect SOE agents.[62] In the final stages of the rout of the German forces, however, when the allies were carrying all before them, this objection became less valid, and forged leave passes and kindred documents were allowed to play their part in disintegrating the Wehrmacht.[63]

The spoken word
As Sir Stephen Tallents pointed out in 1938 radio enabled propa-

[59] FO 898/465 (9.12.44).
[60] *Ibid* (22.9.43).
[61] The success of this ploy is examined in Chapter 9.
[62] FO 898/24 (30.7.44).
[63] See Chapter 10.

gandists to speak to whole enemy populations.[64] Even if it did not give them the unlimited power claimed by D. E. Ritchie of the BBC, who made the 'Colonel Britton' V broadcasts to Europe,[65] there was no doubt that it was a medium of great importance suitable for both open and clandestine use.

The BBC's objective during the first years of the war, when the allies were on the defensive, was primarily to build the greatest possible audience in Europe, to retain its confidence during long periods of seeming disaster, and to sustain morale against the day when its audience could play an active part in throwing out the Germans. In the early days the Corporation did an admirable job in establishing the reliability of its news programmes. It was regarded by the vast majority of listeners not as an instrument of propaganda but as the purveyor of an objective news service run by people anxious to disseminate the truth, however unpalatable it might be on occasion to themselves. This of course made it a first-class instrument of propaganda.

It is true that during the period of the V broadcasts when 'Colonel Britton' was given his head in spite of the misgivings of PWE, the BBC found itself moving dangerously into the realms of loaded propaganda; but with the demise, or rather the execution of Colonel Britton, this tendency was corrected. The BBC thereafter devoted themselves exclusively to the broadcasting of honest news within the limits imposed by the need for security – with the minor exception that their programmes were occasionally broken into to send brief coded messages to resistance groups in Europe.

Honest open broadcasting nevertheless was an instrument of propaganda, and it was PWE's job to see that it was steered in the right direction. This was done principally through a Planning and Broadcasting Committee on which the BBC was represented. It met daily to carry out an inquest on earlier programmes, to discuss the general war situation and to decide how forthcoming broadcasts should be tailored.[66]

A PWE memorandum of November 1942 claims that at the first signs of effective resistance to the German war machine – which was taken to mean the RAF's success in the Battle of Britain and the Germans' failure in the Battle of Russia – broadcasting ceased to be passive and became belligerent. It began to prepare its audience to be active allies rather than grateful listeners. To accomplish this called for careful planning, a marshalling of facts to produce the required effect.[67] Thus even the BBC open broadcasts were slanted, or at least selective. Out of the daily volume of 'truthful' news a selection would be made of

[64] See Chapter 1.
[65] See Chapter 7, 'V'.
[66] FO 898/8.
[67] FO 898/101, p. 528 (2.11.42).

those items most favourable to the allies' objectives in Europe – sustaining the morale of the occupied countries, and attacking the morale of the Reich. Equally, talks and features would be as near as possible to the whole truth, but their subject matter would be chosen to help to achieve the same goals. There was close liaison between PWE and the BBC to ensure that the expertise of the propagandists was made available to the sections dealing with occupied Europe; and the weekly directives which PWE created for their own guidance were passed to the Corporation so that the 'natural' supply of news material could be suitably edited, and talks and features commissioned to support the line of the directives.[68]

Honesty was the best policy for the BBC. Dishonesty was the stock in trade of the secret radio stations. There were three sorts. Genuine freedom stations set up by patriots in their own countries; fake freedom stations operating in one country, but pretending to be in another; and 'freedom of action' stations, which did not try to create the illusion that they were necessarily in any particular area.[69]

PWE saw it as part of their job 'to stimulate or service' the genuine freedom stations, for which their ordinary leaflets provided useful copy. The men who operated them were the real heroes of underground radio. They could not remain safely in the same attic or cellar for any length of time, since sooner or later their signals would lead the Germans to them; and it was a hazardous task to move even their simple transmitters under the eyes of the enemy. Fake freedom stations would occasionally go off the air in mid-sentence to give listeners the impression that the Gestapo had just broken in. When the genuine freedom station was interrupted it was no act designed to hoodwink the listening audience.

In the case of the fake stations the first essential was to convince listeners that it was in their midst – 'that it is sharing the common difficulties and conditions with them, and that it is operating at great risk'. The authority of these stations depended on their success in creating the illusion of risk and locality, otherwise it was impossible to fire the imagination of listeners and persuade them to risk their lives in hostile acts. Those resistance groups which were not in direct touch with the British authorities were less likely to follow orders if they knew they came from the safety of the English countryside.

The 'freedom of action' station had to provide an illusion of authenticity rather than of locality. It had to appear to speak with the authority

---

[68] FO 898/101 (2.11.42).
[69] As time went on PWE's theory became more refined. At the end of 1942 it was claimed that there were two types of freedom station, Opposition, and Counterfeit. The former was subdivided into Representational, Co-operational, and Fictitious; the latter into Official and Unofficial. In practice secret stations could not be pigeon-holed with such precision. (FO 898/51, 15.11.43).

of a group or movement in the country which it was addressing. The actual location of the transmitter need never be specified – but care should be taken to avoid leaving the impression that it was in Britain, and therefore not the independent instrument of the movement it professed to serve, but rather of the self-interested British government. If it spoke for an underground movement it should appear to be underground, even in exile. The value of this type of station was that it could appear to know what was happening in the outside world (unlike the genuine and fake freedom stations which could know no more than what the German censorship passed and what it could pick up from foreign radio) and that it could give an impression of complete independence of any interest – except the movement it served.[70]

The British freedom stations were given the cover name Research Units (RU) and usually were identified by a letter denoting the country to which they broadcast in addition to a popular name. Thus the third freedom station in the series that broadcast to France was F3 (La France Catholique), Y1 the first to Yugoslavia. There were exceptions. Bulgaria was given the letter X, Belgium having already taken B; and the Italian stations were allocated W for Wop. At first the RUs used two shortwave transmitters near Woburn; but they were later supplemented by the high power medium wave station nicknamed 'Aspidistra'.[71]

The RUs worked quite independently of each other, and their personnel were housed separately under conditions of great security. Their only visitors were people with whom they could discuss their work, whose names had to be on an approved list; and they were not allowed to answer the door or use the telephone. Hotels, public houses, and even churches were out of bounds. The staff of La France Catholique were required to use a chapel converted from a bedroom in their own house.[72] Private phone calls were forbidden. If hospitable neighbours called to welcome the new arrivals to the neighbourhood they were given the cold shoulder and told that the newcomers were engaged in secret research work.[73]

There were good reasons for the segregation of the RU staffs. PWE wanted them to believe that each RU was unique and alone enjoyed the facilities provided by the British government to allow them to state their case to their fellow countrymen. Secondly, it was essential that each RU should have its own personality. Segregation precluded conscious or unconscious copying of ideas and techniques which might enable listeners to spot that stations were under the same management. This deception needed careful timing of the use of the specially-built studios in a nearby village where the recordings were made. The staff

[70] FO 898/101, p. 529 (2.11.42).
[71] FO 898/65 (8.4.43).
[72] FO 898/54 (8.5, 2.11.43).
[73] FO 898/51 (27.7.41).

of the numerous RUs must never meet each other, which meant that the cars taking them from Woburn to the studios and back again had to carry out a complicated series of shuttles, making use of the byways of Bedfordshire.

The system failed on at least one occasion. The Socialist F2 staff were recalled to the studios to remake a recording because an important piece of news had just broken, and found themselves in the next studio to the Gaullist F5 where thanks to the inadequate soundproofing they overheard the playback of the Gaullist programme. This was the first they knew of a rival French team. They were outraged by what they claimed to be yet another example of *'Perfide Albion'*, and offered their resignation in a body.[74]

Each team was under a British 'housemaster', a member of PWE's staff who had to ensure that his charges obeyed the very irksome rules. He supplied the team – usually four in number – with the intelligence material needed for their scripts, vetted them, and ensured that when the recording was made they followed the authorized version. As a rule transmissions were recorded, but when a major event demanded an immediate broadcast an RU could get special permission to transmit live, but only in the presence of the Regional Director whose territory was involved. The fact that the broadcasts were recorded meant that they could easily be repeated, and also that there was no danger that the speaker would try to put across something that did not have PWE approval – a real danger having regard to the widely divergent political views of the broadcasters.[75]

The transmission of recorded material led to occasional difficulty. The illusion that a situation was in Germany was shattered if the record arm jumped or the needle ghosted (that is, transmitted background speech from one groove in the record while another groove was playing) since it was axiomatic that the genuine freedom station could not possess elaborate recording gear. These accidents did happen from time to time. Output was independently monitored to assess the performance of the station, and to ensure that it was not departing from the general directives.[76]

The first RUs started broadcasting in May 1940, and by the end of 1942 they were transmitting to 12 countries.[77] Transmissions were made as near as possible to the optimum time for each country, and an official ensured that all the stations were given a fair share of the available transmission time. At first the speakers merely purported to represent opposition groups working against enemy or quisling régimes, but

[74] FO 898/51 (4.10.45)). ('It was recognized that in the long run it would be impossible to keep all knowledge from one group of what the others were doing'. FO 898/1 [31.8.40]).
[75] FO 898/54 (30.5.41).
[76] FO 898/51 (27.10.41).

experience suggested that a more subtle approach might produce better results. GS 1 was a good example of the new method. The pseudo-patriot *Der Chef* denounced corruption, and incidentally showed how easily and profitably government regulations could be disobeyed. Another German RU picked up on a *Hellschreiber* (teleprinter) the transmissions of *Deutsches Nachrichtenbüro,* the German news agency, and was thus able to transmit to Germany local news even before it was printed in the German press. Most of the time this station *(Wehrmachtsender)* broadcast the news faithfully, but every now and then an item would be doctored, or a fictitious item slipped in. The station was modelled on the genuine German *Wehrmachtsenders* – for example, it recorded and played back their musical programmes – and was an ideal medium for spreading false rumours. Under an agreement with General Sikorski a third German RU broadcast news which was used by Polish agents in Poland and Germany to feed pseudo-German clandestine newspapers.

At this time – December 1942 – there were two French RUs. *Radio Inconnue,* 'violent and vulgar in its abuse of Germans and quislings'; and *Radio Patrie,* a combined PWE/SOE venture which was in direct touch with an underground organization in France. Belgium had two stations, one French and one Flemish, which PWE ran in close collaboration with the Belgian *Sureté*. There was a single Dutch station, the existence of which had been revealed to the Dutch government, which co-operated in running it. Its target was the Nazi movement in Holland. The other countries aimed at were Italy, Norway, Denmark, Poland, Romania, Hungary, Bulgaria, Greece, and Yugoslavia. For the last there were three separate stations, addressing the Serbs, Croats, and Slovenes.[78]

There were of course innumerable freedom stations throughout Europe, genuine and fictitious. They included, for example, Radio Himalaya, broadcasting from Italy and pretending to be in northern India; the New British Broadcasting Station (German, with 'Loch Lomond' as its call sign); *Voix Chrétienne* (Russian, aimed at France); Arab Nation Radio (Italy); and more than 170 others.

There was two-way traffic in black radio, as there was in all the propaganda media, and occasionally it got through even PWE's defences, which should have been stronger than those of the British public at large. A news item broadcast by the New British Broadcasting Station in July 1940 said that Major General F. G. Beaumont Nesbitt believed that Sir Campbell Stuart had wittingly or unwittingly allowed the minutes of a certain meeting to be seen by certain unauthorized persons – gross negligence which amounted to high treason. The item went on

---

[77] FO 898/61 (17.12.42).
[78] *Ibid.*

D*

to say that Beaumont Nesbitt was furious with the New British Broadcasting Station and would see to it that 'the blundering jackasses at the Yard and the BBC' were taken off the job of silencing the station. 'Winding up with a magnificent peroration spiced with military and Indian oaths' he said he would handle the matter himself through MI 5.

When the transcript of this item, which had been passed by MI 5 and the BBC, was circulated by the BBC monitoring service PWE were upset and complained bitterly, thereby acknowledging a minor triumph for German black radio. Stephen Tallents defended the BBC by pointing out that these reports had to be circulated quickly if they were to be answered effectively, and that it would be quite impossible to consult everybody named in them. He added that he hoped that this explanation from 'the blundering jackasses at the BBC' would satisfy PWE.[79]

PWE's facilities for broadcasting to Europe were greatly increased when 'Aspidistra' came into operation in 1942. It was a 500-kilowatt medium wave transmitter buried under 30 feet of earth and concrete on the edge of Ashdown Forest near Crowborough in Sussex, with a decoy installation a mile away for the benefit of enemy aircraft.[80] A proposal to broadcast to Germany on German wavelengths had been put to the Prime Minister early in 1941 by the Minister of Economic Warfare. Dalton, as usual, waxed eloquent. Provision would be made for quick changes of wavelength 'so that this ethereal counter-battery may turn its fire from one enemy wavelength to another as occasion requires'; and again: 'the apparatus would create a raiding Dreadnought of the ether, firing broadsides at unpredictable times at unpredictable objectives of the enemy's radio propaganda'. Whatever he thought of Dalton's prose, Churchill liked the idea. He replied more economically: 'Proceed as you propose'.[81]

This was taken to be sufficient authority to buy the transmitter right away – in the United States – which led to the usual inter-Departmental wrangle. The Air Ministry were envious of the new transmitter which was more powerful than anything they controlled, and expressed misgiving about its effect on operational radio, the Wireless Telegraph Board should have been consulted, and so on. Churchill's interest in the ventured revived in September 1942. He minuted Bruce Lockhart: 'First, explain what advantages it gives us (8 lines). Secondly, report every three days the date it is expected to be ready to function'. On 24 September he asked: 'When will it be working full blast?'; and was told 15 October 1942.[82]

The new station greatly increased PWE's scope for black radio; but

[79] FO 898/6 (3.7.40).
[80] FO 898/63 (8.8.42).
[81] FO 898/43 (16, 17.5.41).
[82] *Ibid* (6, 24.9.42).

it did not really come into its own until near the end of the war. Elaborate schemes were suggested for it before this, but none of the more spectacular were adopted. For example, it was suggested in 1944 by the London Controlling Section and Deception Staffs (who were responsible for planning strategic deception) that PWE should use Aspidistra to broadcast to Germany a fake speech by Hitler which would leave listeners in no doubt that he was finally certifiable. The plan was named Operation *Cuckoo* (very aptly, observed the PWE expert who poured cold water on it, implying that it was the sponsors of the scheme rather than Hitler who were certifiable). If Hitler was removed many Germans would be more willing to follow the sane leaders who remained. PWE would no longer be able to maintain that Hitler was ruthlessly sacrificing German lives simply to keep the Nazi Party in power. The BBC could not be used to substantiate the deception since it would mean coupling white with black to an extent that would prejudice the BBC's reputation for telling the truth.[83] So Operation *Cuckoo* was dropped, and Aspidistra carried PWE's normal programmes until it was used for the *Intruder* broadcasts in the last months of the war.[84]

It was of course essential for the secret radio stations to remain secret. Otherwise the average German would derive comfort listening to what were established to be British lies, and the patriot in an occupied country might resent the deception. (In fact, PWE believed that the few people in the occupied countries who did penetrate the secret of an RU were prepared to applaud the deception in the knowledge that it was all part of the allied war effort).

GS 1, the most successful secret station of all, was put at risk at the end of 1941 by a former member of PWE who leaked the truth about it to the *National Review*. A paragraph printed in that paper was picked up by the Germans who made fun of *Der Chef*, the character which Sefton Delmer assumed in his broadcasts, in the weekly *Das Reich*:

> The Chief is speaking! The broadcasts all started with this sentence. Then a Scottish comedian, disguised as a landsknecht, came to the microphone, stuck his good old halberd into some piece of obscenity as perverse as possible, flourished it in the air to demonstrate its juiciness, and then with a vicious plunge, thrust it into the very heart of the German party and home politics . . .

Delmer naturally felt bitter that his work should be thus sabotaged by a former colleague, but nothing was done, in spite of the gross breach of security. However, GS 1 came back on the air after a few weeks, and continued to make an impression on the German listener. Although

[83] FO 898/24 (7.6.41).
[84] See Chapter 8, 'Overlord'.

the authorities knew the station was a fake, they no longer called attention to its existence by making special efforts to stop people from listening to it.[85]

Black radio was supplemented by false rumours (colloquially 'whispers' or 'sibs'[86] to the propagandists) disseminated through the Secret Service and SOE agents. Few ordinary people can resist the temptation to pass on bad news, a human weakness on which the whispering campaign relied for much of its success. The agent who dropped a carefully-constructed rumour might have a hundred unwitting sub-agents working for him in a matter of days.[87]

The specification for the successful rumour was that it should be alarming enough to *have* to be passed on, and credible enough to conceal the fact that it was a fabrication. The impact of whispers varied enormously, according to the credulity of the listener and the ingenuity with which they were composed.

Earlier whispers were usually complicated and sometimes not entirely credible. The rumour that certain doctors had received instructions not to allow aged people in German hospitals to recover, in order to ease the rationing situation, was surely too far-fetched to succeed even in a country where the Jewish extermination camps were taken as a matter of course. This category of rumour, designed to create fear and uncertainty, included a suggestion that Britain had produced a new incendiary bomb, very small and with a long-delayed action. It was dropped in the usual way, and might lodge in pit-head gear, on oil tanks and gasholders, where it would ignite long after the all-clear had sounded. It was therefore necessary to search every foot of ground and roof after an air-raid, which wasted much productive time, and meant that factory workers were never sure what risks they were exposed to.[88]

Again, it was spread around that an eminent Jewish chemist, a refugee from Nazi persecution, had given the British government information that would endanger lives far from the fighting lines. He had carried from Germany details of many secret poison gas dumps which had been confirmed by RAF reconnaissance. These dumps could therefore be bombed at will, and thousands of tons of deadly poison gas would be released all over the country.

Other rumours were intended to start fears about health. Ships arriving in Denmark from the eastern Baltic had brought back a pig disease. This caused reluctance to eat bacon. Typhus was sweeping

[85] FO 898/60 (9.2, 14, 15.3.42).
[86] From the Latin *sibilare* meaning to hiss.
[87] FO 898/101 p. 530 (2.11.42).
[88] In fact, this was almost a description of the Braddock II device, production of which started in 1942 on Churchill's instructions (See Chapter 7). There was always the danger that the inventor of a whisper would hit on something true and secret. It was for the Service Departments to weed out fabricated rumours that came too near the truth.

westward from the destroyed cities of Poland. Inflation and financial collapse were just round the corner. The misdeeds of named individuals were noised abroad. Hatred of the SS was encouraged by rumours that they were given easy and safe jobs at home where they made free with the lonely wives and sweethearts of men away at the war. The morale of the occupation armies was attacked by whispers about the terrible effect of British air raids on their home towns. Rumours aimed at the German navy were spread along the north west coast of Germany where most naval men came from. U-boat crews were subjected to whispers about weaknesses in the construction of their craft and their poor chances of survival.[89]

The production and dissemination of rumours was highly sophisticated. An Underground Propaganda Committee, the existence of which was known only to a few, met weekly at Woburn to examine whispers put forward by the Joint Intelligence Committee, the Foreign Office, the Service Departments, and PWE Regional Directors, and to arrange for those which were approved to be put into their final shape. They would then be sent to the Secret Service and to SOE with suggestions as to where they would most effectively be disseminated. The departments which contributed whispers were required to watch for evidence of reactions so that their success could be evaluated.[90]

At first the output of rumours exceeded the capacity to disseminate them. In November 1940 the Secret Service said that they simply did not have enough agents to handle all the rumours supplied – but they refused to waive their rule, imposed in the interest of security, that a rumour handled by them must not be disseminated through any other channel.[91] About the same time the propaganda department complained that the means of distribution was unsatisfactory.[92] Dalton agreed; but he thought that the rumour-mongers were going for quantity rather than quality, and ordered that production should be cut by one-third.[93] The *Daily Mail* printed a story – based on a PWE broadcast – which confirmed the Minister's assessment. It suggested that some of the material put out by the propagandists was enough to make even a German laugh, in particular the news that 200 sharks had been sent from Australia to be released in the Channel as a defence against invasion.[94]

As a result of Dalton's comments whisper procedures were revised. The authors were instructed to pay closer attention to the general directives which governed the output of PWE as a whole;[95] and the load on the distribution channels was eased by giving the agents authority to

[89] PREM 3/365/11 ff. 1072-80 (16.9.40).
[90] FO 898/9, p. 251 (16.11.40).
[91] *Ibid* p. 244.
[92] *Ibid*, p. 241 (26.10.40).
[93] FO 898/70 (11.3.41).
[94] *Ibid* (30.4.41).
[95] *Ibid* (11.3.41).

create their own rumours without having to clear their proposals with London – so long as they confined themselves to 'low-grade bazaar-talk to counter immediate German sibs', and purely local scandal to discredit Axis sympathisers.[96]

Hitler's invasion of Russia opened up new fields for the rumour-mongers. They were encouraged to give the widest currency to stories about the horror of the winter campaign there. The themes on which they were instructed to concentrate included the intense cold and its effects, the ravages of disease, the impossibility of treating the wounded, the danger from wolves (perhaps this was aimed at timorous wives and sweethearts rather than the men at the front), and the training of vast fresh Russian armies for the spring offensive. The likelihood that epidemics would spread from the east was also to be enlarged upon. Typhus was the best bet, but bronchial pneumonia could be a good second. The citizens of the Third Reich should be urged to bake or boil all pork in order to avoid trichinosis; and it should be hinted that disease was striking most heavily in the Breslau area.[97]

Rumours about allied military plans – strategical whispers – were of considerable importance. They were mainly the concern of the strategic deception experts attached to the War Cabinet Office, and were designed for the ears of service chiefs, ministers and diplomats, but were occasionally handled by PWE, who also provided tactical rumours at the request of the services. In November 1941 the Admiralty badly needed whispers on the theme 'the passage to Libya is equivalent to a voyage into the jaws of death'. Because of the need for speed on this occasion PWE passed the theme direct to agents working in the Mediterranean area with instructions to manufacture and distribute their own inventions. This was followed up with supplementaries prepared in Britain:

> 'You do not see any seagulls now in the Mediterranean.
> They have all been killed by oil from sunken tankers'.
> 'British flame-throwing aircraft are patrolling the
> Libyan coast'.
> 'Thousands of Italians who were sent to reinforce
> Libya have been landed at Messina with terrible burns'.
> 'The Germans have refused the Italians' request for
> tannic acid for the treatment of soldiers burned in
> the great disaster off the Libyan coast.'[98]

Nothing was sacred to the rumour-mongers. They denied the Dambusters credit for their brilliant achievements in 1943, and attributed the destruction of the dams to an international organization of foreign

---

[96] FO 898/71 (4.12.41).
[97] *Ibid* (3.12.41).
[98] FO 898/69 (23.11.41).

workers in Germany who had carried out their first major sabotage operations. The RAF bombing raids were no more than camouflage to enable the saboteurs to do their job. It was likely that the resultant floods would infect all vegetable crops and grain. Dysentery would strike very quickly, to be followed by typhoid in about a fortnight.[99]

Any doubts about the energy, ingenuity, and macabre sense of black humour of the propagandists are dispelled by an examination of the huge volume of creative work they left behind. Something like ten thousand rumours were broadcast to Germany by the secret radio station G 9 alone. These were aimed at first at the general public, but more and more at the armed forces as the allies began to get the upper hand in the field. The whispers poured out by this station were cunningly blended with items of hard news which the listener could verify for himself; and he would find it almost impossible to sort the wheat from the chaff.

An idea of the flavour of these broadcasts may be gathered from a selection chosen from the many hundreds broadcast in October 1943 (when the civilians were still an important target) and in April 1945 (when the whisperers were mainly after the troops).

OCTOBER 1943

It is announced that 12 U-boats have been sunk and 18 are missing. [True]

In Hanau am Main the birth of an elephant has aroused excitement. 'Haruna' is known as the peace elephant because she had her first child in 1871 and her second in November 1918. [False]

Flak ceased firing in Kassel after 15 minutes as they have been short of ammunition since the last air raid. [False]

56 people in Frankfurt am Main have been admitted to hospital suffering from stomach trouble. Of these 23 have died from phosphorous poisoning. State officials have warned people not to drink water from the mains. [False]

60 aircraft took part in a retaliatory raid over England during the night. London had its worst raid for two years. [True]

There is to be an increase in the soap ration in front towns and reception camps. [False]

APRIL 1945

Most planes taking off from fields in the Heimat

[99] FO 898/69 (May 1943).

are simply not coming back any more. They are
probably landing on enemy-occupied German airfields. [False]

Now that the V-1 cannot be fired any more it is being
converted as quickly as possible into a one-man
plane. [False]

There was shooting between members of the *Freikorps*
'Adolf Hitler' and SS-men in Schwerin after Gauleiter
Hildebrandt's announcement that he is standing by the
Führer come what may. An hour later Hildebrandt had
disappeared. [False]

Himmler's brother-in-law Generalmajor Kokott gave
himself up to the British with the remains of his
Division. [True]

A small concentration camp close to the Swiss
frontier at Uberlingen am Bodensee is considered by
the Swiss authorities to be one of the most important
transit and cover stations enabling SS leaders to
cross the Swiss frontier under false names. The SS
leaders disguise themselves as concentration camp
inmates and cross the border as refugees. [False].[100]

[100] FO 898/72.

7
Special delivery

The peasants
The peasant population in Germany and the occupied countries – perhaps a third of the total – was big enough to merit the special attention of the propagandists; but before it could be profitably attacked it had as far as possible to be understood. This called for careful study. What sort of people were the peasants? What part did they play, willingly or unwillingly, in the German war effort? How could the weaknesses of German agrarian policy be exploited in the interests of the allies? The propaganda department devoted a great deal of effort to trying to answer these questions.

They believed that when they came to power the Nazis had made the most of rural discontent, blaming 'the Jewish urban outlook' for the economic difficulties of the countryside. Within the Nazi Party there was a genuine idealist movement summed up in the slogan *'Blut und Boden'* ('Blood and Soil') which preached that whereas the Nazis were passionately keen to foster the interests of the peasants, the British were content that their countryside should consist exclusively of unweeded fields and golf courses. The propaganda department concluded that the agrarian intellectuals had made little headway with the rural community. Nevertheless, the peasants were bound to the Nazi system; and they would probably turn out to be distrustful and unapproachable listeners. Therefore if broadcasts to them were to be successful they must have to do with their personal interest, which they valued above the interest of the state. They had less understanding of 'the higher things' than the middle classes; and on the farms, in contrast to the towns, the tone was set by the older people.[1]

The peasants' principal grievances were considered to be the crushing weight of the Nazi bureaucracy in the towns; the campaign to turn the farmer into a factory-hand working for the Party; the sacrifice of the long-term prosperity of the land in the interest of the war effort; and the transfer of farmers to work in the occupied countries. But before these presumed grievances could be exploited the listeners' confidence must be won by persuading them to believe that in Britain the land really was cared for, whatever the Nazis might suggest. This could be

[1] FO 898/331; 898/338 (25.11.40).

done by giving talks on farming problems, and publicizing the achievements of Britain in agricultural theory and practice.[2] It was accepted that the peasants must play a vital part in feeding Germany; and if they could be induced to worry about the dangers of inflation and shortage, it might lead them to hoard for their own use, and thus reduce the quantities of food available for industrial workers and the armed forces. They would have to be convinced that even if they did agree to sell produce to the authorities it would earn them nothing but worthless paper money; and that if they did not hoard they would go short since there would be nothing to buy in the open market. 'The most efficient Gestapo or Inspectorate' could not ensure that every single one of them delivered his quota.[3]

When the assault on the peasants was first launched in 1940 it was too late in the season to work out a sophisticated programme but it was considered worth while to do something since relatively little produce had been carried forward from the previous season, and the safety margin could not be great. Any interference with supplies might have serious consequences. There were three main objectives. First, German peasants must be discouraged as far as possible from delivering produce to the authorities. Second, to restrict winter sowing farmers should be persuaded that before long many of them would be transferred to one of the occupied countries. No farmer likes to sow a crop knowing that someone else will harvest it. Third, the grievances between the peasants and the ruling classes should be exploited. All this would be accomplished in broadcast talks and by the inclusion of suitable items in the regular news bulletins in German.[4]

The inquest on this programme of broadcasts, held in December 1940, concluded, perhaps a little uncritically, that it had been a success. Some talks – for example, 'My Village' and 'An English Farm' – were just what the German farmer liked to listen to. This may seem surprising. Others had failed because they were concerned with purely British agricultural questions. Others again had got into a muddle in their discussion of German climate, soil, and so on which the speakers had not understood.[5] However, the reaction to the broadcasts showed that they were having some effect. The Nazis told their listeners not to worry – they would continue to be fed. Any shortages were temporary, due to the British blockade, which would soon be ended. Thanks to the German blockade, things were much worse in Britain. The broadcasts were believed to be even more successful in the occupied countries where there was a more eager audience. People had been encouraged to buy all the food they could lay their hands on and store it rather than

[2] FO 898/333 (25.11.40).
[3] FO 898/331.
[4] FO 898/333 (19.8.40).
[5] FO 898/331 (4.12.40).

allow the Germans to strip the country. As a result the controlled press had warned people to buy no more than their immediate requirements.[6]

This experience was used in 1941 to develop a more-carefully planned campaign. Broadcasts were made at dawn, to catch the peasants before they went into the fields, when technical questions were discussed; and on Sunday afternoons when the peasants were resting from their labours they could listen to political discussions of interest to the agricultural community. These talks contained a good deal of criticism of the Nazi food authorities; and they also encouraged the peasant to put his own interests before those of the town dwellers. When spring came the farmers had no time for dawn listening, so a weekly half-hour programme was substituted. Also at this time there began a deliberate attempt to bring the peasants' programmes more into line with those aimed at the industrial workers.

If the hostility between town and country went too far peasants and industrial workers might dissipate their energies against each other when it would be far better for the allies if they were united against the Nazi régime. Therefore direct appeals to the peasants to look after their own interests at the expense of those of the town dwellers were now avoided. Instead reports of passive resistance among the farmers of Germany and the occupied countries were broadcast in the hope that listeners would follow suit. There were also invented rumours of imminent shortages of agricultural requirements (hemp and sacks, for example) and of the danger of using unusual types of fodder – a rare example of the use of BBC open broadcasting as a medium for black propaganda.

The summer programmes continued on much the same lines; but the German invasion of the agrarian Balkan countries gave them a new topicality, and at least in the opinion of those responsible for them, made them more effective.[7]

As time went on PWE's efforts to understand the mentality and circumstances of the peasant became more elaborate. In 1942 the proposition was advanced that whatever his nationality the peasant's first loyalty was to the land on which he lived and worked. He set little store by book learning, because he knew that books did not make crops grow or produce fat bullocks. He hated filling in forms and disclosing his business to government inspectors. Since he was shrewd to the point of cunning he would weigh carefully anything he listened to on the radio, or read. Nine peasants out of ten were agin the government and regarded with suspicion all marketing schemes, price control, and crop regulation. Even more important was the peasant's contempt for the town dweller. He had no desire to be a large-scale producer and fill the bellies of the urban population. All he wanted was to produce enough for his own

[6] FO 898/333.
[7] FO 898/338 (23.9.41).

wants, and a small surplus to enable him to buy the manufactured goods he needed.[8]

There was no doubt much truth in this, but such assessments were the work of one man, or at best a committee. They sought to compress into a few pages the emotions and aspirations of millions of people, or to arrive at a common denominator meaningful enough to point the way to themes which might be profitably adopted in a propaganda campaign; and even if the assessment was miraculously right it could lead different people to quite different sets of themes. The author of the memorandum drawn on above believed that the European peasant could be manipulated not only to further the allied war effort but as a potent force in the reorganization of the world after the war. 'International unity of the men and women of the land from the biggest landowner to the humblest peasant could be a powerful force for good; for it means international unity of the primary producers'. The expert – himself a farmer – was carried away by his own enthusiasm. His colleagues could not agree that the peasants should be encouraged to look after their own interests. The danger of setting country against town still loomed large; and the industrial workers were still potential allies.[9]

In the course of 1942 it became apparent that the Germans were themselves trying to drive a wedge between the farmers and the industrial workers in the occupied countries; and it was considered all the more important that British propaganda should convince the industrial and agricultural workers that it was in their common interest to bring about the downfall of the Nazi régime.[10] The objective was now to make the peasant worry about the future prosperity of his farm rather than to try to help himself at the expense of the town dweller. In theory the end result would be the same – a reduction in the output of food – but it would be achieved in a way less damaging to allied interests.

From now on the main propaganda themes concentrated on the encouragement of good husbandry which would lead to a short-term reduction in output. For example, the importance of using the right balance of fertilisers was stressed, in the knowledge that most farmers would find it difficult to get enough fertilisers in the right proportions. Since it would be a waste of time to use the wrong balance it would be more sensible to sow a smaller acreage fertilized with the right balance. Deep ploughing, which rapidly exhausted the soil when fertilisers were scarce, should be avoided in spite of the Nazis' wishes. In the case of potatoes, beet and turnips, which the authorities were requisitioning in ever-increasing quantities, the farmer should grow only enough for his own needs. He should concentrate only on crops which did not exhaust the soil. In particular he should avoid oil bearing plants, for which there

[8] FO 898/334 (4.2.42).
[9] *Ibid.*
[10] FO 898/331 (30.5.42).

was a very heavy demand, and which needed a great deal of labour, and exhausted the soil. The peasant should try to keep as many calves as possible in the interests of his post-war herds; but pig stocks could be run down since they could be rebuilt quickly. Crops damaged by frost – which were better than nothing so far as the requisitioning authorities were concerned – were not worth the labour of harvesting, and should be ploughed up.[11]

Later in the year it looked as if 'the peasant war' might be turning out well for the allies. A combination of circumstances was making food a major problem for the Germans. The winter of 1941/1942 had been the worst for half a century, the shortage of labour was becoming acute, and fertilisers and seed were very scarce. On top of this Germany had now to export grain to the occupied countries; and she had to import about 10 per cent of her requirements of meat and fat. Everywhere producers were becoming more unwilling to hand over their output. The rationing system was under great strain, and the death penalty could now be imposed for offences against it.

British propaganda spread discouragement and doubt among German farmers, and induced farm labourers in Germany (especially the foreigners who had been brought from the occupied countries) to produce little and to consume much. The occupied countries should be encouraged to keep as much of their own produce as they dared. The difficulties of the food authorities in German Europe should be aggravated, if possible without reducing the quantities of food available for domestic use in the friendly occupied countries. Finally, confidence in the reliability of the food rationing system and the self-discipline which was still restraining people from buying in the black market, should be attacked.[12]

All this would be achieved through a campaign in which both black and white propaganda played their parts. So far as white was concerned the BBC would continue with the 'steady but unobtrusive' reporting of news items, statistics and scientific facts – all carefully presented in a way which concealed the true objective. Great care would have to be taken to ensure that no item revealed ignorance of conditions in Europe; and once again the propagandists were reminded that they must say nothing to the peasants that would tend to turn the town dwellers against Britain. It was up to the individual PWE Regional Directorates in their broadcasts and leaflets to ensure that there was no disharmony between their efforts to influence food production and to exploit food scarcity. It would do no good if the listener was deviously encouraged to limit his output and then in the next breath reminded how near Europe was to starvation. Equally, no link must be allowed to appear between scarcity and the allied blockade. A great deal of blame could be attributed to the

[11] FO 898/331 (16.2, 18.4.42).
[12] *Ibid* (11.6.42).

labour shortage. The farmers had to go short because of the vast demands of the Wehrmacht and the factories.¹³

The black campaign was more vigorous. It demonstrated – mainly through leaflets and the clandestine broadcasts which were now going from Britain to the whole of enemy and enemy-occupied Europe – that the food distribution system was inefficient and corrupt, and that the free market was now being used by everybody. The savage sentences passed on ordinary people caught dealing in it were particularly scandalous, since the Party leaders patronized it freely, and nothing happened to *them*. Farmers were reminded that if they did not sell in the free market the Party officials through whose hands their produce passed would not hesitate to do so. The Nazis' price policy was breaking down, and to avoid the worst effects of inflation everybody should secure their own direct supplies of food. Reports from Germany that people were not getting their full rations were exploited; and it was pointed out that the total amount of food being distributed was being cleverly reduced by the simple device of transferring people from 'heavy workers' rations' to 'workers' rations', and from 'workers' rations' to ordinary rations. Other rationing points were that current rations were insufficient to give protection against disease – this was a good line in towns which had suffered from air raids; and that the rations were badly balanced and must be supplemented from the free market if people wanted to stay healthy. The growing danger of Germany's dependence on foreign agricultural labourers and prisoners of war was also put across whenever possible; and in areas where they were known to be in a majority they were encouraged by leaflets to engage in dumb insolence, and never to speak German.¹⁴

Guidance for the agricultural propagandists who prepared the radio scripts and leaflets was provided by PWE's Central Planning Committee which defined the general lines of policy within which the regional directorates had a reasonable degree of latitude. A study of the central planners' files suggests that they expended a quite extraordinary amount of effort on agricultural problems, seemingly in the hope that they might achieve perfection – whatever that might mean.

In retrospect it is doubtful whether the nature of the end product justified such meticulous care when speed was of the essence and the whole of PWE's staff was under great pressure. For example, a 'phase plan' for agricultural propaganda to Europe was approved on 17 August 1942, to be followed in quick succession by a draft plan of operational propaganda for land workers in German Europe (undated) ; a draft plan for action propaganda (also undated); a draft agricultural plan (30 September); a revision of the last (3 October); a new draft plan for action propaganda (9 October) – described by its principal author as 'a

¹³ FO 898/331 (11.6.42).
¹⁴ *Ibid.*

rather abstract sort of document, a skeleton which will be clothed with flesh and blood in the Working Plan'; preliminary notes for a working plan (15 October); a plan for action propaganda on agriculture (23 October) which was actually approved by the Director General.

The next step in this progress of the perfectionists would have been the drafting and redrafting – heaven knows how many times – of the Working Plan, which would have gone to the Regional Directors to be used as a basis for their own working plans. They would have used their own propagandist sixth sense, the intelligence reports fed to them day by day, and their intimate knowledge of their own region to fashion themes suitable for the country to which they were communicating. In fact, the Working Plan was not completed until 24 February 1943, by which date the Regional Directors, unable to wait any longer for general guidance, were already implementing their own plans. This incredible multiplicity of plans was only the tip of the administrative iceberg. Beneath the surface were committee meetings, discussions with the BBC, the Ministry of Economic Warfare and other government departments. The sum total of the administrative effort (which in this particular instance failed to produce the goods – a general Working Plan) was truly astonishing.

The individual regional plans show how objectives had to be varied from country to country. The German Regional Directorate listed as its main objectives the redirection of farming methods so as to hinder the German war effort; to stimulate illicit consumption; to encourage agricultural sabotage; and to disorganize transport. The French concentrated on criticizing German requisitions of grain and wine from France; and the difficulties facing French agriculture so long as large numbers of French peasants remained in German prisoner of war camps – difficulties which could be mitigated if workers were transferred from the towns to French farms rather than to German arms factories. The Italian region wanted to get the Italian people to think in terms of peace at any price in the course of 1943; and of the desperate situation which would arise for their agriculture as a result of the cutting off of phosphates from North Africa. Inflation had not yet hit Italy seriously, but its potential effect must be stressed. Belgians were to be told that the free market was black only if they traded with Germans; and their farmers were to be encouraged to feed all who were fleeing from the Germans – airmen, members of the resistance movement, and above all those who were trying to escape deportation to work in Germany. The Finns, who were short of food – most of which had to come from Germany – could be told that there were plans to feed European countries including Finland, as soon as the allied troops reached them. The only possible line in Norway was to urge workers through black channels to remain on the land so as to restrict the numbers of men available for work on the German fortifications. Danish farmers were asking themselves whether Britain would buy their produce after the war; so they were to be told that her attitude would depend on the degree of resistance they put up to German attempts to exploit them. Thus propaganda lines were tailored to suit the farmers of all the countries of occupied Europe, including the satellites in the Balkans.[15]

Agricultural sabotage was called for only by foreign workers in Germany, and that as an alternative to their co-operation with the farmers in anti-social activities – hoarding, falsifying statistical returns, illegal slaughtering and so on.[16] In general sabotage was left to the discretion of the men on the spot – assisted and encouraged by SOE agents.[17] The fact that these agents were working in the field was one reason why it would have been unwise to make an all-out call for sabotage. Radio instructions could easily have cut across locally-inspired enterprises.

The propagandists had at their disposal a saboteur's vademecum which would have made nightmare reading for any German farmer. It contained scores of helpful suggestions. Farm buildings might be ingeniously set on fire with a wine glass half full of water, which on a sunny day would act as a burning glass and kindle straw at the distance of two inches. A carafe of water performed the same feat at twice the range. On a dull day – if the barn was not too draughty – a candle planted in oily rags did the trick. Rats were to be encouraged – precisely how was left to the saboteur's imagination – drains blocked, machinery neglected, valves that should be closed left open, and vice versa, roof tiles loosened to let the rain in. Tractors should be left out on frosty nights so that their radiators – filled with the hardest and dirtiest water – would crack.

Livestock were required to play their negative part in winning the war for the allies – which would have upset the RSPCA lobby, had they known. Feed should be seasoned with nails, needles, razor blades, yew, deadly nightshade, laurel or gentian. Foot and mouth disease should be spread at every opportunity. Rams should be castrated before they were put with their ewes – a two-man job, the manual thoughtfully warned. Lean meat boiled in water with a little sugar and brewed for a few days would produce the bacillus from which botulism is formed. These are a few of the ploys offered to the agricultural saboteur.[18]

For the greater part of the war PWE carried on their agricultural campaign on much the same lines, highlighting the conflict between the Nazis' demands and the long-term interests of the peasants, encouraging hoarding, and generally seeking to hinder the German war machine; but

[15] FO 898/336 (3, 23.12.42; 14.1, 17, 24.2.43).
[16] FO 898/338 (5.4.43).
[17] FO 898/337 (16.5.44).
[18] FO 898/333 (14.6.41; 29.7.42).

the opening of the Second Front brought in a new phase in the peasant war. The earlier themes continued to be used against the areas remaining under German occupation; but as the countries of Europe were liberated PWE's message changed. If the farmers were to co-operate with the allies in restoring European agriculture as quickly as possible it would be necessary to convince them that they should pay just as much attention to constructive propaganda as they had done to destructive propaganda in the past; but this new role of the Political Warfare Executive belongs more to the history of peace building than of political warfare.

V

A young Belgian hairdresser fled to England to escape the Gestapo who wanted him for his part in the anti-German demonstrations in Brussels on Armistice Day in 1940. When he was interviewed by Cecil de Sausmarez[19] at the Ministry of Information he urged that some way should be found of proving to his fellow-countrymen that the will to resist was shared by most of them. De Sausmarez mentioned this interview to Victor de Laveleye, a former Belgian Minister of Justice who was in charge of the BBC's Radio Belgique, and suggested that Belgians might be encouraged to chalk some simple sign on walls. In the BBC's Belgian programme on 14 January 1941 de Laveleye asked his listeners to use the letter V as a rallying sign, because it stood for 'Victoire' in French, and 'Vrijheid' in his country's other language, Flemish – and incidentally was the initial letter of his own first name.

No-one expected the response that this simple idea evoked. News of its success flooded in, the first, surprisingly enough, from Prague. 'Multitudes of little Vs had appeared on all sides!' On 2 February the BBC included a reference to the V sign in their Flemish programme which added fuel to the fire. It was evident that the sign had come to stay, and the BBC began to consider how best it could be exploited. The European Intelligence Service produced a paper on 10 March summarising reactions; and de Sausmarez proposed that the remarkable reception which de Laveleye's broadcast had had in France, where it had been picked up by listeners to the BBC Belgian service, should be used as 'ammunition for dealing with other countries which may be reluctant in accepting the scheme for the V sign'.[20]

On 22 March the BBC's French programme *Les Francais parlent aux Francais* broadcast a special feature on the new sign, with even more explosive results. Two days later an American newspaper correspondent at Vichy reported that anti-German inscriptions had become so numerous at Moulins that the whole town was punished. A letter from Marseilles dated 27 March said that walls, pavements, and doors were

[19] Later Regional Director (Low Countries) in PWE.
[20] FO 898/341 (8.10.41).

covered with big Vs – 'there is not a single space without them'; and next day a letter from the Department of Marne spoke of 'nothing but Vs and more Vs, everywhere, on the walls, on the roads, on the telegraph poles'. It was the same all over France. Vs were painted on the door of the Feldkommandant's office in Rouen, on the Feldpost at Nancy, on Wehrmacht cars at Bayonne. From Belgium it was reported 'Never has so much chalk been sold!'

The BBC was quite overcome by this train of events. The European News Department prepared a long paper on 'Broadcasting as a new weapon of war'. Never before had man wielded such power. It could be used to intensify the blockade of Germany. The Germans were short of certain metals, and all over Europe were small metal articles that would be one day requisitioned. A word broadcast from London would see them safely buried in their owners' back gardens. The Germans were short of oil. A word from London would set on fire all their oil storage tanks. A word from London would make life impossible for German soldiers in the occupied countries. There was no limit to the power of the word from London. It would lift the European blackout, drain cafes frequented by German troops of every drop of beer, disorganize road traffic, rot parachute silk. Finally, in this all-conquering campaign, millions of workers in German Europe would go on strike and destroy their factories at a word from London. 'When the British government gives the word, the BBC will cause riots and demonstrations in every city in Europe . . . The above gives a quite inadequate description of what can be done with this unique weapon if it is properly developed'.

To develop this all-powerful weapon, all that was needed was a new committee of BBC officials concerned with the European news bulletins, plus an official of the Ministry of Economic Warfare. Their first objective was to establish a feeling of solidarity between oppressed peoples, and then mobilize them into an underground army. Listeners would be asked to take a mental oath to fight for freedom. Then there would be a moment of silence, followed by the appropriate national anthem. This was only the beginning. Vs would be chalked on walls all over Europe 'not as a vague expression of resentment, but definitely to mark an anniversary. The V that night would be demonstrably *ours*'.[21]

This lyrical document, which seriously attributed to radio the power to end Hitler's war within a matter of months, caused some difficulty in the Ministry of Economic Warfare. Special Operations 1, the black propaganda branch, took the view that the matters referred to were already well taken care of. Further, the BBC overrated the effect of publicly broadcast instructions, as opposed to those secretly communicated, it ignored the danger of reprisals, and the overwhelming importance of keeping utterly distinct both in organization and in one's

[21] FO 898/342 (4.5.41).

mind the difference between secret activities, which involved small bands of picked men, and more open activities in which all sorts and conditions of men can be used.[22] The gist of this, including the unflattering reference to 'all sorts and conditions of men' was passed on to the BBC.[23]

In spite of the hint that they ought to hasten slowly, or perhaps withdraw from the competition, the BBC went ahead with enthusiasm. They believed that their European broadcasts were listened to by a vast audience, millions of whom hoped for a British victory; and they set up a V Committee to co-ordinate programmes to enemy-occupied countries and to show those millions how they could help to bring that victory about. They would create consciousness of a vast underground army, but without encouraging premature risings. They would prove to the British government that this new weapon was so important that it must be made part of the entire war strategy.[24]

So the V campaign carried on, going from strength to strength, while the propaganda department devoted much of its energy at the higher level to organizational problems, casting only a faintly worried glance in the direction of its extraordinarily successful sister body. On 27 June Colonel Britton,[25] who had been invented to lead the V campaign, ushered in fate knocking at the door. Towards the end of his broadcast on that day he said: 'Now, here's a strange thing! There is a V sound ... the letter V, the sign of Victory, in Morse ... three short taps and a heavy one ... and now here is something else ... It's the first few bars of Beethoven's Symphony Number Five. Number Five – do you notice that? Five – the V again. Beethoven's V Symphony, his Victory and Freedom Symphony'.[26] This was a stroke of genius, and it had not been made by one of the professional propagandists.

Kirkpatrick, the BBC's link with the propagandists, told Bruce Lockhart on 8 July that the V Committee 'which so far has had a considerable success within the limits imposed by purely passive resistance' contemplated a special programme for 14 July – Bastille Day – because the withdrawal of some German troops from France and the German attack on Russia had made the peoples of Europe more courageous.[27] A week later Leeper, fearing that the success of the V campaign was about to lead the BBC deeper into subversive propaganda, pointed out that this was SO 1's responsibility and that the BBC must be warned

---

[22] FO 898/342 (8.5.41).
[23] *Ibid* (11.5.41).
[24] *Ibid* (16.5.41).
[25] He was in fact D. E. Ritchie, the author of the document quoted above which claimed that a word from London could change the whole course of the war.
[26] FO 898/343 (23.6.41) (From the first 'V sound' script; FO 898/342 [17.7.41]).
[27] FO 898/342 (8.7.41).

off.[28] Bruce Lockhart promptly appealed to the Foreign Office. He admitted that the campaign had been successful; but it was getting too big for its boots.[29] The BBC was executing a foreign policy of its own creation bordering on incitement to sabotage. Firm guidance must be given at once. In Bruce Lockhart's opinion the V campaign had reached its zenith, and must be slowed down.[30] In particular, he was not impressed by the members of the V Committee. 'There are only one or two very good men, notably Newsome, but there are several wild men, and one wild woman'.[31]

He had no difficulty in getting the Foreign Secretary to act on his advice. On 29 July Eden wrote to Bracken, who had succeeded Duff Cooper as Minister of Information only nine days earlier, saying that he had been giving some thought to the future development 'of the excellent V campaign which is now being conducted in the BBC transmissions'. He understood that it was planned to move beyond the realm of agitation into that of subversive action, and it seemed to him that firm guidance must be given to those in charge of the campaign. They must not go beyond harmless agitation. Also, any future campaigns for maintaining morale in enemy-occupied countries should be kept within the limits of the agreed policy. Finally, suggestions in the press that the V campaign was designed to foment violent action in the occupied territories must be damped down.[32]

Strangely the Foreign Office immediately gave their blessing to the BBC's next proposal – a month-long 'Go Slow' to be launched by Colonel Britton as part of the V campaign, which seemed to go far beyond the 'harmless agitation' authorized by Eden; but the senior men in the propaganda department were still deeply involved in the three-way Departmental battle for power and had little time to spare for tactical moves against the BBC.[33] The new campaign would be brought to a climax in which all the workers of Europe would be asked to go slow for a whole week, when tortoises would join the V signs on the factory walls. Aesop's fable of the hare and the tortoise would be introduced as evidence that the latter would win in the end. The only caveat entered by the Foreign Office was that the 'Go Slow' broadcasts should be integrated with those of the propaganda Department's freedom radio stations.[34]

SOE, however, continued to deprecate the V campaign which they claimed was right outside the BBC's charter, and dealt with matters of which the BBC had little experience – certainly far less than SOE. If

[28] FO 898/342 (15.7.41).
[29] *Ibid* (17.7.41).
[30] *Ibid* (22.7.41).
[31] *Ibid* (25.7.41).
[32] *Ibid* (29.7.41).
[33] See Chapter 1, 'The phoney war, and after'.

the campaign was to continue it should be controlled by SO 1. The point was made in respect of France in particular that the objectivity of BBC broadcasts was of the utmost value. If they concentrated on preaching resistance and sabotage many would cease to listen because of their obvious political bias.[35] On 26 August Ritchie Calder urged that the division of responsibility between SO 1 and the BBC should be redefined. He agreed that the V campaign was ingenious, but it had not been related to covert subversion, or adapted to suit the individual needs of European countries. It was really five campaigns rolled into one: morale making in the occupied territories; morale breaking among the occupying forces; economic warfare; active subversion; and direct sabotage. The last could do no good, and might do considerable harm in the long run.[36]

There was some sense in this; and as soon as the Political Warfare Executive replaced Department EH and the professional propagandists were able to get on with their job rather than squabbling about it, they began to exercise more control over the BBC. A PWE V Committee, on which the BBC was represented, met weekly to determine future V programmes;[37] and a steady stream of misgivings was aired. Ritchie Calder, responsible for PWE's planning, continued to maintain that the BBC's unilateral excursion into operational propaganda raised difficulties which must be quickly resolved. Otherwise the V campaign would become a fiasco and the goodwill it had generated would be lost. Now that overt and covert propaganda had been brought together under PWE's umbrella the relation to them of the V campaign must be clearly defined.

The upshot was that PWE's V Committee continued to meet, making use of the experience of PWE Regional Directors and central planners in evolving V themes;[38] but the steam had been removed from the campaign. The BBC's highly individual approach was made to conform with the policy of 'harmless agitation' which PWE had to work to. The propagandists were allowed to do no more than report objectively the progress of resistance, emphasize the need for discipline and prudence on the part of resistance groups, encourage inflation, hoarding, the embarrassment of the civil administration, the withholding of produce, and go slows in factories, mines and railways.[39] Go slow was also PWE's own order of the day. The Executive Committee ruled on 12 October that guidance to those in charge of the V campaign should be 'in the sense of marking time and going slow'.[40]

This remained the pattern until the spring of 1942. During this period

[34] FO 898/342 (28.7, 1, 5.8.41).
[35] FO 898/297 (13.8.41).
[36] Ibid (26.8.41).
[37] Ibid (24.9.41).
[38] FO 898/341 (3.10.41).

the PWE planners tried to make the V campaign 'a really effective instrument of political warfare'. Ritchie Calder considered that the difficulties which had arisen from time to time were due to the lack of a co-ordinated policy, which was not the fault of the BBC which had relied on bright but sporadic ideas. 'Nor is it fair that we should continue to veto V suggestions without providing a constructive alternative'.[41]

There is no doubt that there had been difficulties. When the BBC chose 14 July as a special V army 'Gala Day' they overlooked the fact that it is a day of mourning in Flanders where it is taken to symbolize the beginning of French hegemony over Belgian affairs.[41] SOE, while not unsympathetic towards the BBC's efforts, pointed out that they had a duty to their agents in the field. They insisted that in the interests of their security they should be consulted about V programmes. Their spokesman said: 'I don't believe the gallant Colonel [Britton] would wish to be even indirectly the cause of embarrassing those to whom we owe such a lot'.[42] There was a case in Holland where a Quisling chief of police who had been denounced in the V campaign became so alarmed that he purged his police force and surrounded himself with an armed bodyguard which 'caused grave inconvenience to SOE'. There was also the fact that some Quislings were *agents provocateurs* for whom the BBC might innocently make trouble.[43] An officer of the Special Branch commented unfavourably on a BBC proposal that Mutual Aid Societies should be set up in the occupied countries 'as a primitive form of cells'. If this were done in the United Kingdom the Special Branch's first act would be to ensure that it was represented in all the societies, so that when the time was ripe the genuine members could be arrested at one fell swoop. No doubt the same would be done in Europe, so that all the BBC was doing was organizing man-traps for any patriots silly enough to take their advice.[44]

Ritchie Calder's solution was the creation of a General Staff to handle the V campaign on which all PWE's regions and the BBC would be represented. Ideally the Allied Governments would also have been represented on the proposed body but they were very sensitive about British propaganda to their countries, and PWE found that in practice it was impossible to get sensible co-operation from them, and the idea of an 'International General Staff' was dropped.[45] A PWE Committee was set up to consider whether open broadcasting could properly be used to encourage sabotage, and surprisingly concluded that 'giving of

[39] FO 898/342 (7.10.41).
[40] *Ibid* (11, 12.10.41).
[41] FO 898/341 (23.11.41).
[42] FO 898/342 (19.10.41).
[43] FO 898/341 (25.2.42).
[44] *Ibid* (31.1.42).

instruction in subversive activity, including sabotage, by means of open broadcasting is likely to result in a considerable increase in militant action in occupied Europe, and that provided this increase is properly directed and controlled it will be of value to the allies'.[46]

This amounted to ratification of the V campaign, but it did not have an enthusiastic reception from the Executive Committee. On 18 March Leeper suggested to the other members – Bruce Lockhart and Dallas Brooks – that the future of the V campaign must be settled one way or the other. Should it urge workers in the occupied countries to commit acts of sabotage, or should it simply report facts about resistance? The campaign had had some success, but there were arguments against carrying it on. Was it right from the safety of Britain to urge resistance groups in Europe to risk their lives?[47]

A fortnight later Leeper again raised the matter. He told Bruce Lockhart 'it is clear to all of us that we can't go on in the present hole and corner way, simply putting a stopper on Colonel Britton without any alternative suggestion'. V had been successful in the occupied countries. Everybody agreed that the campaign should be carried on and made really effective. He thought the best line would be to return to the idea of an Allied General Staff, and that until this had been organized Colonel Britton should be kept as quiet as possible. As soon as the allies had been brought in Colonel Britton could be given his head. 'I really think that in this there is the genesis of a big idea and that PWE would be scoring a very big success at a critical moment in the war . . .' Leeper was sure the Foreign Office would back the idea.[48] On 7 April PWE's V committee considered a proposition that the V campaign must either go forward, or be closed down; and concluded that it must go forward, linked with a general plan for operational propaganda. It was considered unlikely that the allied governments would agree to the proposal that there should be an Allied General Staff, and that for the time being there should be bilateral consultation with the allies.[49]

In spite of Leeper's support for the development of the V campaign, and the recommendation of PWE's V committee nothing was done, for reasons which are not clear on the files. On 20 April Gladwyn Jebb of the Ministry of Economic Warfare wrote to Bruce Lockhart saying that he was very disappointed to learn that the new régime for Colonel Britton's talks and for operational propaganda generally was not yet actively functioning; and asking for an assurance that PWE were not

---

[45] FO 898/341 (20.11.41).
[46] *Ibid* (2.3.42).
[47] FO 898/297 (18.3.42).
[48] FO 898/343 (2.4.42).
[49] FO 898/342 (7.4.42).

delaying matters in the hope of obtaining allied co-operation. The Services, especially the Air Ministry, were asking why the much-discussed extension of the Colonel Britton talks had not yet come into operation. A marginal note on this letter simply says that it was discussed with Gladwyn Jebb[50] on 21 April. There is no indication as to what was said, but it must be inferred that someone in PWE was hostile to the V campaign. Since Leeper, Ritchie Calder and the members of PWE's own V committee were in favour it looks as if Bruce Lockhart or Dallas Brooks, or both of them, wanted the campaign to stop.[51]

Nevertheless when the Foreign Office referred a complaint from the Dutch government that Colonel Britton had been giving orders and making promises to the Dutch without consultation with the Dutch government in London PWE decided that in future the Dutch authorities would be told what Colonel Britton intended to do, but their permission would not be asked. There was no suggestion that the fictitious Colonel had outlived his usefulness.[52]

Three days later Bruce Lockhart wrote to Ritchie of the BBC who had been the main protagonist of the V campaign telling him that circumstances had made it necessary for him 'to suspend the Colonel Britton talks'. It had been unanimously agreed by his policy committee that the V campaign must either advance or retreat; and since it could not go forward as things were it was better to call it off. This was no reflection on Ritchie's contribution. He had done a remarkable piece of work which would have its place in the history of the war, as he – Bruce Lockhart – had told Eden and Bracken.[53] Ritchie replied that he quite understood the reason for the decision – and said he hoped that it would not be too long before the BBC could go on the air again with a strong forward-looking policy.[54] There was however to be no return to the aggressive V campaign for which the BBC had had such high hopes.[55]

Braddock II
Braddock II was the code name for an operation which had its origins in 1942. It was also the name of a special device to be used in the operation.[56] This was a card, six inches by four, a delayed action do-it-yourself incendiary, millions of which would be showered from aircraft. It had been developed by the Special Operations Executive on

[50] Later Lord Gladwyn.
[51] FO 898/342 (20.4.42).
[52] *Ibid* (5.5.42).
[53] *Ibid* (8.5.42).
[54] *Ibid* (9.5.42).
[55] For the operational propaganda aspects of the V campaign see Chapter 3 above.
[56] Braddock I was a saboteur's package containing pistols and explosives to be dropped to resistance groups after D-Day.

Churchill's personal instructions as a result of his reading *The Moon is Down* when it was first published.⁵⁷

Instructions how to set the things off were printed on the card in eleven languages. All the finder had to do was to hide the device, say in a pile of combustible waste in a factory, having squeezed a red spot on the card to start a fuse which half an hour later ignited a tube of petrol gel attached to the card.⁵⁸ This was much more efficient than, for example, the crude wine glass method advocated in the saboteur's vademecum.⁵⁹ If millions of the cards were dropped over Germany in a short period the Germans would almost certainly be compelled to deal with thousands of fires. They would be forced to hunt for the cards to ensure that as many as possible were harmlessly disposed of, which would increase their manpower difficulties.

If the operation was to have the maximum effect it was important to get the timing right. On 4 October 1943 Lord Selborne, Minister of Economic Warfare suggested to the Prime Minister that the time *was* now ripe for 'the operation initiated by you'. Two and a half million Braddocks were ready for use, and the device was being produced at the rate of 300,000 a month. A Lancaster bomber could carry 10,000 up to a range of 600 miles. Selborne pointed out that there were nearly 7 million prisoners of war and forced workers, mostly in Western Germany, and he proposed that at a very early date 5 Lancasters should be detailed to drop Braddocks in this region, and that thereafter there should be weekly showers of 250,000. The morning after the first shower PWE must urge foreign workers, prisoners of war, and anti-Nazis to look out for the devices and use them to strike a major blow for the United Nations at negligible risk to themselves.⁶⁰

In commenting on the suggestion that they should publicize the dropping of the incendiaries PWE agreed that its broadcasts would encourage people to look for them, and that the Germans would be forced to divert scarce manpower to take counter-measures; but they pointed out that there was the objection that wide publicity might inhibit many people from using the devices on the ground that the Germans would know all about them and be on the lookout for their use. Further, the Germans could very well use the broadcasts as justification for reprisals, whereas if PWE kept quiet they might prefer to let

---

⁵⁷ FO 898/397 (4, 16.10.43). By John Steinbeck (1942). ('High in the air the two bombers circled . . . and from the belly of each one tiny little objects dropped, hundreds of them one after another . . . They drifted so slowly and landed so gently that sometimes the ten-inch packages of dynamite stood upright in the snow, and the little parachutes folded gently down around them.')
⁵⁸ *Ibid* (10.1.45).
⁵⁹ See p. 120.
⁶⁰ FO 898/397 (4.10.43).

E

sleeping dogs lie and not draw attention to the new device. PWE therefore recommended that the Braddock II operation should go ahead without publicity. Recipients would then use the device much more freely, and the effect on the enemy would be more disturbing.[61]

The Chief of Air Staff (Sir Charles Portal) agreed that the operation could be mounted, but only as part of a main bombing raid. A small bomber force could not reasonably be sent to the designated areas because of the strength of the defences there. He was also sceptical about the value of Braddock as a weapon. 'We know our normal weapons do great damage, and I do not wish to change to a weapon whose value is entirely problematical until I am assured that such a step is justified', a stick-in-the-mud attitude which ignored the fact that the only way to test the Braddock was to drop it over enemy territory. His conclusion was that the device might most profitably be used just before the launching of *Overlord*. Churchill accepted this, and asked Portal to refer the matter to the Chiefs of Staff so that the Joint Intelligence Committee might study it.[62] At this time Dallas Brooks told Brendan Bracken that PWE's considered opinion was that the operation would be more successful if there was no accompanying publicity, and that he was so informing the Minister of Economic Warfare.[63]

On 9 November 1943 the Joint Intelligence Sub-committee decided that the time was not yet ripe for Braddock II, not for the reasons advanced by the Chief of Air Staff, but because the security forces in Germany were probably still strong enough to prevent the widespread use of the device; and that failure at this stage might prejudice its use later on. They reconsidered the matter in May 1944, on the eve of the invasion of Europe, and this time came to the conclusion that the psychological moment for Braddock would be immediately after *Overlord* had been launched. The Germans would be forced to react violently and even if the incendiary had only a limited success it would cause a serious security problem.[64]

In the light of this recommendation Selborne discussed the next step with SHAEF who said it was wrong to seek the co-operation of allied prisoners of war in exploiting Braddock.[65] Bruce Lockhart confirmed that British propaganda had never urged prisoners of war to carry out acts of sabotage; and indeed propaganda was never directed at them.[66] This did not make much difference to SOE's plan, however, since they were relying mainly on foreign workers in Germany to use the Braddocks. They were more widely dispersed than prisoners of war and had

[61] FO 898/397 (20.10.43).
[62] *Ibid* (10, 16.10.43).
[63] *Ibid* (20.10.43).
[64] *Ibid* (3.5.44).
[65] *Ibid* (17.5.44).
[66] *Ibid* (18.5.44).

access to more vulnerable and important targets. At a meeting with SOE at the beginning of June PWE changed their minds about publicity. They now said that if the Braddock operation was to succeed it must be accompanied by a carefully-thought out propaganda campaign.[67]

Nothing more happened until six weeks after D-Day when Lord Selborne said once again that the time was ripe for Braddock II. There was evidence of rioting in some German towns – although the Secret Service had failed to report it – and he therefore proposed that half a million Braddocks should be dropped right away.[68] However, Bruce Lockhart and Robert Sherwood (of OWI) objected. They wrote to General McClure, head of the Psychological Warfare Branch of SHAEF, claiming that the Braddocks would fall into the hands of the SS and Gestapo 'many of whom are undoubtedly planning to carry on underground activities against the allies during the period of occupation'. Further, it would be a pity to resort to 'terroristic devices' when the war was being won by brilliant strategy and overwhelming force of arms.[69] This was remarkable advice. The two propagandists may be forgiven for failing to foresee the Battle of the Bulge, and thinking that the reoccupation of Europe was all over bar the shouting, but it was hardly fair to brand the relatively innocent Braddock as a terror device. Most foreign workers in Germany would have much preferred a gentle shower of Braddocks which they could have put to good use at leisure, to a string of high explosive bombs over which they had no control. No doubt German civilians would have expressed the same preference.

In spite of the objections of PWE and OWI General Eisenhower (who had been given the last word on the use of Braddock II) decided in the middle of August to drop 200,000 Braddocks nightly. Black radio transmissions would be used to ensure that as many people as possible in Germany knew what was happening and would have a chance of contributing to nationwide arson.[70] Bruce Lockhart agreed, in spite of his earlier objections, that Aspidistra, the high-powered transmitter which had been provided for just such an operation, should pirate German wavelengths to announce the arrival of the Braddocks, and confirmed that this would increase the confusion among the security forces. He pointed out, however, that it had been decided that the Prime Minister's authority was needed before an 'intruder' radio operation using enemy wavelengths could be set in motion.[71] The Chiefs of Staff Committee told General Bedell Smith (Eisenhower's Chief of Staff) that they agreed that Braddock II should go ahead, and also that Aspidistra should be used to support it. SHAEF should get on with their

[67] FO 898/397 (2.6.44).
[68] Ibid (24.7.44).
[69] Ibid (4.8.44).
[70] Ibid (16.8.44).
[71] Ibid (18.8.44).

preparations on the assumption that the Prime Minister's approval would be forthcoming.[72] On 20 August PWE reaffirmed their support, and the Chiefs of Staff instructed their secretary to clear the proposal with the Deputy Prime Minister in Churchill's absence overseas.[73] Everyone was anxious that Braddock II should go ahead without delay.

Alas, all had forgotten that the Minister of Information had a say in the use of Aspidistra – or they had taken it for granted that he would go along with the majority. When Bracken heard belatedly that it was proposed to use Aspidistra without his having been consulted he at once reacted like the wicked fairy who was not invited to the christening. Although he knew that Eden, the Minister of Economic Warfare, SOE, the Chiefs of Staff, and the Supreme Commander were all in favour, and that PWE had agreed to the enterprise, he exercised his veto. He wrote to Eden: 'If we could only stop high military officers and that peculiar organization SOE from making plans affecting the PWE organization without any prior consultation with its Director General, our war effort would benefit.' It was only yesterday (22 August 1944) that he had heard of 'this Braddock II operation' which had been sanctioned by the Chiefs of Staff and the American Bedell Smith, and would be operated in part 'by the busy SOE'. Nobody had thought of asking the Minister responsible for the administration of PWE for permission to use Aspidistra.

Even Bracken had to have some reason for blocking a project which everybody else favoured. He therefore argued that Aspidistra must be held in reserve for some future intruder operation. He considered that it would be premature to use it at this stage, just as Britain's use of tanks in the first war had been premature. The Minister of Information knew better than everyone up to and including the Supreme Commander.

This was quite shameful petulance. For one thing, PWE had been consulted about Braddock II and had given their support; and they had argued earlier that the operation would be more successful if it were not accompanied by propaganda. But the wicked fairy's *amour propre* was upset. Aspidistra was *his* football, and nobody else was going to play with it, whatever it meant to the war effort.[74]

---

[72] FO 898/397 (19.8.44).
[73] *Ibid* (20.8.44).
[74] *Ibid* (23.8.44). This was not the only time Bracken's existence as a Minister was overlooked. In May 1944 the Defence Committee (of which he was not a member) decided to set up a special organization under a Minister to intensify propaganda encouraging the French to evacuate danger areas. They also issued instructions direct to PWE. When Bracken learned this he wrote an angry minute to Churchill. To appoint another Minister was putting the clock back to the days of the Standing Ministerial Committee. Chaos would return. 'Ill health and other reasons make me anxious to leave the Government as soon as I can. And I shall be glad of the freedom

Three months later Selborne ventured to suggest yet again that Braddock II should be launched. Eisenhower had called urgently for special measures to injure German morale and Braddock seemed to be tailormade for the purpose. Churchill referred his suggestion to the Chiefs of Staff, who asked Bruce Lockhart to discuss it with SHAEF. Perhaps having in mind his own aversion to a 'terrorist device' and his Minister's tantrum about Aspidistra he persuaded SHAEF that the time was not yet ripe – although he told McClure that since Braddock II was Churchill's own idea it was bound to be used sooner or later.

He was wrong. Small quantities of Braddocks were dropped from time to time, without any accompanying propaganda, and were used to start fires in the towns where they landed; but the plan to drop millions in a short space of time was never used – to the great disappointment of General Gubbins, head of SOE. He remained convinced that a full-scale Braddock II might have yielded a valuable dividend.[75]

---

to beat up Bevan and his tribe of vicious critics'. Churchill replied briefly: 'I agree. You are the Minister. If Bridges had asked me to amplify I should have said this'. It seems clear, however, from the Defence Committee minutes that they did intend to make a new appointment, perhaps having forgotten that Bracken had anything to do with propaganda; and that Churchill was covering up. (PREM 3/365/11 ff. 1011–13).
[75] FO 898/397 (28.11, 30.12.44; 2, 5, 22, 25.1, 19.3, 17, 26.4.45).

8
Hard sell: Propaganda in military operations

Operation *Torch*
Propaganda in support of military operations came fully into its own in Operation *Torch*, the Anglo-American expedition designed to give the allies control of French North West Africa in November 1942. In spite of the liaison between the military wing of PWE and the Services, which was supposed to make each side aware of the help they could get from the other, the most had not been made of the few chances to exploit military success in the first years of the war. Some golden opportunities were lost, of which the most unfortunate was the small but highly successful combined operation against the German submarine base in the French port of St Nazaire on 28 March 1942.

News of this daring exploit could have been used to raise the morale of Britain's supporters throughout Europe and to demonstrate to the world at large that the allies had the ability to strike hard at the enemy; but simply because it had occurred to no-one to exploit the political warfare possibilities of the enterprise the first that PWE heard of it was when the news came through that it had taken place. Many of the people of St Nazaire concluded that it must be the first wave in the allied invasion of France. They became unnecessarily involved and suffered heavy casualties. The German propagandists were quick to seize on this fact and led the French nation to believe that the British had taken measures against the people of St Nazaire for their own nefarious purposes. It took PWE twelve hours to find out exactly what had happened and to decide how best to make use of the incident; but by that time the Germans had completed an admirable publicity job. What should have been an outstanding British propaganda success story became almost a German victory.

Those concerned with the political warfare aspects of *Torch* were well aware how easy it could be to produce a comparable propaganda boomerang – but on an infinitely greater scale – if something went wrong with the landings; and indeed they assumed that even if the operation went entirely according to plan there would be great disappointment in Britain, the United States and particularly in France when it became known that the allies' first major operation had not been launched in Europe. It was feared that some Frenchmen would think that the choice of French North Africa meant that the allies were seeking territorial conquest rather than taking a first step towards the liberation of Europe.

There was another important difficulty, however. The expedition was to be announced as an American operation, on the ground that the French in North Africa were more likely to welcome the Americans with open arms than they would the British. For a variety of reasons the British were unpopular with the French, not the least because they had fought on when the French had surrendered; and German propaganda had fostered this unpopularity. It was believed that if *Torch* could be shown to be purely American there was a good chance that the French troops would join forces with the invaders. Therefore, although the Royal Navy and the RAF and substantial contingents of the army were due to play an essential part in *Torch* their mere presence was denied by the early propaganda.

This necessary deception was considered to be an invitation to the Axis propagandists to make play with their slogan that *this* time the British were fighting to the last American. PWE were also faced with the problem of keeping a balance between the idea that *Torch* was just as good as a 'Second Front' to sustain the morale of those who had been waiting desperately for the allies to land in Europe, and the idea that sooner or later the real Second Front *would* come to their rescue. Again, PWE could encourage the waverers in the invaded territory to co-operate either by emphasizing the invincible power of the expedition, or by playing down the idea of force and suggesting that the Americans were coming as friends. Yet again, should an appeal to the French be based on nationalist 'anti-Boche' sentiments, or should a class-distinctive anti-Fascist element be introduced?

These were some of the questions which the propagandists – British and American – discussed among themselves on the eve of *Torch*. PWE thought that the provision of the right answers might well be the deciding factor 'in an issue which will closely affect the course of the war, namely whether the French nation as a whole decides to embrace the allied cause, or whether a portion of it embraces that of the Axis, or tries to remain neutral'. This may have been something of an overstatement; but there is no doubt that the Executive were right in their belief that the peculiar political warfare difficulties raised by *Torch* could be overcome only if propaganda was related to strategy throughout the planning of the military operations and during the time they were in progress.[1]

General Eisenhower entirely agreed with the propagandists, although his reasons, as summarized in a telegram in August 1942, may seem to be slightly backhanded. He said 'subversive activities, propaganda, and political warfare are not only inappropriate but a positive menace unless

[1] FO 898/131 (11.10.42).

carefully and completely co-ordinated with all military plans, and therefore must be passed on and approved by the Supreme Commander'.[2] No doubt the propagandists would have wished that this observation had been more happily phrased and that the Supreme Commander might have given them credit for a more constructive role than his words implied; but it is probably true that his heart was in the right place. At any rate his order, whatever the reason for it, meant that the propagandists were deeply involved in the planning of a major operation, perhaps for the first time in the history of warfare.

Eisenhower had just attached to his headquarters a Political Section to advise him on political warfare and subversive activities, among other things. It was headed by Mr W. H. B. Mack of the Foreign Office, with seven other members including one from each of OSS, OWI, PWE and SOE, and under the Supreme Commander was responsible for finalizing the *Torch* political warfare and subversive activities plans, making use of the expertise of the British and American agencies. Propaganda to enemy and enemy-occupied countries was looked after by PWE working in co-operation with the London representatives of OWI. PWE was solely responsible for propaganda to Spain, Portugal, Spanish Morocco and Tangier – which had to be reassured at the earliest safe moment about the objectives of *Torch* – but again there was the closest consultation with the Americans. The plans were approved by the Foreign Secretary before they went to the Political Section, then by Eisenhower, and finally on to the War Department in Washington for approval by them and President Roosevelt. The consultative arrangements could hardly have been more elaborate and this may well be why the *Torch* propaganda was an outstanding success.

A general directive provided guidance for the working propagandists. It stated unequivocally right at the beginning: 'This is an American operation'. There must be no reference to the co-operation of British forces until their presence was referred to in the communiqués. The purpose of the operation was to defeat the Axis forces in North Africa and to frustrate the occupation by German troops of French North Africa. The expedition must not be represented as the opening of a Second Front. (In spite of this the Prime Minister and President Roosevelt later agreed to a press communiqué for issue after the landings had begun which said that the operation was in effect the commencement of a Second Front. This was spotted by Bowes-Lyon, head of the PWE Mission in the United States, and removed).[3] Every effort would be made to avoid the shedding of French blood unless Hitler and his agents in France made it inevitable. If there was a clash between the French and allied navies, then the Germans must take the blame. Although

[2] FO 898/129 (6.8.42).
[3] *Ibid* (31.10.42).

Torch marked the beginning of the liberation phase of the war it was on no account to be presented as a signal for revolt in Europe; and every precaution must be taken to damp down premature risings in occupied countries. In particular there must be no incitement to general or local revolt in France. The indirect encouragement of undetectable sabotage, however, especially in the field of transport, should continue. A parallel directive for use in the Far East stressed the fact that growing American strength now allowed United States forces to operate in both the European and Pacific theatres.⁴

Of the subordinate political warfare plans the most important was aimed at France and the French Empire. The basic theme was that the liberation of French territory had begun. An American Expeditionary Force more powerful than that which came to France in 1917 had now set foot on French soil. Propagandists were instructed to distract attention from any resistance which the invasion force met at the hands of the French, and to convey the impression that the Americans had been welcomed as allies, their principal objective being to join with the French North African forces to start an offensive that would end the war. As soon as it was confirmed that the planned internal pro-allied *coup d'état* had taken place and that the Americans *were* in fact welcome, the emphasis of propaganda would shift. The new themes would include: 'The most loyal and responsible elements of the French North African army have assumed responsibility for the defence of French overseas territory against threatened Axis invasion. They have appealed to the President of the United States for military support and a powerful allied force is now in process of landing'.⁵

There was of course no guarantee that the hoped-for *coup d'état* would take place, or that the invading force would be welcome, and alternative propaganda themes had to be planned on the basis of alternative assumptions. The *coup d'état* might be only partially successful, and insufficient to suppress resistance at all the landing places, in which case the basic theme – that the liberation of French territory had begun – would be repeated as long as might be necessary. If the French completely refused to co-operate and there was considerable military resistance, then it would be necessary to fall back on counter-propaganda on the lines: 'We have arrived as allies to defend you, and we are greeted with bullets ... How can you bring yourselves to shoot on your oldest allies, and against the truest interests of France and yourselves break a friendship which is 150 years old. We have no designs whatever on your territory which is and will remain French'.⁶

The presumed success of *Torch* was to be exploited in propaganda to Italy, along with the British success in the Western Desert. It would be

⁴ FO 898/131 (3.11.42).
⁵ *Ibid* (15.10.42).
⁶ *Ibid* (15.10.42).

stressed that the allies' offensive was gathering momentum, and that the day of reckoning would soon be at hand. Now was the time to choose between the hated Führer and his tools – Mussolini and his gang – on the one hand, and the British and American promises, which would certainly be fulfilled, on the other.[7] Plans were also prepared to reassure Spain and Portugal about allied objectives in North Africa. Neither country would be involved in hostilities as a result of the American expedition.[8]

Whispers were to be allowed to make their risky contribution to deceiving the enemy. Agents throughout Europe busied themselves putting round rumours that supposedly came from inside allied headquarters, and led to the conclusion that the British were about to invade Sicily. At the same time the dissemination of all rumours relating to North West Africa was abruptly halted. In retrospect this use of a whispering campaign may seem to be a two-edged weapon. It has much in common with the three-card trick in which the victim's chances of 'finding the lady' are statistically good so long as he refuses to believe the evidence of his eyes. It would have been simple enough for the German High Command similarly to refuse to believe the evidence of their ears and to guess that a spate of rumours about the impending invasion of Sicily, and total silence about North West Africa meant that the next target must be North West Africa – unless of course the perfidious British were engaged in a double bluff and all the time intended to invade Sicily.[9]

An impressive set of leaflets, several bearing the Stars and Stripes in full colour, was prepared to support PWE's radio propaganda. These included a message from President Roosevelt which began: '*Aucune nation n'est plus intimement liée, tant par l'histoire que par l'amitié profonde, au peuple de France et à ses amis que ne sont les Etats Unis d'Amerique*'; another from Eisenhower, which ended '*Tous ensemble, on les aura!*' which was to be dropped over the main cities of Metropolitan France as well as in North Africa; another with the text of the announcement which Roosevelt had recorded for broadcasting on D-Day; and an *Avis au Peuple Français,* in the name of the British and United States governments explaining the objectives of *Torch.* There was also a 48-page illustrated booklet devoted entirely to the part the Americans had played in France in 1917/18, including a photograph of the young Roosevelt, who as he proudly pointed out in one of the leaflets, had been associated with the American forces in France in the first war; and a handbook for members of the expeditionary force with advice about the climate, health hazards, and social behaviour in North Africa ('You must *not* talk to Moslem women. Never. Under no cir-

---

[7] *Ibid* (13.10.42).
[8] *Ibid* (24.10.42).
[9] FO 898/71 (3.1.43).

cumstances ... Bargain on prices ... Be generous with your cigarettes ... Be kind to beggars').[10]

Eisenhower tried himself to make a contribution to the content of the leaflets, but it was rejected. Perhaps the propagandists thought that the Commander in Chief should stick to his last, and leave them to get on with the job that they were paid to do. His idea was that to remind the French people of the long-standing connection between France and the United States a picture of Lafayette, who had played a part in the American War of Independence, should be printed on the leaflets. His proposal was submitted to PWE for study, when they disposed of it by pointing out that while Lafayette's name might be well enough known in the United States, his part in the War of Independence was virtually unknown in Metropolitan France, and his very existence was unknown in French North Africa.[11]

All the leaflets – over 30 million of them – and large numbers of posters and miscellaneous documents in French and Arabic, for example forms for claiming compensation from the United States for damage to property, were printed by PWE in a remarkably short space of time. The highly complicated plans for disseminating them in accordance with a very demanding time schedule and for setting in motion the various radio transmissions called for action in Gibraltar, from which certain of the leaflets were to be despatched to North Africa; Washington; North Africa itself; and London, where the Foreign Office, the War Cabinet Office, the Admiralty, and PWE were to arrange for the recordings made by Roosevelt and Eisenhower to be transmitted throughout D-Day (alternatively, if the operation was postponed they had to announce the fact in coded messages to SOE in North Africa so that their subversive activities, including the stimulation of the *coup d'état*, would be held over until the revised D-Day); and to set in motion the dropping of leaflets by US aircraft over unoccupied France (main targets, Vichy, Lyons, Marseilles, and Toulon) and by the RAF over occupied France (main targets, Paris, Lille, Roubaix, and Tourcoing).[12] The whole vast operation was carried through without a hitch, and when the operation was safely over the American High Command showered congratulations on PWE.

There is on the file a curious grumbling note by Bruce Lockhart dated 15 October 1942, nearly three weeks before D-Day (7 November 1942), in which he plays down PWE's contribution. The Executive had been a mere handmaiden to the Americans in planning and executing the political warfare plans for *Torch*. They had done no more than place their experience and resources at the disposal of the Americans who had been responsible for all the policy decisions – although it was

[10] FO 898/130.
[11] FO 898/129 (24.9.42).
[12] FO 898/131 (31.10.42).

true that PWE had achieved the impossible by winkling 36 officers and men out of the British forces in as many hours at the request of the Americans – specialists who would join the *Torch* psychological warfare teams in the field. He concluded: 'I have grave misgivings as to the quality of the Americans' work and the efficiency of the existing organization. In particular it is clear that OWI's relations with the American military authorities are not nearly so happy as are ours with the British.' He telegraphed the whole of his grumble to Bowes-Lyon in Washington, for no apparent reason; and equally oddly he made a point of reading it, first to Eden and then to Bracken – but did not leave a copy with either Minister.[13] It almost looks as if he was afraid that the political warfare contribution to *Torch* was going to be inadequate, and that he was seeking to disclaim in advance any responsibility. In fact, PWE did play a very big part in the preparatory work, even if the final decisions belonged to the Americans, and the staff fully deserved all the praise they later received.

The political warfare plans for *Torch* may have gone like clockwork; but for one of PWE's officers attached to the Expedition things went less smoothly. He – Colonel K. Johnstone – sent back vivid reports about the landing and the early days of occupation which included 'frank remarks about the British Navy and the American Army' which it was decided were unsuitable for general circulation within the Executive. In one passage he referred to the fact that the execution of field propaganda is the task of military political warfare companies. 'Enquiry shows that in this most political of all possible operations there was no such company attached to the troops who would make the first vital contact with the French, and who would probably therefore decide whether our objective was to be achieved with greater or lesser bloodshed or perhaps without bloodshed at all. My duty therefore seemed clear. As you know, I have always strongly held that if Political Warfare wants to get itself taken seriously by the army as "the fourth fighting arm" which it likes to term itself it must sometimes take a soldier's risks'. Johnstone pointed out to the American commander that it was essential to have someone who could communicate with the first French troops they ran into, and volunteered to accompany the landing troops for this purpose.

Everything went wrong with the landing arrangements, so far as Johnstone's contingent was concerned. 'I have never known any scheme turn out so utterly unlike its intention. With our faces duly anointed with soot and vaseline, wearing American helmets, slung megaphones (the symbol of our trade) and heavy Commando boots with rubber soles we duly took our places in the boats at half-past ten on Saturday night the 7th. There was a considerable but not excessive swell, the night was

[13] FO 898/129 (15.10.42).

clear and starry but not too bright and the lights of the suburbs of Algiers could be seen eight miles away across the sea'. It had been intended that flotillas of 9 or 11 boats should make for the beaches four miles west of Algiers, and that the actual landing should take place at 1 am on 8 November, but nothing went right. A series of mishaps delayed the departure of the boats for 1½ hours. When Johnstone's 'flotilla' eventually moved off it comprised only 4 boats, one of which broke down, and the other two got lost, so that when his boat reached the beach it was on its own. 'You may imagine that the BBC's subsequent tribute to the perfect timing of this part of the operation was greeted with some wry smiles!'

In Johnstone's assessment the delay in getting the troops ashore might have proved very serious in that those who had engineered the *coup d'état* were relying on getting full scale American support long before they did; and there was a danger that in the meantime the *coup* would be reversed.[14] If this is true, it means that the success of what was very largely a political warfare operation backed up by troops was put at risk by the troops' performance. Johnstone reckoned that quick military success was the thing that really mattered. Next in importance came the visible presence of a large force, the re-opening of trade with the outside world, and the re-education by propaganda of the people so that they could see world affairs again in their true proportion. There was a good deal of evidence of the success with which the Germans had indoctrinated the people of the region. Johnstone cites the case of two Frenchmen who were overheard to exclaim in genuine surprise as they watched some American troops: *'Tiens! Ce ne sont pas du tout des types juifs!'*[15]

Operation *Husky*
In March 1943 General Eisenhower asked that plans for psychological warfare to help Operation *Husky* – the allied invasion of Sicily – should be drawn up. In particular, he wanted to know what line to follow up to the moment of the assault, and after the assault had begun. Eden told Churchill that in the first phase a tough line with no promises should be maintained. Thereafter a ray of hope might be held out to the Italians. The allied forces could then be presented as liberators rather than as conquerors. Eden had already discussed with the Americans a plan in which at first the war against the Italians would be prosecuted with all possible vigour, passive resistance and sabotage would be encouraged, and the Italians would be reminded of the utter hopelessness of their position: then the allies, without making any specific commitments, should hold out the hope that after the defeat of the Fascist government the Italian people would survive as a nation.[16] Churchill agreed with

[14] FO 898/131 (15–25.11.42).
[15] *Ibid*

this general line; and on 16 April the Combined Chiefs of Staff, with the approval of the State Department and the Foreign Office, confirmed to Eisenhower that propaganda to Italy would be hard up to the assault on Sicily, and soft thereafter.[17]

Shortly after this the Commanders-in-Chief in the Middle East, not knowing what was being done about propaganda for *Husky* (with which they were not directly concerned) sent a long signal to the Chiefs of Staff in London setting out their views. They justified their intervention on the ground that over a long period they had become expert on the morale of the Italian armed forces. They believed that they would fight with much more determination in defence of their own country than they had done in North Africa, and considered that an intensive propaganda campaign (the ingredients of which they provided) must therefore be an essential part of *Husky*.[18]

While the lead on political warfare for the invasion of Sicily was thus being taken by the Supreme Commander and senior Ministers the Political Warfare Executive was carrying on with the groundwork on which broad policies could be built. As the Executive had become more experienced its propaganda campaigns were drawn up with ever-increasing mathematical precision. If the plans are examined critically they may seem to be absurdly detailed and optimistic. They read as if the trends and future events which they presuppose are inescapable, so long as the right propaganda themes are put across.

There was of course no intention on the part of those in PWE who drew up these plans that the working propagandists should take them at their face value, that they should dole out their specifics – whether in the form of radio broadcasts or leaflets – exactly according to the detailed prescriptions with which they were provided by the planners. The elaborate assumptions were no more than guidelines within which the propagandists were to operate in order to ensure that they all thought on the same lines and spoke with the same voice. If this is not recognized it must seem that the propagandists engaged not in the possible art of political warfare, but in a totally improbable pseudo-scientific exercise in which wishful thinking was the main ingredient.

This is illustrated by a memorandum on PWE's 1943 military tasks – its tasks designed to help the allied military effort – in which the cardinal aim of Anglo-American strategy is taken quite simply to be the defeat of Germany in 1943.[19] How this goal can be attained is then set out in a logical progression of plans. So far as Italy is concerned, political warfare will seek to render it impossible for the Italians to continue to fight,

---

[16] PREM 3/365/2, ff. 242–4 (10.3.43).
[17] *Ibid* f. 199 (16.4.43).
[18] *Ibid* ff. 227–9 (26.4.43).
[19] Studied by the Chiefs of Staff Committee on 29 March 1943 (CAB 79/62, f. 232).

by exploiting the naval, military and air operations against them, by aggravating all the causes of internal disruption, by exacerbating the mutual distrust of Italians and Germans, and by waging a war of nerves on the peoples in the Mediterranean area and the Axis troops there.

More particular objectives are then developed, for example the surrender of the Italian forces, or such a reduction of Italian morale that the Germans will no longer dare to rely on Italian troops or Italian administrators. It is contemplated that these objectives will be attained by instilling four convictions into the minds of the Italians, namely: that by prolonging the war, they are ensuring the devastation of their country; that they will shorten the war by refusing to co-operate with the Germans and Fascists; that it is in their interest individually and collectively to get out of the war; and that it will not be degenerating for them to do so.

There is yet one more stratum of planning to come. The prescribed convictions will be sown in the minds of the Italians by stressing the overwhelming military and industrial superiority of the allies, the increasing threat from the air to Italian cities, and by suggesting that the Italian forces were well aware of their responsibility to their country, and that it was open to them to save it by stopping the war.[20]

While PWE was thus fashioning the nuts and bolts of propaganda. Eisenhower suggested to his masters in London and Washington tha they had not paid enough attention to his earlier points. On 17 May he again stressed the importance of the psychological warfare aspects of *Husky*. In view of the toughness of the operation he considered it essential that every effort should be made in advance to weaken the enemy's resistance. All the indications were that the Italians would fight bravely in defence of their own territory. It would not be enough to threaten them. If they were not offered some way out, they had no alternative but to rally round their leaders – which was exactly what he wanted to avoid. The assurances which he had been authorized to give about Italy's future were not explicit enough, and in any case, to withhold them until immediately before the invasion would deprive them of all value so far as the operation was concerned.

He proposed that soft propaganda should be fed to the Italians right away. It must be drummed into them that if they stopped fighting the allies would regard it as 'evidence of good judgement', entitling them to 'peace with honour'; that the allied governments pledged full nationhood to Italy after the defeat of the Axis; and that the only obstacle to an honourable peace was the Fascist government. A statement on these lines would enable the Italians to balance the advantages of surrender against the consequences of continued resistance, and to place the blame for their having to carry on fighting squarely on the Fascists.[21]

[20] FO 898/349 (30.3, 28.4.43).
[21] PREM 3/365/2, ff. 230–2 (17.5.43).

In London the Vice-Chiefs of Staff strongly supported Eisenhower. They told the Chiefs of Staff – who at this time were in Washington with the Prime Minister – that the success of *Husky* was by no means a foregone conclusion, and that if Eisenhower believed that soft propaganda should be brought in immediately, he should have his way. They added that while the Foreign Secretary did not agree with them he accepted that the military viewpoint should be given full weight.[22]

Eden certainly did not agree with the military experts. At a meeting of the War Cabinet on 20 May (presided over by the Deputy Prime Minister Clement Attlee in the absence of Churchill) he explained that although it had been agreed with the United States government that there should be no change in the nature of propaganda to Italy until immediately before the invasion of Sicily, Eisenhower was now urging that the change should be made right away. The Vice-Chiefs of Staff, who were anxious that everything possible should be done to help the troops in what was bound to be a most difficult operation, agreed. The Foreign Secretary, who had circulated a memorandum on the hard/soft propaganda issue, thought that Eisenhower was wrong.

Brendan Bracken, the Minister principally concerned with propaganda, was caught out. He complained that he had only just seen Eden's memorandum, and therefore could not express an opinion – which shows how much he was in the hands of his officials when it came to policy-making. In the absence of a contribution from the Minister of Information the War Cabinet decided to sleep on the matter.[23] Next day Bracken did rather better. He proposed that the change to a soft line should be left as late as possible. He was supported by the Home Secretary (Herbert Morrison) who said that any promises to the Italians would divide public opinion in Britain and the United States. Against this the Vice-Chief of Naval Staff (Vice-Admiral Sir Henry Moore) argued that everything possible must be done to weaken the resistance of 'the garrison in Huskyland', preferably through the soldiers' families, which would take time. Therefore the sooner a soft line was adopted the better. The Minister of Economic Warfare (now the Earl of Selborne) agreed and pointed out that the Special Operations Executive, which was of course on the spot in Italy, also favoured a longer softening-up period. However, Eden had his way. The War Cabinet concluded that the shorter period was to be preferred, and it was left that the Foreign Secretary would so inform the Prime Minister.[24]

PWE had earlier analysed the proposition which Eden disliked instinctively. Would a political pronouncement weaken Italian resistance? Who would make it? When should it be made? If a big enough induce-

---

[22] PREM 3/365/2 ff. 213–4 (19.5.43).
[23] CAB 65/34, f. 98; 65/38, f.23 (20.5.43).
[24] CAB 65/38, ff. 27–9 (21.5.43).

ment could be offered to the Italians their will to resist would be affected; but current policy ruled out any such inducement. Any declaration must be made by the highest authority. PWE was satisfied, however, that any statement within the existing policy would be shot to pieces by enemy propaganda. It might even be taken as a sign of weakness, which would hearten the Italians. Therefore the change should be deferred as long as possible – otherwise the policy statement would evaporate instead of soaking in.[25]

On 22 May Eden sent a telegram to the Prime Minister which was an exact reflection of the PWE assessment. An announcement now would be shot to pieces by enemy propaganda, and be regarded as weakness. A statement of policy would evaporate instead of soaking in.[26] The Executive must have been gratified to see how closely the War Cabinet followed their advice. Whether it was sound advice is another matter. PWE were accustomed to mount year-long campaigns in which an idea would be put over again and again, on the principle of dripping on stone. Yet in this case, when they were presented with one of the most saleable ideas of the whole war – which the military experts advocated – they feared that it would evaporate. A technical appraisal based on their usual principles would surely have confirmed the views of Eisenhower, the commanders in the Middle East, and the Vice-Chiefs of Staff.

However, even before the War Cabinet had come to a firm conclusion, the President and the Prime Minister had agreed that the earlier plan would stand. They both took exception to Eisenhower's reference to 'peace with honour'; and Roosevelt said 'we cannot get away from unconditional surrender'.[27]

In spite of the rebuff Eisenhower made another attempt to ease the path of the men under his command by exploiting the fourth arm. On 29 June he told the Combined Chiefs of Staff that he was considering the use of black radio to spread a rumour that Italy had asked for and been granted an armistice. He was much attracted by the idea, as was Alexander. Even if it was only partially successful it could confuse and discourage the Italians at a critical stage of the assault on Sicily. The only snag was that the black broadcasts would be picked up in Britain and the United States, where people would also be given false hopes. The British Chiefs of Staff examined the idea on 1 July and agreed to recommend it to the Prime Minister. The Foreign Secretary again expressed doubts, but said that on this occasion he was not prepared to press his 'instinctive opposition'.[28]

The matter was further discussed at a Staff Conference on 2 July presided over by the Prime Minister. The Foreign Secretary and

[25] FO 898/349 (21.5.43).
[26] PREM 3/365/2, ff. 194–5 (22.5.43).
[27] *Ibid* ff. 196, 198.
[28] FO 898/349; CAB 79/62, f. 119 (1.7.43).

Minister of Information were also present. The Conference approved the proposal and the British Chiefs of Staff told Eisenhower that so far as they were concerned he could go ahead, subject to certain conditions. For example, only black shortwave stations in Britain should be used, supported by rumours and black leaflets from North Africa. They were not worried by the danger that the British and American press would get hold of the fake story. If they did they would be told that it was a legitimate *ruse de guerre*.[29] This telegram was hastily cancelled the following day. In a further message the Chiefs of Staff said that they did not now think that the armistice rumour would have much effect on *Husky*. They were also advised, presumably by PWE, that the ruse was bound to be found out, since various agencies in Britain and the United States monitored all black broadcasts. British radio would therefore be discredited. 'Nevertheless, with the approval of the Prime Minister, we are prepared to agree that the ruse should be tried, if the commanders on the spot feel that it will make a material contribution to the success of *Husky*'.[30]

Sefton Delmer, PWE's leading exponent of the black art, took up with great gusto the idea of a bogus armistice announcement. He suggested that it should be made on as many enemy transmissions as could be counterfeited. PWE's black radio stations, however, must not carry the actual announcement, but simply carry on with their two-month-old campaign of news and rumours hinting that there was in Italy a strong and active peace party anxious to come to terms with the allies. Delmer pointed out that the Admiralty radio station at Cleethorpes naturally tended to interfere with the transmissions of one important German longwave station (DNB) and suggested that if this jamming were deliberately intensified it would force a large part of DNB's longwave audience on to the DNB shortwave transmission which PWE would in fact be pirating.[31]

The Minister of Information was lukewarm about the whole proposal, perhaps because it had not been thought up by one of his professional propagandists. When he submitted a draft of the fake proclamation prepared by PWE he said that both he and Bruce Lockhart thought it was deplorable, much too long, when what was wanted was a news flash. (Why then, one might ask, had the Minister not submitted a news flash?) He went on: 'I assume that the Generals responsible for this bright idea . . . have given proper consideration to the reactions that this declaration will create in the event of a United Nations reverse in the *Husky* operation. They will be the laughing stock of the world and many a day will pass before British propaganda will be taken seriously

[29] CAB 79/62, f. 153; PREM 3/365/2, f. 156; FO 898/349 (2.7.43).
[30] PREM 3/365/2, f. 150; FO 898/349 (3.7.43).
[31] FO 898/349 (3.7.43).

... but if the Generals want it, we'll do it against our better judgement'.[32]

This was a Ministerial performance of a very low order. The good Minister makes his mind up as to the proper course of action, announces his decision, modestly accepts credit if he is proved right, and unquestioningly accepts blame if he is proved wrong. He does not attribute the decision to others so that when things turn out badly he may say 'I told you so'. Eden hedged his bets in much the same way. He made it quite clear that he was against the proposed announcement, but he was not prepared to veto it.

Churchill, who had already given his blessing, was impressed by Bracken's lack of enthusiasm. He at once sent a telegram to Dill, who was in Algiers, saying that the armistice announcement would not have much bearing on the actual fighting. When it became known that the allies had spread the rumour the future credibility of British and American broadcasts would be suspect. 'We should consider whether the price to be paid does not exceed the advantage likely to be gained. On this I am prepared to be guided by Eisenhower and Alexander'.[33] So Churchill too was not prepared to say yea or nay.

Anthony Bevir had observed this transaction with misgiving bordering on horror. Finally, he could no longer keep quiet. He wrote to Leslie Rowan,[34] the principal private secretary: 'I must say I think this is frightfully dangerous. The Italians think they are an honourable people, oddly enough. Equally oddly, there is respect for the House of Savoy'. If the British government stooped to forging the name of the King of Italy for this purpose it would bring them even lower than the Germans in the eyes of the Italian people. Bevir consoled himself with the hope that Churchill's telegram to Dill 'will be enough to choke them off'.[35]

Rowan allowed himself to forget for a moment that private secretaries are seen and not heard. Bevir's letter found its way on to the Prime Minister's desk. Churchill read it, and saw the light. He remembered that it is the job of the Minister, and in particular of the Prime Minister, to take decisions. He immediately dictated three telegrams about the fake armistice. To Dill he said: 'Further reflection on this dodge convinces me against it'; to Alexander: 'I hope it will be squelched locally'; and to Eisenhower: 'We shall certainly not agree to it here, believing that it would do far more harm than good. Every good wish'. Eisenhower replied that no further action would be taken. 'Sincerely appreciate your good wishes'. Churchill, perhaps thankful that at the eleventh hour he had side-stepped a major gaffe, rounded off the ex-

---

[32] PREM 3/365/2, f. 153 (2.7.43).
[33] PREM 3/365/1, f. 118; 3/365/2, f. 152 (3.7.43).
[34] Later Sir Leslie.
[35] PREM 3/365/2, f. 149 (3.7.43).

change on 5 July: 'Thanks very much. Trust all is focussing well. W.S.C.'[36]

The last word was with Leslie Rowan. He sent a note to Bevir which suggests that they may have had an earlier difference of opinion about his contribution to the discussion: 'You won hands down. Just see what yer done!'[37]

Overlord

It is impossible in a few pages to describe all that PWE did in connection with Operation *Overlord*, the allied invasion of Europe. In the months before and after D-Day the propagandists were active in three main spheres. They continued their output of white and black propaganda with the objectives of lowering the morale of the enemy and raising the morale of the occupied countries. Secondly, there was intensive study of probable conditions in the liberated territories – in consultation with the allied governments – so that material could be prepared well in advance to accelerate rehabilitation. Separate contingency plans were evolved on three different assumptions – that the Germans would leave without putting up a fight, that there would be a short conflict in which not too much damage was done, and that there would be a long and bitter struggle. PWE's main objective was to get the facilities with which they were most directly concerned – radio and the press – back on their feet as quickly as possible.

Thirdly, there was work in support of *Overlord* itself, one of the most important elements of which was a contribution to strategic deception. During the six weeks prior to the Normandy landings PWE's radio programmes carried repeated warnings to fishermen on the Western seaboard of Europe from the North Cape to the Pyrenees, and to all people living near strategic railway junctions to expect heavy aerial bombardment. After the landings huge quantities of leaflets were dropped over the Pas de Calais and West Flanders to reinforce the belief held by some of the German High Command (which the allies knew about through the Ultra decyphering machine)[38] that a second invasion would be launched in that area.

PWE were also concerned with the training of officers to be dropped behind the enemy lines as the allies advanced; and the direction of political warfare agents waiting in the occupied countries to play their part in the liberation of Europe. These men – political warfare men as distinct from the saboteurs of SOE – co-operated with local resistance groups in five principal campaigns: the demoralization of the enemy; the sowing of mistrust between rival Quisling organizations; the denial of labour to the German war machine; preparation for interference with

[36] PREM 3/365/2, ff. 139–40; 143–5 (4–5.7.43).
[37] *Ibid* f. 142 (4.7.43).
[38] See *The Ultra Secret*, Ch. 15.

road and rail communications after D-Day; and generally undermining the administration of the occupied countries.

PWE managed a substantial publishing enterprise. The Executive produced huge quantities of what became known as 'the D-Day Publications'. These were designed to boost Britain – as can readily be deduced from their titles – at the earliest possible moment after liberation. There were about a dozen altogether: 'Britain – Citadel of Liberty'; 'The Battle of Britain'; 'The Battle of Sea Communications'; '500,000,000 People: the Empire at War'; 'Keeping the Base'; and so on.[39] There were also soldiers' guides to the occupied countries, complete with useful phrase supplements and do's and don'ts. The French guide began 'A new BEF, which includes you, is going to France'; and in the behaviour section it commanded 'Do salute civilians when you talk to them – they expect it of you'; and 'Don't pull up vine stumps for firewood. They may look dead, but they're not'.[40] Thirdly, there was a series of basic manuals for the use of the natives of the occupied countries telling them what to expect when the invasion came, and how best to look after their safety.[41] All this involved a huge amount of writing, editing, translating, and printing.

There were also *ad hoc* jobs to be done from London, for example, propaganda to dissuade the Germans from flooding Holland before they withdrew; and the dropping of leaflets warning them that if they took over for their own use food parcels parachuted to the people of the occupied countries they would be regarded as war criminals.

A very confident PWE paper of February 1944 claimed that relationships established with groups in France and Belgium would enable the Executive to make an important contribution to the success of the invasion. They were less hopeful about Holland, where the government had been obstructive; but the people of Holland, Belgium, and France had already provided ample evidence of their capacity to respond to instructions from London under much less favourable conditions than would obtain at D-Day. The will and ability of the organized groups had been confirmed by regular contact between political warfare staff and the resistance leaders. In particular, use would be made of the many clandestine newspapers which were directed from London.[42]

One of the special tasks assigned to PWE, working with the Americans, was to plan a covert attack on the morale of the German forces in Norway, Denmark, Holland, Belgium and France. Although the German soldier had shown himself capable of stubborn resistance in battle, the occupation troops, relaxed by long periods of inactivity, should be good subjects for propaganda. If they were keyed up by the

[39] FO 898/474.
[40] FO 898/478.
[41] FO 898/484.
[42] FO 898/376, ff. 117-8 (12.2.44).

expectation of imminent invasion their discipline would improve; but if propaganda induced a 'sitzkrieg' mentality, like the phoney war attitude which had contributed to the fall of France, it would pay off.

German troops should also be led to believe that the High Command would make their real stand along the borders of the Reich, leaving the outlying troops to their fate. Another possibility was to engender a general escapist 'to-hell-with-the-war attitude', in which the men would constantly be reminded about conditions in Germany, the vulnerability of their families to bombing, and the danger of a rising by the foreign workers. Resentment against their officers and the Nazi Party would be fostered. These themes would be put across through covert radio, black leaflets and rumours; and with luck the Germans themselves would spread them around by word of mouth. There must be no link between this plan and overt propaganda; and if the covert attack was to succeed the level of overt propaganda in the five countries must not be raised. If it was, the enemy would become more vigilant, and the weakening effect of the covert plan would be negatived.[43]

As D-Day came nearer, relations between PWE and its sister organization SOE improved – fortunately, since both were due to contribute to the allies' final effort. PWE was constrained to acknowledge the improved relationship in a memorandum of July 1943. SOE was now much more favourably disposed towards 'the concept of subversive action of a political kind jointly with, or on behalf of, PWE'. It was recorded, however, that one of the consequences of the earlier friction was that PWE's Regional Directors were tending to take less interest in the operational side of subversion.[44]

The closer co-operation between the two organizations is reflected in the outline plans for political warfare in support of *Overlord*. The operations were listed under three headings: mainly PWE, with SOE support; mainly SOE, with PWE support; and joint. The areas in which SOE took the lead included immobilization of transport and communications; the arming of prisoners of war and political prisoners; general guerilla activities; and attacks on grounded aircraft and enemy headquarters. There was to be joint responsibility for 'depriving the enemy of the services of collaborators' – which could be interpreted in more ways than one; attacks on enemy food stocks, ammunition, and fuel dumps; and the mobilization of police and local government workers. PWE was to take the lead in destroying records useful to the enemy; stirring up the foreign workers; undermining troop morale; and gathering local intelligence.[45]

These activities were planned in painstaking detail. The attack on transport and communications, which in the earlier part of the war

[43] FO 898/376 (31.1.44).
[44] *Ibid* p. 133 (8.7.43).
[45] *Ibid* ff. 3-7 (14.9.43).

was intended to harm industry, would now be aimed at the armed forces. Hundreds, even thousands, of places should be attacked at the same time – the Germans could not possibly guard every mile of the main road and rail routes, let alone the subsidiary networks; but before D-Day PWE's work must be educational and organizational. The value of any act of sabotage carried out before D-Day would be a fraction of its value on or after D-Day. Instructions how to make road and rail blocks should be communicated to the occupied countries; and contact should be made with patriotic organizations among railwaymen, lorry drivers, bargees and lock-keepers.

The aim of propaganda must be to create a clear understanding of the crucial importance to the Germans of all forms of transport. News stories of successful transport sabotage in Russia and the Balkans should be used to show people what could be done. This oblique educational campaign would be run through white radio and leaflets; but the covert radio stations would talk quite frankly about what should be done at the time of the invasion – by every able-bodied person. Black printed material would give simple instructions in graphic form.[46]

PWE's plan for strikes claimed that during the crucial week or ten days after an allied landing they could help to obstruct the movement of supplies in the tactical and strategic back areas. They would impose an unrehearsed and therefore incalculable strain at a critical stage in the invasion. It was believed that even without help from British propaganda spontaneous and unorganized strikes were likely. If reprisals were to be avoided their conduct would be of great importance. Picketting would play straight into the enemy's hands and must be ruled out. Advance arrangements must be made for the supply of food and money to the strikers. There would have to be a thorough investigation of the groups to be encouraged to strike; and then both black and white propaganda should be used to urge the value of solidarity and concerted action.[47]

A third plan out of the many prepared at this time concerned strategic deception. This was really a matter for the Chiefs of Staff, but it was well established that PWE and SOE activities were carefully watched by the enemy and therefore could be used to mislead him. If the General Staff wanted the Germans to think that the allies were more likely to invade one country than another there could be intensified SOE activity there and an increase in the number of cryptic messages sent to it (PWE did not enlarge on the possibility that the enemy might equally decide that the increased activity was a bluff, and a clear indication that the selected country would *not* be invaded). There should be a study of the tricks used by the Germans in 1940 to see if they could be used or improved on; and of the rumours which were

[46] FO 898/376, pp. 8–12.
[47] *Ibid* pp. 13–36.

used to create civil and military confusion. White radio was useless for this sort of deception; but black could be used with great effect. What was also needed was 'the fake Staff Officer at the crossroads, the despatch rider with forged orders to retreat, the simple old man or little child with their false information'.[48]

An attempt is made in the following chapters to evaluate PWE's overall contribution to the defeat of the enemy; but it is virtually impossible to evaluate any aspect of the Executive's work. This is just as true of the part it played in *Overlord* as of its other contributions. Little evidence was committed to paper at the time. When people are fighting a battle there is seldom an opportunity to write about it; and the sum total of the official accounts which do survive does not amount to very much.

A report of the adventures of a Captain in the Special Air Service (one of the British political warfare agents trained to operate behind the enemy lines after D-Day) who was dropped 25 miles north of Bourges shows that he was almost more involved in quarrels with the Americans than with helping the French. He had the misfortune to break an arm when he landed and had to be carried through German-occupied villages to a maquis hospital. When news of the liberation of Paris came through there was general rejoicing and the neighbouring villages declared themselves liberated in spite of the presence of German troops. When it was proposed to mount an assault on Bourges the Captain vetoed the enterprise on the ground that it was too strongly held. Although the local resistance groups had liberated the district without help from the allies the Americans insisted that the Germans should surrender to them, which infuriated the French, and won them the Captain's sympathy; but when he tried to lodge a protest with Bruce Lockhart about the general behaviour of the Americans his American opposite number refused to send his telegram. It was March 1945 before Bruce Lockhart saw his written report.[49]

It is difficult to know what to make of a report like this. It seems that the Captain's only positive achievement was to restrain the local patriots from attacking Bourges – which may or may not have been the right thing to do. It seems likely that if the historian is presented with a hundred or a thousand comparable episodes he will still fail to arrive at a firm verdict.

An idea of the activities – and the problems – of the radio propagandist in the field may be gathered from a letter from Commander Donald McLachlan to Sefton Delmer written in Luxembourg in December 1944:

> The situation is a unique and amusing one. The editor, chief

[48] FO 898/376, pp. 23–6.
[49] FO 898/358 (5.3.45).

writer, intelligence officer and production chief is . . . me! . . . The next two things are to build up railway intelligence and air intelligence. In the former the prospects are excellent. A high railway official captured as a private at the front is sitting near here pouring his heart out to the railway experts at Bradley's HQ. He knows the lingo and can recite whole chapters of the German Bradshaw by heart. He is a dream . . . The first generation Americans sit and cluck their tongues when they hear a slip by the readers. Tremendous arguments go on over idiom and the use of words, and there is a general tendency to regard the white boys [ie the open propagandists] as a kind of coloured trash which I find most amusing . . .
No one had any ideas about the form of the programme, its length, its style and character. We literally had to build round the signature tune. We had one professional actor; one old chap from the Pfalz with the ambition to address Social Democratic speeches to his old colleagues; one rather dumb seller of women's clothes with the rank of corporal who has a good voice, a Dusseldorf twang, and bad nerves . . . The real sweat is the writing. The news and special items go through as many processes as synthetic rubber.[50]

One *Overlord* operation carried out by PWE appears to have been particularly successful. This was the 'Intruder' operation in which the high-powered Aspidistra transmitter was used to implement a curious reversal of allied policy with regard to the evacuation of German civilians from the forward areas.

As the allied armies moved eastward the Germans encouraged evacuation from the Rhine and Ruhr areas of people who were not engaged on industrial work, so that they might be re-employed in agriculture, industry, or in the building of fortifications further to the rear, and thus help to maintain the level of production and improve the country's defences. Allied propaganda sought to counter these measures by urging German civilians to evade compulsory evacuation by hiding in cellars or nearby woods. Those left behind would contribute nothing to the economy and would in due course be overrun by the allied advance. This policy was in marked contrast to the line taken by the Germans in 1940 when they did everything they could to terrify civilians into fleeing, so that they would obstruct allied troop movements.

PWE in fact believed that it would be more profitable to stimulate panic evacuation, but were overruled by PWD. In November 1944, however, they suggested that the policy should be changed. Refugees would block enemy lines of communication, they would spread panic to the rear of the German armies, and they might even force the Wehrmacht to take action against them.[51] SHAEF had no doubt that a panic evacuation could be achieved by 'political warfare bombing'; but again

[50] FO 898/208 (11.12.44).

decided against it on the ground that the allies' own progress might be held up by the refugees 'since no British or American soldier could be induced to use German methods of machine gunning and manhandling civilians'. Therefore standstill propaganda was still the right line.[52] Evidence was accumulating that many civilians who might have been evacuated to useful jobs elsewhere in Germany had been lost to the Reich.[52]

This policy carried on unaltered until the beginning of March 1945, when the Voice of SHAEF was still urging doctors to remain with their patients and frustrate Himmler's game of creating a zone of disease behind the retreating German armies; miners to stay put to protect their mines and future employment, and to keep their possessions out of the hands of the SS; the police to remain at their posts to prevent looting by the SS and party toughs; and the farmers to follow the example of 50,000 of their fellows and dodge compulsory evacuation.[53]

Then during a visit to SHAEF in the first week of March the Prime Minister 'insisted that the resources of propaganda should be used to make the German civilian evacuate, instead of staying put, as had hitherto been advocated by SHAEF'. This was very much deprecated by the working propagandists attached to PWD who bitterly complained: 'As has happened on previous occasions with regard to paramilitary matters his view was accepted without serious resistance on the highest level'. PWD were dismayed by the decision, which would mean an embarrassing *volte face* in both black and white propaganda. In particular white propaganda, which was due to carry the commands of the military government to the German people after the cessation of hostilities, was being asked to play a black trick, namely to instruct civilians to do something that would result in loss of life, great suffering and disorganization. They saw that the only hope was to make representations to Churchill. McClure therefore asked Crossman, who was now on his staff, to get PWE to ask their Ministers to approach the Prime Minister.[54]

PWD's case was that the 'stay put' policy involved resistance to the German evacuation plans, and therefore to the Nazi Party; and there was ample evidence of its success. PWD recognized that PWE had always favoured evacuation, and conceded that there might have been a case for evacuating the relatively scattered population on the west bank of the Rhine well ahead of the allies' advance and close-support bombing, in their own interest. 'Now we are asked to urge evacuation under shellfire and bombing immediately behind the front, into a hinterland with no natural defences. For two months we have been describing

[51] FO 898/395 (16.11.44).
[52] *Ibid* (7.3.45).
[53] WO 219/1346.
[54] FO 898/385 (7.3.45).

graphically, both on black and white, the consequences of such evacuation in Eastern Germany. The German propaganda line will be: "The allies are planning another Dresden".[55]

The new Deputy Director General of PWE (General W. H. A. Bishop) did not enlarge on PWD's plea when he told Eden and Bracken of SHAEF's decision. He did point out, however, that it meant a complete reversal of policy; but it had been decided 'by the highest political and military authorities [presumably Churchill and Eisenhower] as the means whereby PWE can make the greatest contribution towards the immediate end ie the defeat of the German forces in the field'.[56] He confessed that it would take great ingenuity to make such a violent change so quickly, but it could be done. Eden agreed with the new policy. Bracken agreed with enthusiasm. He said that every effort must be made to implement the decision – which was long overdue.[57]

The change was anathema to the BBC. The instructions to stay put had been broadcast most vigorously and reinforced by every argument of German self-interest. News of German civilians in captured towns had been used to illustrate the happy results of refusing to evacuate. 'An attempt to reverse all this will cost us our reputation and will also prove ineffective'.[58] Thus Douglas Ritchie. But the highest political and military authorities had spoken – and argument was irrelevant.

A special PWD directive was issued on 15 March 1945. The Supreme Commander had decided that 'a drastic change in policy' relating to evacuation was essential if political warfare was to give maximum support in the next and vital phase of allied military operations in the west. A SHAEF directive of the same date signed by General McClure does not refer too pointedly to a drastic change but simply amends and brings up to date the directive in force, and refers to changes in the military and political situation. It indicates helpfully how the propagandists may execute their enforced somersault without appearing too foolish to their listening audience. It was considered that there would be no real problem for the black propagandists, who were a law unto themselves; but the white would be considerably embarrassed. Their audience must be told that while nowhere in Germany was any longer safe, the Ruhr was much less safe than elsewhere. The only hope was to stop the war as soon as possible.[59]

The new policy made possible the use of Aspidistra in the sort of operation for which it had been primarily installed. In January 1945 Bruce Lockhart discussed with his Ministers Aspidistra's contribution

[55] FO 898/395 (7.3.45).
[56] Ibid.
[57] Ibid (7, 8.3.45).
[58] Ibid (11.3.45).
[59] Ibid (15.3.45).

to the final phase of military operations in Europe. It was mooted that at the moment of a decisive allied breakthrough an attempt should be made to end the resistance of the German armies in the west by putting out a fake German announcement that their High Command had sent emissaries asking for an armistice. The Combined Chiefs of Staff recommended against the idea in rather woolly terms. They thought that it would be unwise to implement it 'unless there appears to be a high probability that the military results derived from it are such as to justify the risk involved'. The English translation of this gobbledygook is 'a good plan if certain to succeed'. They conceded, however, that when the collapse of Germany was imminent Aspidistra might be used in a major deception;[60] and the chance came with the reversal of the evacuation propaganda policy.

PWE considered on 15 March the implementation of the new directive. It was agreed that a lurid picture should be painted of conditions in the battle area, in contrast with the safety of the interior of the Reich to which the Party were escaping. Aspidistra would be used to intrude on a station serving the Frankfurt area with fake instructions from the German authorities ordering immediate evacuation. The impression would be given that the Party could no longer hold the people back. Black leaflets would also be used.[61]

The Intruder programme began on 24 March shortly after eight o'clock in the evening. For fifteen minutes announcements of the movement of allied aircraft were transmitted on the special German air raid warning wavelength; and then the Reich Defence Commissioner for Dusseldorf came on the air to say that it had been decided to evacuate Zones 4 and 5 immediately, but only those liable for military service and age groups 29–31 would be allowed to go. As far as possible the movement of other people would be prevented.[62]

Soon after the supposed Defence Commissioner had finished speaking an 'important announcement' was broadcast on Cologne's wavelength: 'In the night of 23/24 March strong British formations launched the expected large-scale offensive on the Lower Rhine on both sides of Wesel . . . the British assault columns which are reaching the eastern bank are being smashed immediately in hand-to-hand fighting.' A few hundred British troops had been landed by transport aircraft and gliders. An immense battle would start shortly. Transport was paralysed, and evacuation impossible, except for those who would carry on the struggle in the interior. Others would have to stick it out, and if need be face death bravely. Instructions about reporting to assembly points followed. It was suggested that small handcarts,

[60] FO 898/395 (15.3.45).
[61] *Ibid.*
[62] FO 898/47.

bicycles or wheelbarrows would make it easier to carry personal belongings.[63]

The following night the black propagandists got down to it in earnest. The German home radio programme was picked up from Vienna, and then when Frankfurt had to close down because of the approach of allied bombers Aspidistra stepped in with the home programme on Frankfurt's wavelength. So far as Frankfurt's listeners were concerned their normal service had carried on without interruption. Then the relay was broken into at intervals with a series of alarming announcements. Those due to evacuate must move off immediately. Enemy armoured cars had just passed through Oberramstadt. Red Cross nurses in the Kassel district to report for duty. An army car with four passengers in German uniform, presumably enemy agents, was travelling towards Gelnhausen. The car must be stopped and the occupants arrested. If they resisted they should be killed. All butchers in Kassel to report to the slaughterhouse 'to help in the execution of emergency measures'. (Was this choice item inserted by a PWE man with a macabre sense of humour?) Handcarts, wheelbarrows and prams should be taken at once to the assembly points. So it went on hour after hour, with air raid warnings scattered among the other announcements.

The transmission was interrupted at intervals to establish that Frankfurt radio was still silent; but apart from these interruptions – of half a minute or so – the enemy wavelength was successfully used from 8.43 in the evening of 25 March to noon on 26 March; and for shorter periods on three or four of the following days. Many of the announcements were picked up by agencies monitoring German radio and were sent out in their news services. This heightened the illusion of truth – and also gave the world, and many people in Britain, a false impression of the progress of the allies. Very few people had been let into the secret and many in authority, including those concerned with intelligence, had to be warned after the event to take what they had heard with a pinch of salt.[64]

There is no doubt that Intruder was launched at the psychological moment and had a considerable success. As usual the contemporary evidence is not extensive, but there was one illuminating report from a *Gauamtsleiter* (district administrator) to his superior. He said that the intrusion of enemy radio announcements had caused great confusion and unrest. Whole neighbourhoods had been terrified by the news of the approach of enemy tanks and armoured cars, emergency evacuation orders, etc. The enemy were seeking to create chaos in the transport system, and to set up targets for terror attacks from the air (this Nazi, at least, assumed that the allies would play according to the German

---

[63] FO 898/47 (24.3.45).
[64] *Ibid.*

rules). German radio should have followed up each fake transmission with an explanation and a correction – but this had not been done until 28 March, four days after the deception had begun. The German radio programmes had, in fact, caused great irritation: in these momentous days the citizen expected to hear something other than jazz and swing music. (Perhaps *Gotterdämerung* would have been more to the official's taste). It was remarkable that there had been no attempt to answer the Jewish lies of the enemy transmitter.

Unless something positive was done within the next few days, catastrophe was inevitable. Rumours, strengthened by the enemy pirating of German wavelengths 'do all that remains to finish off the fighting spirit of the troops and the endurance of the people. The individual feels deserted and betrayed . . . He cries out for an unvarnished explanation from the German leadership . . . The politically-conscious in the Party and amongst the people still believe firmly in the historic change promised by the Führer; but the weaker elements are growing restless and beginning to doubt'.

The report concluded with a passage which would have cost the author his job, and probably his liberty, only a short time before: 'The argument is brought forward that the eternal favourable colouring of reports, and parade-ground displays have darkened the perception of the Führer and cut him off from the people . . . Month after month and year after year we have been consoled for the misery of the enemy air war with "equal reprisals". Our patience has also been exploited endlessly with allusions to a change through the use of decisive weapons and discoveries. So far nothing has happened and no bond has been kept. That is what the people are saying everywhere'.[65]

In his own humble way the *Gauamtsleiter* had written the epitaph of the Third Reich.

[65] FO 898/47 (29.3.45).

9
Customer reaction: The effect of propaganda

Ideally this and the concluding chapter would evaluate the contribution of the propaganda department to the total war effort; but any such evaluation is impossible. There is a vast store of evidence; but for every fact in the files of PWE and elsewhere there are a thousand uncertainties. For every individual documented reaction there are a thousand unknowns. Even the documented reaction must often be suspect; for example, the testimony of the prisoner of war. The mere fact of his capture meant that he was no longer the man PWE had been aiming at, and even if he answered all the interrogator's questions honestly he probably gave a false impression of the extent to which he had been influenced by propaganda. Sometimes he may have tried to give the answers he thought his captors wanted to hear; and it was then up to the political survey officer who interrogated him to make his own judgement of what he *did* say. Even if the state of mind of the individual prisoner was accurately assessed, it remained to decide how it had been arrived at. What effect had propaganda really had? The perfect propaganda line was one which the prisoner swallowed without knowing that it *was* propaganda; and even the most sophisticated computer could make little of that sort of negative evidence.

Prisoners of war were one thing. At least they could be examined face to face. It was much more difficult to assess the effect of propaganda on people hundreds of miles away in enemy, satellite or occupied countries. Most of the reports the propaganda department received were second hand; but the real difficulty was that the original report was inevitably subjective. The man who read a leaflet and then proceeded to say what he thought about it really ceased to be the individual at whom it had been aimed. He had unconsciously aligned himself either with those responsible for dropping it, or those at whom it was directed. For a leaflet to succeed it had to be read, the message assimilated, and the piece of paper forgotten. If a recipient took the trouble to write to PWE or to some third party about it, it had failed in its intended purpose. Leaflets had the greatest impact when they influenced thinking subliminally; but there was virtually no chance of direct measurement of that impact. In assessing their success month by month

PWE had instead to rely on the flimsiest of straws in the wind.

Most authors are sadly aware that the sum total of their reviews may be culled to establish that a book is both the best and the worst ever written. So it is with judgements on the early British propaganda campaign.

A report from an agent in Bavaria said that if leaflets continued to be dropped 'one can reckon they will make an impression on people'. A traveller returned from Trier to Paris: 'The flood of leaflets dropped by the RAF has had a great effect on the population'. A memorandum from Copenhagen: 'Trouble which the authorities had in Hamburg, Chemnitz, and other towns near which leaflets were dropped confirms that they were having an effect'. A Dutchman who visited Germany from time to time assured the British government that Germans in the big towns were anxious for further news to be dropped by the RAF. A letter written to New York said that when British planes dropped leaflets near Berlin the Germans were astounded – first to find that the Nazis had fooled them when they claimed that the RAF would never reach Berlin, and second that the British dropped paper instead of bombs, because they did not want to destroy the Berliners. A German industrialist told the British Consul General in Zurich that the distribution of leaflets from aeroplanes should be kept up. Germany should be swamped with them.[1]

It might be concluded from these six pieces of evidence that the early leaflet campaign was successful, and worth every penny it cost.

However: a report from an agent in Bavaria said that 'leaflets which have been dropped are absolutely no good ... there are very few people in Germany today, even those friendly to Britain, who believe the leaflets contain the truth'. Another report from Bavaria: 'The English leaflet aeroplane propaganda, so far from having done good, has done harm'. The British Chargé d'Affaires at Tallin recorded that leaflets attacking Hitler had been very badly received in Germany since the people as a whole were still solidly behind him. An American working with the Red Cross in Poland ('a man of sense and judgement with no axe to grind') was 'entirely sceptical about the value of leaflets at the present time. So long as Germans were unshaken by a single military reverse leaflets were useless. They might even set up a resistance to British propaganda which would be a handicap at a later date'. Another American: 'I fear that Germans have been taught to discount the leaflets you have been distributing. They discount most of their own news as propaganda, and probably regard your leaflets in a similar light'. A Danish journalist returned from Germany said that generally speaking British leaflets had had very little effect.[2]

[1] FO 898/462.
[2] Ibid.

CUSTOMER REACTION

It might be concluded from these six pieces of evidence that the early leaflet campaign was a failure and not worth the money spent on it.

In these circumstances all that can be done is to set out some of the evidence and leave it to the reader to try to make up his own mind. In the early days one of Department EH's tests was the reaction of the German leaders. The more they reacted the more successful was British propaganda. In the first week of the war Göring said 'Ridiculous propaganda pamphlets have been dropped by British planes, but heaven help them should they exchange propaganda for a bomb'. He added that the fact that the leaflets were written in good German proved that they were not written by an Englishman, but by a German Jew determined to destroy Germany – thereby using the British leaflets (which in fact were not in good German) for his own propaganda purposes. A month later he claimed that the 'stupid and silly' leaflets dropped over German towns and villages would not affect morale. In Germany no-one listened any more to the hostile outer world, but only to the voice of the Führer. In a speech at Munich Hitler claimed that every British balloon that dropped a few intellectual leaflets was proof that nothing had changed in Britain in the past twenty years; but every reaction from Germany would demonstrate to the British how things were moving in the Reich. A lull in the delivery of leaflets in October 1939 inspired a flight of fancy on German radio about the tactics of the British Ministry of Misinformation. Lord MacMillan (then Minister of Information) had had to replace his warplanes with balloons – beautifully designed, charming playthings for his grandchildren, the fabric of which could be made into first-class anoraks, warmer than the best sable. Bigger and better balloons from Lord MacMillan would be most welcome. All this suggests that the Germans knew that they were in such a commanding position that the British propaganda effort was neither here nor there; but the members of Department EH could and did argue that because Hitler and Goebbels took the trouble to reply to their leaflets they must be at least slightly worried about their effect.[3]

A curious Secret Service report of January 1940 supported the idea that British propaganda was getting under the Germans' skins. It purported to provide an assessment of the German authorities' views on the relative merits of enemy leaflets and radio propaganda. Both the Gestapo and Ministry of Propaganda regarded leaflets as more dangerous. If a German citizen deliberately tuned to a foreign station on his radio he knew that he was committing an offence; but if he saw a piece of paper on the ground it might be no more than an advertisement for liver pills. The Ministry of Propaganda considered leaflets to be dangerous because the average German got so much propaganda thrown at him on the radio during the day that he became tired of the spoken

[3] FO 898/462 (9.9, 6, 10.10, 8.11.39).

F

word, and switched on his radio at home only for music – a rather defeatist position for the Ministry of Propaganda to adopt. The same average German was attracted by any kind of printed matter – he had a great penchant for reading. But this did not mean that either the Gestapo or the Ministry of Propaganda underrated the importance of radio as a propaganda medium. This report, which said very little at great length, was solemnly read out to the War Cabinet by the Foreign Secretary, and the unknown agent had earned his keep.[4]

A month later Dallas Brooks tried to sum up the effectiveness of British propaganda in the first six months of war. He wisely accepted that it was difficult to come to a firm conclusion; but saw some significance in the recently-increased sentences on people caught listening to enemy radio or reading leaflets, in the jamming of British broadcasts, and in the Nazi leaders' constant references to foreign propaganda in their speeches. (It is of course hardly surprising that they should have devoted a good deal of effort to the war of words at this stage, since it was virtually the only war being waged.) There was evidence that British radio was widely listened to, and British leaflets read with interest; but Brooks admitted that they were not yet having the full effect that had been hoped for. In particular there was no sign of an early revolt in Germany; and it was clear that the Wehrmacht would have to suffer a reverse before there was any chance of an uprising. The Nazis' control was far too tight, and there was no-one outside the army, which was very loyal, capable of leading a revolt.[5]

It was much easier for PWE to measure reaction to their propaganda in the occupied countries, since people regularly escaped from them to Britain with first hand accounts of the state of affairs, and since there was closer contact with these countries through agents than there could be with Germany. They were singularly fortunate in the case of Belgium from which Paul Struye (who became President of the Senate after the war) sent them a survey of public opinion by secret courier every six months or so. These were invaluable for the creation of new propaganda themes, and for the study of the reactions to those already in use. They covered many different aspects of public opinion, but the sections on propaganda and the Belgian attitude to Britain were of particular importance to PWE. They showed how opinion was changing – or being moulded – during the occupation.[6] Thus:

After a year (June 1941): nearly all Belgians listen to the BBC, in spite of the penalties. Those who don't, pick up the BBC news at second hand. Neutral stations are listened to – Sottens, Ankara, Boston, for example – but it is the BBC that really matters. Yet the people regard

---

[4] CAB 65/11, f. 199 (29.1.40).
[5] FO 898/3, ff. 275-8 (25.2.40).
[6] The surveys were published under the title *L'évolution du sentiment publique en Belgique sous l'occupation allemande* (Brussels, 1945).

Britain with mixed feelings. They still resent the passage of British troops through Belgium in May 1940, and the destruction they caused. The great majority, however, profoundly admire the courage of the British people in fighting on, although few believe their claim that they are the champions of the small nation. It is simply a war between two imperial powers. Britain was wrong to urge Poland to resist and France to go to war when her own forces were so painfully inadequate. Some believe that Churchill has no love for Belgium. Why has he not publicly guaranteed her empire?[7]

After twenty months (February 1942): the whole of Belgium hears the transmissions from London – those who don't dare to listen are quickly brought up to date by those who do. The German-controlled press is fighting against the BBC's propaganda and its influence on the people. Most listeners want to hear news about the progress of the war rather than allied propaganda. They admire the objectivity with which the British announce their reverses and losses, and trust their communiqués much more than those of the Axis; but they are critical of the exaggerations and fantasies of some commentators who are badly informed about the position of the occupied countries. The people don't want their heads to be stuffed with propaganda, whether by friend or foe.

After two and a half years (December 1942): public opinion is now resolutely anglophile, but this is largely because people believe that their liberation depends on a British victory. Severe criticism of Britain's imperialism and her selfish policies is not uncommon – even from those who devoutly hope for an Anglo-Saxon victory. Churchill's prestige has greatly increased in recent months. Some of his earlier speeches, especially those addressed to neutral countries, have left a nasty taste in the mouth; but today public opinion pays tribute to his great personality and abounding energy. It shows increasing admiration for the British people as a whole – in spite of their faults. They are now seen as a great nation with a brilliant future.[8]

After three years (June 1943): anglophilia is increasing by leaps and bounds. Earlier this was linked to Belgium's hope of liberation, but today there is more of a pro-British feeling. All sectors of the population admire Britain's recovery from the debacle of 1940, and the way the people have faced up to adversity. Churchill's prestige is very high. Nearly every Belgian regards him as the man of the age, whose actions are directly influencing the course of history. The fact remains, however, that in spite of these anglophile sentiments most people believe that Britain is still fighting for her empire; but they now also believe

---

[7] *L'évolution du sentiment publique en Belgique sous l'occupation allemande*, pp. 51–3.
[8] *Ibid* pp. 88, 111.

that Belgian and British interests coincide, and they accept that British rule is tolerant and tolerable, which German rule is not.[9]

After forty-four months (February 1944): anglophilia continues to be the first article of faith of occupied Belgium. American and Russian victories are of course hailed by everyone, but British victories are acclaimed as if they were our own. Many Belgians are learning English. At the beginning of the occupation ten German books were sold for every English book: now it is the other way round. Churchill is more popular than ever – people were very worried by his recent illness.[10]

The last months (September 1944): paper shortage has reduced the size and circulation of the newspapers; but no-one is in the slightest influenced by the controlled press. They read it avidly, but only because the Belgian must read his newspaper every day. The clandestine papers come out more or less regularly. The miniature newspapers dropped by the RAF, especially *l'Arc en Ciel* are read more and more widely. The BBC is still the principal source of news and is listened to openly. German propaganda has intensified. Colour posters appeal to the people to join Nazi formations, and warn of the dangers of Bolshevism.[11]

The condensation of a single theme into a few paragraphs cannot convey an adequate impression of the value of Struye's contribution to the work of PWE; but it gives an inkling as to how public opinion moved in Belgium during the occupation. The surveys, which are brilliantly judicial, are of particular value since they were made at intervals over a period of years. They do not suffer from the hindsight which creeps into post mortems made by PWE after the war; and although they are the work of one man, he was a shrewd observer in touch with all sections of the community – a relatively small and compact community which could be observed much more closely than most European nations – and they probably get as near the truth about public opinion as is humanly possible. It remains to decide, however, how far PWE's activities were responsible for moulding that public opinion. The clear inference from Struye's surveys is that it was the BBC that really mattered, with some support from the clandestine press, which itself depended largely on news from the BBC. Leaflets of the 'mini-newspaper' type played their part; but the British clandestine radio stations are not mentioned at all.

Conditions varied considerably in the other occupied countries, but the broad pattern of Belgium was roughly repeated elsewhere. There is no doubt that the straight BBC news was the important thing. So far as Denmark was concerned, for example, 'It is hardly possible to over-

---

[9] *L'évolution du sentiment publique en Belgique sous l'occupation allemande*, pp. 142–3.
[10] *Ibid* pp. 168–9.
[11] *Ibid* p. 185.

estimate the importance the BBC had for occupied Denmark ... The ordinary, and until 1940 largely unknown letters BBC acquired in the course of a few weeks almost magical qualities ... No account, however detailed, could completely attest to the vital significance for Denmark of the broadcasts from London.'[12] At the end of 1944, while still under occupation, the Norwegians paid a generous tribute to the BBC in the Christmas number of a newspaper they published in Stockholm: 'At the turn of the year all listeners, and in particular Norwegians, wish to send their warmest thanks to the BBC, which in its wholehearted understanding of the importance of victory over Nazism has placed all its resources at the disposal of the occupied countries.'[13]

It was the same in France, where any important news broadcast by the BBC was common knowledge within a few hours of the transmission. This was made possible by the use of illicit radios by listening groups, the formation of which was encouraged by PWE. At first the French, like most of the rest of Europe, were suspicious of news from London, and assumed that it must be no less distorted than the 'news' they heard from other combatant countries; but it was established with the passage of time that the BBC was not covering up bad news and was cautiously underplaying the good.

PWE held its own inquest into reactions in France during the whole war in April 1945. This was based on the widest possible survey of opinion among the French resistance, other Frenchmen from all walks of life and all over France, and recorded opinions in the papers of SHAEF, the BBC, PWE and OWI. The difficulty of measuring the effect of PWE's contribution is freely acknowledged. 'It is extremely difficult ... to point to an achievement which was without doubt solely the result of some operation of ours.' Having said this the memorandum goes on: 'It can perfectly safely be said, however, that the work of PWE was of immense value, and yielded a dividend which enabled General Eisenhower's armies to romp through France unexpectedly quickly and with an unexpectedly light casualty list owing to the work of the resistance men and women who had been so much helped by us'. The evidence cited to support this verdict includes the fact that the French Ambassador in London gave a luncheon for the French sections of PWE and the BBC, and that resistance leaders 'made pleasant references to their work' – perhaps not the hardest of evidence.

The broad conclusion of the inquest is that the British propagandists – PWE in their own right, and through the BBC – were completely successful in supplying accurate news, and thus combatting the dis-

---

[12] Jørgen Haestrup in the foreword to *British broadcasting and the Danish resistance movement 1940–1945* (J. J. N. Bennett, Cambridge, 1966), pp. xi–xii.
[13] Asa Briggs, *The war of words* (vol. iii of *The history of broadcasting in the United Kingdom*, Oxford 1970), p. 689.

torted versions of world events put out by Vichy and Germany; and in building up a disciplined population capable of playing its part in the liberation of France. They were not very successful in projecting Britain to France, because the Frenchmen in the BBC were afraid of appearing to be too anglophile for their audience's taste. The French people were never given a true picture of Britain's war effort and sacrifices.[14]

What of the propagandists' other activities *vis-à-vis* the occupied countries? Compared with radio propaganda leaflets counted for very little, and sometimes even did harm. For example, the *Avis* series (warnings dropped to the people of France) 'because they all too frequently ordered the impossible, or urgently warned when no action followed'.[15] The miniature newspapers were an exception, however. *l'Arc en Ciel* in Belgium, *Le courrier de l'air* in France, and *De Wervelwind* in Holland, all made an important contribution to morale building. The only criticism was that there were seldom enough of them. Late in 1942 one of the principal Dutch underground newspapers said: 'since April this year thousands (but far too few!) Whirlwinds have fluttered through the darkness every month. We rejoice at it . . . this 32-page beautifully-illustrated colour magazine is excellent . . .'[16] In 1943 the Dutch Prime Minister spoke of 'the moral strength derived by the population from *De Wervelwind*', and asked that its circulation should be increased.[17]

It is more difficult to find concrete evidence of the value of PWE's numerous propaganda campaigns carried out through radio and leaflets: for example, the attempt to make the farmers withhold their produce from the Germans, the encouragement of local government employees to lose papers and generally cause 'the inevitable red tape to become scarlet',[18] the interference with the transfer of industrial workers to German factories, the 'go-slow' in which people working directly or indirectly for the enemy were urged to do as little as possible. Even if it were possible to establish how many workers in scores of villages and towns throughout occupied Europe succeeded in dodging the columns which were marched to Germany, there is no way of telling how many were encouraged to do so by what they heard from PWE; but surely the great majority must have made up their own mind – to go quietly to Germany, or to go into hiding – totally uninfluenced by armchair exhortation from London.

PWE seem to have considered that the 'go-slow' was their most successful campaign; but again the evidence is unsatisfactory. Many

[14] FO 898/420.
[15] *Ibid.*
[16] FO 898/464 (late 1942).
[17] *Ibid* (13.5.43).
[18] FO 898/420.

would have gone slow on principle – the practice is not unknown in normal times – without encouragement from propagandists sitting in comparative comfort in a foreign country.

The same difficulty of measurement applies to PWE's efforts to restrain the occupied countries from having a go at the Germans before D-Day, and to prepare them to play their full part when the invasion started. There was no major uprising, and therefore PWE claim a success; but it may be that the majority of the patriots would have elected to lie low in any case.

Finally, it is slightly easier to judge PWE's success when it comes to the practical operational activity which they undertook in collaboration with the resistance groups. This was in effect the establishment of secret PWE outposts to carry out propaganda on the ground, particularly after D-Day, using nationals of the occupied countries, with a few PWE agents playing a minor but important role. There is evidence that this groundwork was done well, in difficult circumstances. It included the management of elaborate radio networks in the occupied countries, the despatch by air of propaganda material to reception committees, and the dropping of agents, several of whom were executed as spies. Whether the second stage of this activity – the actual dissemination of propaganda – paid a meaningful dividend it is impossible to say.

The propagandists' white messages probably had no effect at all on the German civilian population. They may have accepted the force of much that was said both on the radio and in leaflets, but it did not cause them to take up arms in the cause of freedom. Although large numbers were executed for their hostility to the régime, that hostility must as a rule have been readymade, and not the product of British propaganda; but even if it was all the result of British propaganda it amounted to very little in the total war effort.

Black propaganda probably had more bite in it, so far as the German civilians were concerned; but once again it is difficult to believe that it changed the course of the war at all. The devices thought up by the black propagandists were ingenious, and they were implemented with infinite patience and skill; but if it is asked, would the war have been prolonged by a single day if these black games had not been played it is difficult to justify any answer but no.

Perhaps one of the most successful black ploys, or at least one where the reaction is well documented, was the dropping of forged food ration documents over Germany. The objective was to disrupt the distribution of scarce food, to throw the rationing authorities into confusion, and to land in prison – or worse – those who used the forged cards to draw extra rations. The Germans reacted vigorously to this campaign. They tightened up the rationing system, and warned people that if they took advantage of this manna from heaven they would suffer heavy punishment, in serious cases the death penalty. The British had chosen to drop ration cards because they believed that German food supplies were precarious, their greatest miscalculation of the whole war. Compared with the previous year the position was 'almost luxurious'. If, however, anyone endangered the public interest by drawing rations to which he was not entitled 'he is playing a game which may prove very dangerous for him'.[19]

Large numbers did play this dangerous game to the detriment of their fellow citizens, being often ignorant of the fact that the cards were a gift from the enemy, so good were the forgeries; and a good many were brought to trial. Their numbers increased during 1944, in spite of the alleged abundance of food, and PWE's files abound with court cases. In August 1944 a Berliner was sentenced to two years' penal servitude and his wife to fifteen months for trying to use forged cheese and sausage coupons. A woman in Dortmund got two years. In Essen a man earned four years' penal servitude for picking up ration cards dropped by the enemy and passing them on to his fiancée – who got eighteen months. Death sentences were usually hidden away in an inconspicuous corner of the newspapers, but in *Der Neue Tag* of 15 February 1944 a sentence of death on a man who had tried to use forged ration cards was given headlines. These are a few of the cases which were reported; and on the principle of the tip of the iceberg PWE concluded, probably rightly, that a great many people were using the forged cards and getting away with it. The German authorities were very worried and made special arrangements to cope with the threat. The courts had found that defendants frequently claimed that they had acquired the fake cards in some legitimate way – for example, from a soldier on leave – which was no longer susceptible of proof or disproof. *Gauleiters* were instructed that whenever there was news of ration cards being dropped in their district people should be warned of the fact and reminded of the penalties for using them so that those brought before the courts would find it difficult to plead ignorance.[20]

Another reaction in the rationing field may be noted in passing. Some of PWE's black leaflets suggested that '*Diplomatenverpflegung*' ('diplomatic rations') were issued to numerous Party officials, which meant that they were much better fed than the man in the street. This rumour became so widespread that Martin Bormann had to issue a denial in which it was explained that diplomatic rations were allowed only to the representatives of foreign powers in Germany in accordance with the usual diplomatic practice.[21] Soon after this DNB reported that a woman at Halle had been sentenced to six months' imprisonment

[19] FO 898/465 (16.3.43).
[20] *Ibid* (13.11.44).
[21] *Ibid* (18.1.44).

for saying in a beer cellar that German officials were still enjoying diplomatic rations.[22]

Although these were undoubted successes in the propaganda war against the German citizen, they were no more than pinpricks. Even when all the similar successes are brought into the account it is difficult to believe that they blunted the German war effort by more than a tiny fraction of one per cent.

Most of PWE's leading propagandists accepted that those at the receiving end of propaganda are more affected by it when at the same time they are suffering military defeat:[23] but this is not a universal truth. Some, soldiers and civilians alike, will be spurred on to resist more stubbornly by an enemy who tells them that they are finished; but the vast majority do not react in this way. The student is again faced with the impossible task of separating and evaluating the reaction to the shooting war on the one hand and the war of words on the other. A German prisoner of war captured in Italy in January 1944 illustrated this point when he talked about the surrender of his unit. Morale and nerve had been shattered by clever surrender leaflets, backed up by heavy artillery fire. The fighting quality of the men had been sapped by hunger – they had little or no food and what they had was cold – and by their youth. Although the soldier – or was it his interrogator? – put the propaganda leaflets first, it is possible that the shells and the lack of food were solely responsible for the decision to surrender.[24]

PWE attacked the morale of the Wehrmacht after D-Day through all the media at their disposal. In the weeks before D-Day the main objective had been to concentrate the attention of the German soldier on the enemy within (that is, the Party) rather than on the enemy without. After D-Day the themes were switched to the hopelessness of continuing the war, the folly of useless sacrifice, and the incompetence of Germany's leaders. The soldier was reminded constantly of the military disasters on the Eastern front, the decline of German war production, the impotence of the Luftwaffe, and the breakdown of authority. There is ample evidence of reaction to this attack, and the fact that it seriously worried the German High Command.

The grey radio station *Soldatensender Calais*, which broadcast on

---

[22] FO 898/463 (31.1.44).
[23] Goebbels enunciated an extension of this principle in his propaganda directive of 5 February 1945. After admitting that morale had collapsed in certain units of the Wehrmacht, he said he had always maintained that domestic propaganda was easy enough when things were going well, but not when they were going badly. The leadership now had a chance of showing its moral and political strength – this would be the great hour for German propaganda (FO 898/532 [13.7.45]).
[24] FO 898/469 (7.1.44).

the high-powered medium wave Aspidistra, supported by three short wave stations, was perhaps the most successful medium. It was causing trouble long before D-Day. A German report in March 1944 said it was creating great unrest and confusion by the news it was putting out about the military situation and the home front, which included verbatim transmissions of the official German news service (DNB) with a number of 'more or less tendentious items mixed in'. People were showing ever-increasing trust in the station's news because as a rule its reports turned out to be accurate.[25] The army became even more alarmed by *Calais's* performance after D-Day, and put out warnings about it. 'The station broadcasts false items interspersed with genuine news, mostly without any commentary, so that they stick in the minds of the listeners because of their conciseness. Another trick is the broadcasting of pleasant music between the news items to enable slow minds to digest what they have heard'. An example of the ingenious false news broadcast was given. It was reported that reassuring news for parents had been received from the children's evacuation camps. The weekly number of deaths from diptheria had decreased from 548 to 372. 'There is reason to believe that the number of deaths will be kept at this comparatively low figure in spite of the great lack of doctors and drugs'. The report pointed out that this news item was a complete fabrication, but its objective presentation 'sticks like a venomous thorn in the heart of every soldier who has taken it for true and who may have his own children in one of the evacuation camps'.

It was pointed out that the station had adopted the conclusions of Adolf Hitler who had written in Chapter Six of *Mein Kampf* 'Propaganda should not be addressed to the intellectual, for propaganda is as far removed from science as an advertisement is from art; but always to the mass of the people, speaking more to the heart than to the mind. Propaganda must be popular and on such a low level that it can reach right down to the dullest person'. Officers must talk to their men in small groups and explain to them that *Soldatensender Calais* is an enemy station, and how they can identify it. The German soldier should have a strength of character which enemy propaganda cannot touch. 'We are too pure spiritually to be concerned with such dirt'.[26]

The widespread and angry reaction to the transmissions of *Calais* leaves no doubt that it was having its effect on morale. At this time more than half the prisoners of war including men from infantry, armoured, and artillery units and the SS admitted to having listened to the station. General von Schlieben and other senior officers listened to *Calais* as a source of news during the siege of Cherbourg; and when they were interrogated as prisoners of war they used 'certain key phrases

[25] FO 898/420 (16.3.44).
[26] FO 898/391 (26.8.44).

and themes of our propaganda ... suggesting that they may have been absorbed into their ordinary line of thinking'. U-boat officers listened both in port and at sea. There was a large audience in the Luftwaffe who listened quite openly in the mess.[27]

The grey propaganda of *Soldatensender Calais* was paralleled by the white Voice of SHAEF which issued instructions and warnings – in effect a continuation of the *Avis* broadcast to occupied France. These announcements, which had the full authority of the Commander in Chief, were put out in five languages. They 'were always sensible and never asked the general public to do more than was well within the possibilities' – unlike the *Avis*.[28] After 16 June 1944 it was laid down that the Voice of SHAEF must be used sparingly and reserved for messages from the Supreme Commander with specific or general instructions 'of real military significance'.[29]

Of the leaflets, the fake German forces newspaper *Nachrichten für die Truppe* was the most ambitious and the most successful. Between 250,000 and 750,000 copies were dropped daily from United States' aircraft. The paper exploited genuine news by slipping in occasional false items with an edge to them – as did *Soldatensender Calais*. Reactions to *Nachricten* were highly satisfactory – from PWE's point of view. A German officer captured at the beginning of July 1944 said that the rank and file should not be allowed to read it. They did not yet believe it, but sooner or later it would begin to make its mark. The men would regard the tissue of lies as pure gold, and throw away their weapons. 'In such matters one must be firm from the start otherwise the seeds of lies shoot up like weeds.'[30]

This may have been unduly flattering – perhaps the officer wanted to please his captors – but there is no doubt that the German High Command was seriously worried by the daily deliveries of the fake newspaper which were made with the precision of clockwork. An order was issued against it on 29 July 1944. The news-sheet was so deceitful and defeatist that it could 'disturb the spiritual bearing of some of our less well-educated men'. The order goes on to give a general pep talk. The guiding hand of the German officer must show itself. It is his duty to make the Nazi philosophy clear to his men, in private conversations, or in group meetings. 'The officer will find strength in his own national socialist attitude which knows no doubt, and his unshakeable faith in his Führer to be a leading example and thus have the good fortune to be trusted by all his men'. But he must not just issue orders – he must speak from conviction. It was easy to convince men in times of victory

[27] FO 898/64 (3.8.44).
[28] FO 898/420.
[29] FO 898/391 (16.6.44).
[30] FO 898/465 (6.7.44).

that the Nazi philosophy constitutes the power from which these victories result. To remain stalwart in times of need and reverses, in order to transfer the faith to others – that is true leadership.[31]

Nevertheless, *Nachrichten* went from strength to strength, partly because it was delivered more efficiently than the Germans' own troop newspaper, the *Frontkurier*. When there was heavy fighting *Nachricten* was the only paper the German troops received, which strengthened the implication in its columns that the war was for all practical purposes over. In November 1944 a loyal Nazi begged his headquarters to speed up deliveries of *Frontkurier* in self-defence. He pointed out that *Nachrichten* brought yesterday's news punctually to the front line, and even the most zealous soldier was tempted to read it, especially since *Frontkurier* arrived anything up to four days late. 'There must be some way to bring the news to our men earlier in order to kill the soldiers' curiosity'. There was not. The Germans did not have the aircraft to deliver newspapers. The allies did – another aspect of the proposition that the winning side finds it easier to put across its propaganda.[32]

Leaflets which also had a marked success were the malingering booklets and the desertion leaflets. The former were referred to in an order by von Rundstedt which said: 'Recently cases of self-mutilation have been increasing on a scale that cannot be tolerated. In future, in all wound cases it must be established whether there is any question of self-mutilation ... Moreover, an increasing number of soldiers are suffering from skin diseases. It is learned from enemy propaganda and confirmed by medical specialists that these are caused by injecting petrol which leads to very persistent skin disease. In both types of case the strictest examination must be made; and men found to be guilty should be summarily tried and shot'.[33]

PWE's booklets made much of simulating and stimulating skin disease, and there is little doubt that credit must go to them. In October 1944 a prisoner of war who had prolonged his stay in hospital by opening his wound with a knife seven times later obtained a copy of PWE's booklet *Krankheit rettet (Sickness saves)*. He bought the drugs and equipment prescribed at a chemist and contrived to return to hospital for another nine weeks.[34] In February 1945 it was reported that cases of self-mutilation were still on the increase. 'Young soldiers at the front for the first time, 4-Fs, stragglers, members of units no longer existing, are easily tempted to perform acts of self-mutilation to escape the front line'. It was claimed that they usually got the idea from talking with other soldiers, but the enemy contributed suggestions for feigning

[31] FO 898/391 (29.7.44).
[32] FO 898/465 (10.11.44).
[33] *Ibid.*
[34] *Ibid* (26.10.44).

various types of illness. The offence was tantamount to desertion, and equally merited death.[35]

Reaction to rumours was probably greater among civilians than among the armed forces, but nevertheless the German High Command found it necessary to take special measures to control rumour-mongering. A booklet issued by the Army High Command in 1941 included 'rumours' as one of twenty themes which company commanders should use when talking to their men. Rumours were a particularly effective enemy weapon. They were disseminated by black wireless stations, leaflets, and by word of mouth by secret agents. They spread with extraordinary speed, working 'as a creeping poison, like an influenza epidemic'. The enemy relied on rumour-mongers to spread lies 'concerning alleged conflicts between the Wehrmacht and the Party, illness, disease, embezzlement, racketeering and so forth'. Guidance prepared for officers in February 1942 said that they should make themselves familiar with the enemy's technique in spreading rumours. This was done according to a prepared plan in which London and Moscow co-operated. The rumours put out were cleverly adapted to the weaknesses of the German people, which included guilelessness, and the urge to show off. The guileless German might discount 90 per cent of what he heard, but he would still be left with 10 per cent of poisonous enemy fare. Many people felt themselves to be important when they knew something special, and they liked to make an impression when passing on unpleasant news; but when the officer knew the tricks of enemy propaganda he could quite easily spot the rumours – and ensure that they were not repeated.[36]

The ultimate triumph of the propagandist was to persuade a member of the enemy force to desert. Surrender leaflets (surrender is a pleasanter term than desertion) had been used in Italy and in North Africa where they were popular with the Italian troops. So popular that, 'it probably sounds like a fairy tale, but during the later stages of the Tunisian campaign the Arabs actually started an Italian surrender leaflet black market, and sold our surrender passes to the Italian troops'.[37] After D-Day allied desertion propaganda was stepped up. A report from the 7th Army said that the enemy propagandists were very active, using leaflets dropped from aircraft and fired from guns, and loud hailers. The messages were topical and skilfully worded. Their main purpose was to undermine the German soldier's morale by pointing out the difficulties of the war situation and the mistakes of his leaders. Special appeals were directed to Austrians, Poles and Russians serving in the German forces.[38]

[35] FO 898/465 (17.2.45).
[36] FO 898/63 (18.7.42).
[37] FO 898/469 (8.3.44).
[38] FO 898/391 (10.7.44).

A battalion commander recorded that the effect of these tactics on morale was beyond all doubt, and cited the case of a corporal who had deserted in spite of the fact that he had won the close combat medal, the infantry storm medal, and the medal for the wounded.[39] The commander of the 2nd Panzer Division issued an order against desertion on 18 July 1944. Members of his Division had deserted to the enemy thereby committing the most despicable crime a soldier could commit. They had broken their oath to the Führer and Fatherland. 'I have made certain that such traitors shall never again, even after the war, tread on German soil without being handed over to the rigour of the law. Further, I have notified the criminal authorities in Germany of their names so that appropriate action can be taken against their relatives and fiancées. The families of traitors do not belong in the German community'. The commander had no doubt that the reason for these desertions was the flood of enemy leaflets. 'We must prevent this lying venom from falling into the hands of irresolute comrades'.[40] In November 1944 a captain said that the showers of leaflets had turned his men into 'a bunch of neurotics' . He therefore decided to throw his hand in and come over to the allies.[41] In March 1945 a circular for the 9th Panzer Division referred to the enemy's 'vile and cunning methods' for inducing men to desert. 'He realizes that he cannot win the war against the Nationalist Socialist State, in spite of his material superiority and masses of troops . . . A defeated Germany will be used as cannon fodder for the protection of England.'[42]

These examples can be multiplied many times over. There is no doubt that the interaction of clever propaganda and military superiority seriously damaged the morale of the German troops in the last nine months of the war; but there is no way of segregating the relative importance of the two elements. The officers of the Psychological Warfare Division of SHAEF did what they could to measure the decline in morale, so that future propaganda themes could be suitably adjusted, but it was very difficult to come to a firm conclusion. For example, at the beginning of July 1944, when the Germans were successfully resisting the allied advance in the St Lô–Carentan sector of the Cherbourg Peninsula 126 prisoners were asked a series of questions; and a month later, when the allies had broken through a further batch of 195 were

---

[39] FO 898/391 (8.7.44).
[40] Ibid (18.7.44).
[41] FO 898/469 (15.11.44).
[42] FO 898/465 (1.3.45). German surrender leaflets (which claimed that to help the Bolshevists to win the war would be fatal to Britain's future and promised that deserters would not be regarded as prisoners-of-war) were considered to pose no threat to allied morale – another example of the relationship between military success and propaganda (WO 219/1345).

asked the same questions.[43] The comparative figures for four of the questions were:

	Percentage of prisoners answering 'Yes'	
	Before breakthrough	After breakthrough
Do you believe that Germany will win, or at least achieve a stalemate?	22	11
Do you trust German propaganda?	34	19
Do you have faith in National Socialism?	56	29
Do you support Hitler?	76	53

No doubt the professional psychologist could make much of this sort of statistic, which shows a rapid decline in morale; but it is virtually impossible to assess the part played by propaganda. There is no doubt that it helped, but how much can never be said with certainty.

[43] FO 898/391.

10
Conclusion: Profit or loss?

The permutation and combination of departmental functions is a game much relished by those who design the machinery of government – witness the endless chopping and changing of responsibilities in Whitehall since the end of the Second World War. The game may not matter much in time of peace (although this is debatable); but it is desirable in time of war, and indeed before a war begins, to provide machinery which will ensure that the functions of government are carried out with the maximum efficiency. There is evidence in the preceding chapters that the propaganda and psychological warfare functions of the British government were seriously impaired, especially in the early years of the war, by organization and management that could hardly have been worse. Pressure of events cannot be blamed. The government gave itself four comparatively leisurely years – as compared with the war years – to prepare a blueprint for an efficient propaganda department. Why did it fail?

A related, and more important question, is why did it not establish the single department of propaganda and subversion which many advocated?

A sub-committee of the Committee of Imperial Defence was charged in 1935 with the task of preparing plans for the formation of a wartime Ministry of Information. At its first meeting the sub-committee clearly had in mind that propaganda to enemy countries would be one of the functions of the new Ministry. It studied the performance of the organizations which had controlled information in the First World War: the Official Press Bureau, formed in August 1914 which was concerned with censorship; the Ministry of Information which in March 1918 was developed out of the Department of Information established a year earlier to influence opinion at home and abroad; and the Department of Enemy Propaganda set up in February 1918. It was found that there was confusion over the responsibilities of the Ministry of Information and the Department of Enemy Propaganda; and also that the latter, for reasons which no one understood in 1935, had dealt with propaganda to Britain's ally Italy. There was thus a good precedent for the muddled responsibility which caused trouble in the Second World War; and it might have been expected that the sub-committee

CONCLUSION: PROFIT OR LOSS?

would see the danger signal and try to avoid the same mistake.[1]

It was accepted that the Department of Enemy Propaganda had done a good job. Its objective had been to convince the enemy of the hopelessness of their cause and the certainty of allied victory; and it was given credit for the withdrawal of Bulgaria from the war, the break-up of the Austro-Hungarian empire, and the final defeat of Germany – with the help of the kindred organizations in France and Italy. With this record of presumed success in mind the sub-committee might well have devoted a good deal of attention to the propaganda function of the new Ministry, but in fact it was hardly discussed after the first meeting – at which the Foreign Office objected to the creation of a Ministry of Information at all, on the ground that they had a perfectly competent News Department 'composed of experts who had learned the technique of propaganda'. The Treasury representative dismissed this point of view as being 'narrow and parochial'.[2]

The broad outline of the new Department had taken shape by the middle of 1936. Provision was made for a Publicity Division which would exploit 'all the various media of modern publicity and propaganda' and experiment in methods improvised to meet wartime conditions.[3]

This was not good enough for Sir Stephen Tallents, whose appointment as Director General designate of the new Ministry had been mooted in 1936 and was confirmed in March 1938.[4] Tallents was convinced that propaganda to enemy countries would be one of the more important functions of his Ministry, and wanted to be allowed to press on with the preparatory work. In September 1938 he introduced a paper in the sub-committee arguing that the German people should be provided with economic evidence of the folly of their going to war, and assessing the susceptibility of various classes of the German population to British propaganda. Although he was not the author of the paper he adopted it as his own; but it cut no ice with the sub-committee, which merely 'noted it' – the code word for consigning it to the wastepaper basket.[5]

However right his ideas may have been, Tallents had simply no chance of implementing them. The Foreign Office were against him because they wanted to preserve their empire. Chamberlain's invitation to Campbell Stuart in September 1938 to start planning a shadow propaganda organization[6] – which was apparently never communicated to Tallents in spite of the fact that it had great significance for the structure of his new Ministry – meant that Campbell Stuart was com-

[1] CAB 16/127, ff. 100–1.
[2] CAB 23/99, ff. 9–10.
[3] *Ibid* f.203.
[4] CAB 16/127, f. 34.
[5] *Ibid*, f.

G*

mitted to fight secretly against Tallents's aspirations in the field of propaganda. Most important of all, the mandarins of Whitehall believed that propaganda to enemy countries was an idea that should be swept under the carpet until war had started. Horace Wilson, Warren Fisher, and Bridges – respectively the Prime Minister's principal adviser, the Secretary to the Treasury, and the Secretary to the Cabinet – all wanted to put off the evil day when Britain would have to contemplate engaging in foreign propaganda.

Campbell Stuart saw Wilson on 19 October 1938 and told him that Tallents had prepared a report which said much more about the organization of propaganda to the enemy than Stuart deemed advisable. According to Wilson, Stuart took the view (which Wilson thought was shared by most of those who had studied the subject) that propaganda should not be much spoken about, and should not be written about at all: a truly remarkable example of planned muddle-through. For good measure Stuart added that Tallents was interesting himself excessively in propaganda to the enemy 'to add to the importance of those who are concerned with other aspects of the Ministry of Information' – a singularly uncharitable observation which is not supported by any of the contemporary evidence.[7]

Wilson, being aware of Stuart's commission from the Prime Minister, accepted that Tallents must be defeated. He mentioned the point to Warren Fisher (chairman of the sub-committee dealing with the new Ministry of Information) so that he might also ensure that Tallents's report got nowhere. He suggested that Campbell Stuart should be appointed to the sub-committee 'to express his views and give assistance'.[8] So are the forces that win the battles of Whitehall recruited and deployed. In a note of 2 December 1938 he recorded that the sub-committee should be steered towards appointing a small nucleus of one or two officials to carry out the planning of the new Ministry; and that 'the minimum activity about propaganda in enemy countries should be displayed now'. The question of propaganda in time of war was an extremely delicate matter and must be dealt with only when the time came.[9]

By now Tallents must have been aware that he was up against it, for he called on Bridges on 5 December to discuss his position. According to Bridges 'Sir Stephen was very expansive' about the work which still remained to be done in connection with the planning of the Ministry of Information; but he (Bridges) refused to be drawn and simply said that the matter would have to be discussed at the next meeting of the sub-committee, which of course he knew had been rigged. '. . . as a

[6] PREM 1/374, f. 24.
[7] PREM 1/388 (20.10.38).
[8] *Ibid.*
[9] *Ibid* (2.12.38).

CONCLUSION: PROFIT OR LOSS? 179

result of further discussion between us, in the course of which I came definitely to the idea that we should regretfully have to part with him, he said that he would of course be very sorry, but that there would be no ill-feeling on his part'.[10] There the matter was left, pending the meeting of the sub-committee.

At the meeting Warren Fisher expressed the view that there should be a nucleus of two or three officials to do the preparatory work – only a slight departure from the script which Wilson had provided. 'He would deprecate the formation of a nucleus on any large scale, and he was convinced that it should not usurp in peacetime the functions of existing agencies or Departments'. Tallents pointed out that there was a great deal of preparatory work still to be done; and suggested that it would be facilitated if the intention to set up a new Ministry could be announced.[11] Both Wilson and Warren Fisher disagreed. It was all right to announce the plans for a new Ministry of Supply, or a Ministry of Food, but a Ministry of Information would inevitably be associated with the question of propaganda in enemy countries. So it must be kept secret.[12]

Thus, the answer to the first question posed above – why did the government fail to prepare a blueprint for an efficient propaganda department which could have gone into action at the beginning of the war? – is quite simple. The three most influential civil servants of the day, for reasons which in retrospect seem to be entirely unconvincing, refused to give Tallents his head. Propaganda was a dirty word and the less it was thought about before hostilities started the better. Campbell Stuart's secret one-man-band in Electra House was the thing: the all-out preparation which Tallents wanted to undertake was to be avoided at all costs. The real failure, however, was not the mandarins' success in keeping propaganda out of sight until the war started, but their inability to see the manifold advantages of a single department concerned with subversion in all its aspects.

Why, then, did the government not establish a single department? This question is touched on by Professor M. R. D. Foot in *SOE in France* in the light of the papers of the Military Intelligence, Research Branch (MI R) which are still closed to non-official historians. A meeting on 1 July 1940 chaired by the Foreign Secretary (then Halifax) came very near to a firm recommendation that there should be a single department. The draft minutes record: 'After some discussion of the multiplicity of bodies dealing with sabotage and subversive activities there was a general feeling voiced by Lord Lloyd [now Colonial Secre-

[10] PREM 1/388 (5.12.38).
[11] The Home Secretary said in Cabinet some months later that secrecy had hampered the preparatory work for MOI and asked that Parliament should be brought into the picture (CAB 23/99, f. 325).
[12] PREM 1/388 (14.12.38).

tary] that what was required was a Controller armed with almost dictatorial powers.' On 16 July Churchill invited Dalton to take charge of subversion; and on 19 July Chamberlain signed SOE's charter.[13]

This document is still closed but it appears from later references to it that it did not of itself rule out the establishment of a unified subversion department. Indeed, it intended that all propaganda – open and covert – should go to SOE, which was prevented only by Duff Cooper's intransigence, and Dalton's failure to insist on his rights. During the twilight period between 16 May 1941, when it was agreed in principle to have a Ministerial Triumvirate, and 27 August 1941 when Dalton and Bracken suggested the 'complete fusion' of the propaganda department there was still a chance that a unified subversion department might be set up. It is not clear what Dalton and Bracken meant by 'complete fusion'. Probably they didn't know themselves. The Executive Committee shot their idea down by claiming that Woburn's activities must be kept separate and secret; but it is conceivable that Bruce Lockhart and his colleagues, had they believed in the idea of a single department, could have used SOE's charter to persuade Ministers that propaganda and active subversion should go hand in hand under one leader. That they did not may be attributed to their wish to avoid a further period of Ministerial wrangling; or perhaps to the fact that if a single department had been set up they would have found themselves smaller fish in a larger pool.

What might have been, indeed what should have been, is now only of academic interest, since it is axiomatic that the lessons learned in one war have little relevance in the next; but it is nevertheless of interest to consider the design of a 'Fourth Arm' organization – if only to measure the cost of the government's failure to do something which at least some of its advisers favoured.

One of the general arguments against the fourth arm conception is that it would have tainted the BBC. It is widely accepted that there was great virtue in an independent BBC; and that British overseas propaganda would have been less effective had it been believed that the BBC was not an independent body but was taking its orders from a Minister of Propaganda. In fact, this argument does not stand up. How many of the millions who listened to the BBC in occupied countries were aware of the constitutional niceties in the relationship between the British government and the Corporation? Precious few. In enemy countries where it was even more important to get the British message across, they were even fewer. To these millions – friend and foe – it was the British government and not the BBC that spoke to them; and the reason that what was said on British radio had a great impact was not that it came from a body known to be independent, but that years of

---

[13] *SOE in France* (London, HMSO, 1968), pp. 6–10.

CONCLUSION: PROFIT OR LOSS?

wartime listening persuaded listeners that what they heard was the truth. It is to be presumed, or at least hoped, that if the BBC had been directly under the control of a Cabinet Minister, instead of a Board of Governors, its output would not have been one word different, nor would its credibility have been one iota less.

However, while it is true that the truth subverts when it is pitted against lies, the BBC would not have been a component part of The Fourth Arm. It would have been allowed to go its own way, subject only to the controls imposed by military security, and a modicum of liaison with The Fourth Arm organization to ensure that the truth – the BBC's stock in trade – would not undermine some line being propagated by the subversionists. The BBC for its part would have to eschew anything like the V broadcasts which were tantamount to operational propaganda. *That* sort of activity would have to be left to the discretion of The Fourth Arm, in agreement, where possible, with the allied governments in exile.

Richard Crossman, eight years after the end of the war, said how wise it had been to maintain the BBC as an independent organization, which seldom saw eye to eye with PWE. 'Indeed, our meetings between the PWE and the officials of the BBC took the form of long bitter fights. Quite properly, the BBC officials were determined to do nothing beyond reporting the straight news . . . Our job was to inject the highest percentage of propaganda content we could into the news service of the BBC. If we had been given complete control of the BBC the percentage we should have injected would, I think, have been far too high. It was a healthy thing to have this permanent war between the independent BBC fighting for its "straight" news and the Psychological *(sic)* Warfare Executive struggling to corrupt the BBC for the purpose of winning the war!'[14]

This is a strange comment. Was it right that the balance between straight news and propaganda should be determined, not by the normal processes of Whitehall, in which (more often than not) reasonable people sit round a table and come to a reasonable conclusion, but simply by the relative strengths of those who represented the two organizations? It follows that, had PWE been stronger and the BBC weaker (or vice versa) the balance would have been wrong; and much damage might have resulted before the Minister of Information who shared Ministerial responsibility for PWE and answered for the BBC in the House of Commons was forced to step in to put things right. This danger would have been averted if the BBC and the subversionists had been separate, each with their own clear terms of reference.

If the BBC is set on one side, the Fourth Arm would have taken in leaflet propaganda – black and white – black radio, and all the activities

[14] *Journal of the Royal United Service Institution*, vol. 98 (1953), p. 353.

of the Special Operations Executive.[15] Hugh Dalton argued the case for such an organization during his battle with Duff Cooper in 1940. He pointed out that those who claimed that all propaganda should be under the control of one Ministry were wrong. 'There is much greater weight in the proposition that all subversion should be under one control.' Propaganda to enemy and enemy-controlled countries was undoubtedly subversion, but propaganda within Britain, to the Empire, to the United States and many other neutral countries was not. Further, some forms of propaganda were by their nature so secret that they must be handled by a secret Department. He went on to claim that subversive propaganda must be linked with subversive action. 'It must form part of our war strategy, must be closely related to the revolutionary movements against the enemy, and planned in constant co-operation with the Chiefs of Staff.'[16]

The logic of all this was unanswerable. Unhappily, Ministers are human beings first and logicians second. Duff Cooper eventually agreed that Dalton was right – but if there was going to be a Fourth Arm, the Minister would be Duff Cooper. So there never was a Fourth Arm. It is difficult to decide whether he, who refused as long as he could to surrender open propaganda, or Dalton who must have won the battle had he not thrown in the towel, or Anderson who was given the chance of making sense out of a nonsensical situation, was most to blame for the failure to establish a unified subversion department. Perhaps Anderson was most at fault. When Churchill instructed him to settle the dispute between Dalton and Duff Cooper in December 1940 he (Churchill) told him that as he saw it there were three alternatives: to leave things as they were; to give all propaganda to MEW; or to give it all to MOI.[17] Since it was obvious that to leave things as they were would merely perpetuate the squabble, one of the other alternatives had to be chosen. The best option was to give everything to MEW, and Anderson, having for all practical purposes been armed with the Prime Minister's prior approval, could easily have recommended it. He missed his chance and as a result the efficiency of both propaganda and subversive activities suffered.

This is illustrated by the numerous cases of friction between PWE and SOE cited above. Had there been unified control both Executives would have done their jobs much more effectively. The ridiculous confusion which could arise in the management of the two bodies is

---

[15] In practice the white radio aspirations of the allied governments (which would not have accepted the directives of the BBC on the ground that it was not a government department) would have militated against this form of organization.

[16] INF 1/893 (15.12.40). General Wavell also advocated a 'Fourth Arm' – see p. 57 above

[17] PREM 3/365/7, f. 786.

CONCLUSION: PROFIT OR LOSS? 183

illustrated by an episode in 1943 when Brendan Bracken, the Minister of Information, who was partly responsible for PWE, told Lord Selborne, the Minister of Economic Warfare, that he was sending the PWE liaison officer in MEW (Leonard Ingrams) to Algiers to replace Richard Crossman in the Psychological Warfare Branch. Selborne objected. Bracken swiftly replied that he could not object since Ingrams was *his* man. He had been on PWE's payroll since 1939. Selborne would have to get on without him. Not so, said Selborne. PWE might think that Ingrams was a PWE man, with an interest in SOE, but he was in fact an SOE man with an interest in PWE. The fact that PWE had been paying him for the whole of the war was part of his cover.[18]

Taken in isolation this is merely amusing, but if such friction is repeated over and over again, it becomes serious. In June 1942 one of PWE's senior staff wrote: 'Is it in the charter of SOE to indulge in this amateur political mystery-making independently? Are they absolutely incapable of ever co-operating in any particular with any department? We do our best to put everything at their disposal and to take them as far as possible into our confidence, and we receive in return intrigues and obstruction and cutthroat competition . . .'[19] In May 1943 there was a row between PWE and the BBC about the propriety of allowing a certain man to broadcast to Austria. It took Newsome of the BBC five pages of injured prose to set out his version of the dispute, and a major crisis in the nation's affairs was averted only because the broadcaster-designate had had his teeth out and could not speak.[20] On 7 March 1944 there was a row between PWE and SOE about the arrangements for delivering propaganda material to PWE's agents in Belgium, which SOE carried out on an agency basis. On 24 March 1944 there was a row between PWE and SOE about the use of transmission time for messages to French resistance groups. On 21 April 1944 there was a row between PWE and SOE about the supply of PWE material to Stockholm for the use of the underground press in Norway.[21] Differences of opinion would inevitably have arisen between the propagandists and the subversionists had they belonged to the same organization, but it is ten times easier to resolve such differences when the decision is in the hands of one Minister.

If the organization of political warfare was less successful than it might have been, so was the management. Bruce Lockhart, who was in charge for most of the war – first as chairman of the Political Warfare Executive, and then as Director General, was anything but a dynamic leader. He seems to have been more interested in finding reasons for

[18] FO 898/25 (12, 22, 25.11, 7.12.43).
[19] *Ibid* (10.6.42).
[20] BBC Written Archives (Minute by N. F. Newsome, 3.5.43).
[21] FO 898/25 (7, 24.3, 21.4.44).

not doing things than in taking the lead in shaping the policies of the Executive. A member of the staff of the Office of War Information in London prepared a dossier on the senior staff of the Executive for the information of a member of the American Secret Service visiting London. He naturally wanted to get as near to the truth as possible, and he had nothing to fear from the law of libel. Bruce Lockhart 'is essentially an "outside operator" with no real sense of executive or organizational work or loyalties. He was once an extremely aggressive person but for various reasons including his "personal habits" he is a shell of the man he formerly was. He was named to his post in order to remove the confusions and the ineffectiveness of a three-man board made up of himself, Leeper and Brooks. In fact, he has shown himself to be weak and unable or unwilling to take over effective control. He depends slavishly on Eden and tries to build up his strength by undercutting the strength and authority of his former colleagues.'[22] There is nothing in the hundreds of PWE files that would lead to disagreement with this assessment.

The compiler of this dossier was well aware of the civil war which raged between the agencies concerned with propaganda ('while the Bracken-Dalton feud was going on it was so intense that MOI men and SOE people were not permitted to talk to one another'); and he also claimed to have inner knowledge of the domestic strife within PWE. Bruce Lockhart 'pigeonholed Bowes-Lyon's *ad interim* report from Washington, did not even show it to Leeper, and let it be assumed that Bowes-Lyon was merely idling and sending in no material from America'. When Bowes-Lyon was accused at a big official meeting of all sorts of shortcomings including irresponsibility, Lockhart completely failed to back him up or even to defend him. 'I do not think Lockhart is motivated by personal animosity. He merely is an essentially weak man trying to nip in the bud all possible competition.'[23]

Even if the evidence of this report, which deals with Dallas Brooks and Leeper in equally unflattering terms, is discounted, there seems to be little doubt that the Political Warfare Executive was less well directed than it might have been. It is difficult to measure the effect on its overall performance – the working propagandists probably got on with the job of drafting leaflets and speaking into their microphones without giving too much thought to what was going on at the top; but it is tempting to think that with younger and more dynamic leadership PWE would have seen the force of Dalton's case for a 'Fourth Arm' and supported it with all the energy they could command.

So much for what might have been. As to judgement on what actually was – the open broadcasting of the BBC came through with flying

[22] RG 208 OWI Box 74.
[23] *Ibid.*

CONCLUSION: PROFIT OR LOSS?

colours. This fact has been testified to in many places, and need not be further stressed.

In the early days PWE believed that the Fourth Arm could play a major part in an allied victory. With remarkable optimism Dallas Brooks said in April 1940: 'the propaganda weapon might well prove decisive in securing victory if it could be successfully exploited to encourage the German land forces to attack.'[24] This must rank as one of the most splendid howlers of the war; and no doubt Brooks revised his opinion a few weeks later when the Germans attacked of their own volition, unprovoked by British propaganda.

As time went on the propagandists became more humble. In an essay on black propaganda written in July 1942 Leeper wrote: 'It is highly dangerous for the propagandist to exaggerate the part he has to play. In serious propaganda over-acting is not only amateurish but dangerous. The propagandist must be content to be the forerunner of those who will claim the prize'.[25] By the beginning of 1944 the wild enthusiasms of 1940 have been conveniently forgotten. A PWE memorandum records in February of that year: 'Our hope never was to produce decisive political results by propaganda. It was always felt that the repressive machinery in Nazi Germany was far too powerful to allow of any popular movement against the Nazi régime until all controls broke down. To hope for such a movement as a result of our political warfare was unrealistic.'[26] This was hindsight of a high order.

There is no doubt that propaganda in support of military operations was successful – but just how successful no one can say. The better a campaign is going, the more effective the accompanying propaganda will be. Duff Cooper enunciated this principle in the House of Commons in July 1941, a shade too fulsomely: 'The power of propaganda, as of all other weapons, must depend very largely upon the time when it is used. In the early stages of a war its weight is not so great as in the last stages, when it can prove decisive. There is no dispute about the fact that propaganda against victory in arms is powerful, but when victory in arms is on your side, propaganda can press the results of victory miles further.' He believed that propaganda could bring victory months, and even years nearer.[27] The same point was made more soberly by Richard Law, Parliamentary Under-Secretary to the Foreign Office in November 1942, speaking in the Commons about the success of Operation *Torch*: 'Political warfare, as I believe, cannot be effective by itself. It can only be effective when it is combined with military action. Words by themselves can do little good'.[28]

[24] FO 898/4 (3.4.40).
[25] FO 898/63 (18.6.42).
[26] FO 898/101, ff. 3–4.
[27] Hansard (Commons) vol. 372, col. 1536.
[28] *Ibid* vol. 385, cols. 149–50.

Yet again, a draft report (which was never completed) on the work of the Psychological Warfare Division: 'The concensus of military observers seems to have been that the varying influences of strategical and tactical propaganda were inextricably linked, and that in general neither could conceivably have been effective without an impressive display of the force of allied arms. Experience was that only when the final military assault was closely co-ordinated with that of psychological warfare could the latter hope to be an important aid to the Force Commander.' The same report concludes: 'The first fact that must be written in the hatband of every psychological warrior is simply this: "Psychological warfare of itself will win no battles for the allied cause".'[29]

It must, however, be accepted that 'military' propaganda – black and white, leaflets and radio – did pay a dividend, the size of which increased with the allies' successive victories in the field; but it is quite impossible to compute the percentage of that dividend.

If there is no doubt about the value of the BBC's open propaganda, there is a great deal of doubt about PWE's black radio activities – other than those directly related to military operations. Richard Crossman did not think much of them. He said: 'Although we found the left-hand activities enormous fun, although a vast amount of talent went into them, although I am sure they entertained the Gestapo, I have grave doubts whether black propaganda had an effect in any way commensurate with that of straightforward propaganda from the enemy to the enemy.' With the benefit of hindsight his advice would be 'Put your best talent on to the white propaganda: do not be diverted into the vastly entertaining and endless delicacies of the black varieties.'[30] Kirkpatrick wrote in 1942 that the Research Units were important but they did not have a large audience. The voice of the various dissident groups was not as authoritative as the voice of London.[31] Carleton Greene said after the war 'the programmes of *Soldatensender Calais* were so funny that I have sometimes wondered whether they did not raise rather than depress morale.'[32] PWE's own inquests into the success of black propaganda never claimed very much for it; and it seems clear that Crossman's conclusion was right. Black propaganda was fun for those who dispensed it; but it achieved very little.

It is possible to make out a case that the most effective wartime propaganda would be complete silence – no propaganda at all. The side that is winning a war pays little attention to anything that the loser may say. The more the loser protests he will win in the end, the more

---
[29] WO 219/4751 (10.10.44).
[30] *Journal of the Royal United Service Institution*, vol. 97 (1952), pp. 321-2.
[31] FO 898/35 (23.1.42).
[32] Quoted in Briggs *op. cit.*, p. 434.

the winner is encouraged by what he hears, believing it to be empty talk. Equally, if the winner shouts from the housetops that he is winning, the loser wonders why that is necessary. If he needs the help of words, his weapons cannot be all-powerful. So, much of the propaganda aimed in wartime at whole populations may be no more than a costly ritual which is self-defeating.

If the rule that the lessons learned in one war do not apply in the next is momentarily suspended, and if it is accepted that only military propaganda – that is, propaganda directly related to the conduct of military operations – helped the allies to win the Second World War, it would seem to follow that the Political Warfare Executive's successor body should be required to limit its activity to that type. It should be left principally to the BBC to disseminate the only other propaganda, by far the most powerful – truth, which above all things beareth away the victory.

Appendix
Manuscript sources

(a) Public Record Office

AIR MINISTRY

AIR 2/4189–91	Files of registered correspondence of the Air Ministry
AIR 13/131–2	Files relating to organization of Balloon Command

CABINET

CAB 16/127	Ministry of Information: plans for establishment
CAB 23/96, 99	Cabinet conclusions (1938–39)
CAB 24/281	Cabinet memoranda (1938)
CAB 65/1, 5, 10–11, 18, 34, 38	War Cabinet conclusions and confidential annexes
CAB 66/10, 13, 17	War Cabinet memoranda (WP and CP series)
CAB 67/3	War Cabinet memoranda (WP[G] series)
CAB 68/1	War Cabinet memoranda (WP[R] series)
CAB 69/4	War Cabinet Defence Committee (Operations) minutes and papers
CAB 79/15, 62	War Cabinet, Chiefs of Staff Committee, minutes of meetings

FOREIGN OFFICE

FO 371/21711	Propaganda co-ordination committee
FO 371/21791	British propaganda in Germany
FO 395/597, 602, 605	Co-ordinating publicity abroad

APPENDIX

POLITICAL WARFARE EXECUTIVE

FO 898/1, 3, 4, 6, 8, 9	Preliminary organization
FO 898/10–12	Formation of the Executive
FO 898/23–5	Liaison with other Departments
FO 898/30, 35, 37	Political Warfare Intelligence Directorate
FO 898/43, 47, 51, 54, 60	Radio propaganda
FO 898/61–5, 69–72, 84	Underground propaganda
FO 898/98–9, 101	Training School
FO 898/104, 118, 124	Missions abroad
FO 898/129–31, 137	Mediterranean theatre
FO 898/177–8, 181, 183, 194–5, 208, 241	Germany and occupied countries
FO 898/252	Neutral countries
FO 898/286, 297, 331, 333–4, 336–8, 341–3, 349, 358	Directorate of Plans and Campaigns
FO 898/376, 391, 395, 397	Preparation for the invasion of Western Europe
FO 898/420	Post-war planning
FO 898/450, 457–9, 462–6, 469, 474–8, 484	Leaflets
FO 898/531-2	Captured enemy documents and civilian intelligence

MINISTRY OF INFORMATION

INF /1474	Transfer of staff to Political Warfare Executive
INF 1/893, 895	Propaganda relating to enemy and enemy-occupied countries: relations with Ministry of Economic Warfare and Political Warfare Executive
INF 1/898	Propaganda to enemy and enemy-occupied countries: minutes and papers for Standing Ministerial Committee for Political Warfare

PRIME MINISTER'S FILES

PREM 1/272	Sir R. Vansittart's committee to consider government publicity in foreign countries
PREM 1/374	Propaganda in enemy countries

PREM 1/388   Proposal for Ministry of Information in time of war
PREM 3/365/1   Joint declaration by Prime Minister and President to Italian people
PREM 3/365/2   Psychological warfare in connection with Operation *Husky*
PREM 3/365/4–5   Examples of leaflets dropped over enemy territory
PREM 3/365/7   Arrangements between Foreign Office and Ministry of Economic Warfare.
PREM 3/365/9   Anglo-American Political Warfare Co-ordinating Committee
PREM 3/365/10   New Delhi Political Warfare Emergency Committee
PREM 3/365/11   Propaganda: various

Military headquarters' papers:
Supreme Headquarters Allied Expeditionary Force

WO 219/1340   Operation *Overlord*: draft directive on psychological warfare
WO 219/1343   Allied propaganda broadcasts to the German people and foreign workers in Germany
WO 219/1345   German leaflet propaganda inviting allied troops to defect
WO 219/1346   Psychological warfare against Norway and Germany: policy

(b) United States National Archives

RG 208/OWI
Papers of the Office of War Information.

Select Bibliography

J. J. N. BENNETT: *British broadcasting and the Danish resistance movement* (Cambridge, 1966).

ANDREW BOYLE: *Poor dear Brendan* (London, 1974).

ASA BRIGGS: *The history of broadcasting in the United Kingdom*, vol. iii *The war of words* (Oxford University Press, London, 1970).

SIR R. BRUCE LOCKHART: *Comes the reckoning* (London, 1947). *Giants cast long shadows* (London, 1960).

HUGH DALTON: *The fateful years: memoirs, 1931–45* (London 1957).

SEFTON DELMER: *Black boomerang* (London, 1962).

A. DUFF COOPER: *Old men forget* (London, 1953).

THEO FLEISCHMAN: *Ici Londres* (Brussels, 1948).

M. R. D. FOOT: *SOE in France* (London, 1966).

JOHN STEINBECK: *The moon is down* (London, 1942).

SIR C. STUART: *Secrets of Crewe House* (London, 1920). *Opportunity knocks twice* (London, 1952).

PAUL STRUYE: *L'évolution du sentiment publique en Belgique sous l'occupation allemande* (Brussels, 1945).

VICTOR DE LAVELEYE: *Ici Radio Belgique* (Brussels, 1949).

Journal of the United States Institution vol. 97 (1952); vol. 98 (1953).

United States army in world war II: The European theatre of operations: the supreme command (Washington DC, 1954).

F. W. WINTERBOTHAM: *The Ultra Secret*.

Index

Admiralty, 22, 95, 110, 139, 146
Agents, 37, 109
　PWE, 43, 86, 148, 183
　SOE, 51, 80-1, 91, 96, 98, 100, 108, 173
Agriculture, 113-21
Aircraft, 13, 29, 44
　Flying Fortress, 91, 92
　Lancaster, 129
　Wellington, 44
　Whitley, 44
Aircraft, Production Ministry, 92, 93
Air Ministry, 89, 95, 98, 106, 128
Air Staff, 90
Alexander, General Sir Harold (later Field-Marshal Earl Alexander), 147
Algiers, 39, 141, 147, 183
Allied governments, 53, 54, 55, 56, 126, 182*n*
Americans, 92, 135, 152
Anderson, Sir John (later Viscount Waverley), 20, 182
　'Anderson Award', 20-22
Anglo-American Psychological Branch, 38-9
Anglo-French Propaganda Council, 28-9
Anglo-German Fellowship, 16
Ankara, 162
Appeasement, 9, 11, 16
Armée secrète (Belgian), 86
Ashdown Forest, 106
Asia, 41-2
'Aspidistra', *see* Radio
Atlantic Charter, 48
Attlee, Clement (later Earl Attlee), 132, 144
Australia, 109
Austria, 11, 70, 183

Austrians, 173
Austro-Hungarian empire, 177
Avis, 171
Axis Powers, 57, 110, 135, 143, 163

Balkans, 30, 70, 115, 151
Balloon Development Establishment, 93
Balloons (leaflet), 13, 14, 93, 161
　description of, 93-4
　manufacture, 94
　operation, 94-5
Baltic, 108
Bangkok, 57
Barman, T. G., 55
Bartlett, Vernon, 11
Battle of Britain, 71, 72, 101
Battle of Russia, 101
Battle of the Bulge, 131
Bavaria, 160
Bayonne, 122
BBC, 11, 18, 19, 24, 30, 45, 52, 55, 60, 65, 67, 78, 119, 141, 162, 165, 180, 186-7
　black propaganda, 101
　Central News Room, 63
　European Intelligence Service, 63, 64
　European News Dept., 122
　European Record Unit, 63, 64
　foreign language news, 9, 14
　incitement to sabotage, 51
　monitoring, 61, 106
　nature of broadcasts, 69
　News Information Bureau, 64
　Overseas Research Unit, 63, 64
　Regional Editors, 33
　Religious Broadcasting Dept., 84-5
　success of, 71, 164-5, 184-5
　'V' broadcasts, 121-8, 181

Beaumont Nesbitt, Major-General F. G., 105-6
Beaverbrook, Lord, 22, 23
Bedell Smith, General Walter, 131
Belgian government, 54, 56, 105
Belgium, 7, 53, 54, 63, 88, 89, 94, 96, 105, 122, 149, 183
  reaction to propaganda, 162-4
Benson, 95
Berlin, 13, 14, 80, 81, 160
Berne, 47
Bevan, Aneurin, 133n
Bevir, Anthony (later Sir Anthony), 21, 147
Bilbao, 95
Birchington, 94
Bishop, General W. H. A., 155
Black market, 51
Blake, William, 69
Blankenberg, 94
Blockade, 114, 117
Board of Trade, 34
Bolshevism, 62, 164
Bormann, Martin, 168
Boston, 162
Boulogne, 13
Bourges, 152
Bowes-Lyon, David, 26, 136, 140, 184
Bracken, Brendan (later Lord Bracken), 25, 26, 34, 92, 124, 128, 132n, 140, 144, 155, 183
  appointed to MOI, 24
  attitude to *Braddock II*, 130, 132
  attitude to *Husky*, 146-7
Braddock I, 128n
Braddock II, 128-33
Bradley, General Omar, 153
Bremen, 44
Breslau, 109
Bridges, Sir Edward (later Lord Bridges), 132n, 178-9
British Council, 9, 10, 11, 14, 15
British Empire, 77, 182
Brook, Norman (later Lord Normanbrook), 21
Brooke, General Sir Alan (later Field-Marshal Viscount Alanbrooke), 58
Browett, Sir Leonard, 64, 65
Bruce Lockhart, Sir Robert, 25, 26, 32, 37, 55, 56, 64, 76, 106, 119, 146, 152, 155
  Chairman of Executive Committee, 24, 31
  Director General, 34
  'V' broadcasts, 51-3
  on GS I, 81
  and leaflet bombs, 93
  and 'V' campaign, 123-8
  opposes *Braddock II*, 131
  and *Torch*, 139-40
  weakness of, 183-4
Brussels, 121
Bulgaria, 30, 105, 177
Burma, 57
Burma Office, 40
Bush House, 7, 35, 64

'C' (head of Secret Service), 82
Cadogan, Sir Alexander, 9
Cairo, 37
Calabria, 40
Calder, Ritchie (later Lord Ritchie-Calder), 31, 36, 50, 51, 125, 126, 128
Canada, 38
Carentan, 174
'Cesar II', 86
Chamberlain, Neville, 10, 12, 16, 17, 44, 74, 180
  appoints propaganda committee, 9
  sets up 'Electra House', 177-8
Chemnitz, 160
Cherbourg, 170, 174
Chief Diplomatic Adviser, *see* Vansittart
Chiefs of Staff (COS), 41, 47, 56, 58, 77, 131-3, 142, 144, 145, 151
  liaison with, 31, 57
  favour militant propaganda, 52
Chief of Staff, Supreme Allied Commander (COSSAC), 39-40
Churchill, W. S. (later Sir Winston), 7, 34, 76, 81, 83, 91, 132n, 136, 141, 144, 145-8, 155
  establishes SOE, 17, 19, 180
  and Dalton/Duff Cooper feud, 20-6
  praises PWE, 41
  and allied government propaganda, 53
  opposes soft line with Italians, 77
  interest in 'Aspidistra', 106
  Belgian attitude to, 163
Cleethorpes, 146
Collaborators, 79
Cologne, 81

INDEX

'Colonel Britton', 52, 101, 124, 126, 127, 128
   and see Ritchie
Colonial Office, 40
Combined Chiefs of Staff, 39-41, 142, 145, 146
Committee of Imperial Defence, 176
Copenhagen, 160
Courtrai, 7
Coventry, 88
Cranborne, Viscount (later Marquess of Salisbury), 24
Crete, 77
Crewe House, 9, 9n
Cripps, Sir Stafford, 81, 82
Croats, 105
'Cross-listening', 70
Crossman, Richard, 32, 73, 154, 183
   on propaganda to Germany, 73-4, 76
   on BBC and PWE, 181
   on black propaganda, 186
Crowborough, 106
Czechoslovak government, 24, 54
Czechoslovakia, 70, 90, 96

Daily Herald, 60
Daily Mail, 109
Dallas Brooks, Major-General (later Sir Dallas), 26, 52, 127, 162, 184 185
   appointed to Executive Committee, 24, 31
   Deputy Director General, 34
   Chairman, Political Warfare (Japan) Committee, 40
   on propaganda to Germany, 75-6
   on US political warfare, 90-1
   and *Braddock II*, 170
Dalton, Hugh (later Lord Dalton), 22, 24, 25, 26, 33, 46, 48, 54, 73, 106, 109, 180
   given charge of SOE, 17
   duel with Duff Cooper, 18-21, 182
   goes to Board of Trade, 34
   attitude to Germany, 76-7
   argues case for Fourth Arm, 184
Dam Busters, 110
Danes, 119
Danzig, 12
Das Reich, 107
Davis, Elmer, 41
D-Day: *Overlord*, 43, 85, 86, 91, 95, 128n, 131, 148, 150, 151, 152, 167, 169, 170, 173
   Torch, 138, 139
'D-Day publications', 149
De Bosis, Lauro, 96
De Gaulle, General Charles, 73n, 78
de Laveleye, Victor, 121
Delmer, Sefton ('*Der Chef*'), 80-1, 105, 107, 146, 152
Department EH, 17, 29, 30, 49, 56-7, 60-2, 74, 84, 161, 179
Department of Enemy Propaganda (1918), 28, 60, 176-7
Department of Information (1917), 176
Der Neue Tag, 168
de Sausmarez, Cecil, 7, 121
Desertion, 173-4
Deutsches Nachrichtenbüro (DNB), 105, 146, 168, 161
De Wervelwind, 166
Dill, General (later Field-Marshal) Sir John, 147
Diplomatenverpflegung, 168
Dominions, 72
Dominions Office, 40
Dortmund, 168
Dresden, 155
Duff Cooper, Alfred (later Viscount Norwich), 17, 18, 19, 20, 22, 23, 26, 47, 48, 56, 73, 124, 180
   and post-war Europe, 46
   duel with Dalton, 18-21, 182
   replaced by Bracken, 24
   on propaganda, 185
Dunkirk, 78
Dunstable, 35
Dusseldorf, 156
Dutch government, 54, 105

Economic Warfare Ministry, 17, 18, 24, 33, 34, 40, 46, 61, 119, 122, 182
Eden, Anthony (later Earl of Avon), 9, 21, 22, 25, 40, 52, 76, 83, 91, 128, 136, 140, 155, 162
   resigns or Foreign Secretary, 10
   thinks Ministerial Committee failed, 34
   and allied governments, 54
   attitude to GS 1, 81
   asks for aircraft for PWE, 90
   and 'V' campaign, 124
   and *Husky*, 141, 144, 145, 147

Eisenhower, General Dwight D., 38–41, 77, 131–2, 138–9, 141, 144, 145, 147, 155, 165, 171
  on propaganda, 135–6, 143
Elba, 12
English Channel, 109
Essen, 168
Europe, 46–9, 54, 56, 60–1, 83, 85, 90, 96, 101, 117, 127, 134, 137
  invasion of, 148
Evening Standard, 73

Far East, 40, 41, 57, 94, 137
Fécamp, 29–30
Federation of British Industry, 15
Films Council, 10
Finland, 119
Finns, 119
Fisher, Sir Warren, 10, 16, 178–9
Flanders, 126, 148
Food Ministry, 179
Foot, Professor M. R. D., 179
Foreign Office, 11, 14–17, 22, 24, 31, 40, 47, 52, 55, 81–2, 124, 127, 136, 139
  News Dept., 9, 10, 15, 16
  Political Intelligence Dept., 18, 61
Foreign Secretary, see Eden; Halifax
Foreign workers, 130, 150
'Fourth Arm', 18, 57, 180, 181, 182, 182n
France, 46, 70, 77, 85, 89, 94–6, 98, 105, 125, 134, 149, 150, 165–6
Frankfurt, 94, 111, 156, 157
French, 74, 135, 140, 152
French Empire, 77, 137
French government, 54
Frontkurier, 172

'Gaby', 86
Gelnhausen, 157
George II, King of the Hellenes, 82
German High Command, 67, 71, 138, 148, 150, 156, 169, 171, 173
Germans, 72, 74, 92
Gestapo, 66, 67, 98, 131, 161, 186
Glenconner, Lord, 37
Goebbels, Dr Joseph, 45, 67, 161, 169n
Goering, Marshal Hermann, 88, 161
'Go-slow', 51, 52, 58, 124, 166–7
Greece, 77, 82, 83, 105
Greek government, 54, 82
Greene, Hugh Carleton (later Sir Hugh), 186
Grenoble, 28
Gubbins, Major-General Sir Colin, 133

Halifax, Earl of, 10, 14, 15, 30, 45, 179
Halle, 168
Hamburg, 44, 160
Hamburger Fremdenblatt, 88
Hanau, 111
Harris, Air Chief Marshal Sir Arthur, 87, 92
Harrow, 35
Hellschreiber, 105
Henderson, Sir Nevile, 10, 45
Henley-on-Thames, 95
Himmler, Heinrich, 99, 112, 154
Hitler, Adolf, 11, 13, 16, 45, 62, 66, 67, 69, 70, 72, 83, 84, 97, 99, 107, 136, 138, 160, 161
  objects to Vansittart's committee, 10
  invades Russia, 110
  on propaganda, 170
Hitler Youth, 67, 80
HMS Ganges, 59
Hoare, Sir Samuel (later Viscount Templewood), 45
Holland, 60, 63, 89, 90, 94, 95, 96, 105, 149
Hood, Lord, 20–1, 48
House of Commons, 19, 185
Howe, Ellic, 7, 35, 99
Hungary, 105

Imperial Communications Committee, 17
India, 36, 105
India Office, 40
Ingrams, Leonard, 183
Ismay, General Sir Hastings (later Lord Ismay), 52
Italians, 36, 72, 97, 110, 119, 141, 142, 143, 144, 147, 173
Italy, 70, 77, 90, 91, 97, 105, 119, 137, 142, 143
Information Department (1917), 176
Information Ministry (MOI), 12, 13, 15, 16, 18, 22–4, 30–4, 40, 45–8, 61, 121, 124, 144, 182
  establishment of, 21
  reorganization, 23
  Far Eastern Bureau, 40
  Foreign Publicity Divn., 31

INDEX

Information Ministry (French), 30
Japan, 40
Jebb, Gladwyn (later Lord Gladwyn), 127, 128
Jerusalem, 37
Joint Intelligence Committee (JIC), 31, 84, 109, 130
Johnstone, Colonel K., 140-1

Kassel, 111, 157
Keynes, John Maynard (later Lord Keynes), 47
Kiel, 67
King-Hall, Stephen (later Lord King-Hall), 12
Kirkpatrick, Ivone (later Sir Ivone), 33, 34, 123, 186
Krankheit rettet, 172

Lafayette, Marquis de, 139
L'Arc en Ciel, 164, 166
La Revue de la Presse Libre, 98
La Revue du Monde Libre, 98
Law, Richard, 185
Leaflets, 12-15, 28, 30, 34, 38, 44, 45, 53, 54, 67-9, 87, 142
  artillery, 97
  black, 98-100, 156
  delivery techniques, 87, 96-7
  influence of, 17, 98, 159-62, 169
  leaflet bomb, 71, 91, 92, 93
  metal, 88
  numbers dropped, 95-6
  operational, 98
  production, 15, 16, 35, 54, 59, 97, 100
  tactical, 90
  timeless, 89, 98
  strategic, 90
  surrender, 97, 169, 173, 174n
Le Courrier de l'air, 89-90, 95, 98, 166
Le Courrier Illustré, 98
Leeper, Rex (later Sir Rex), 18, 26, 54-5, 123, 127, 184
  Heads of News Dept., 10, 16
  joins Executive Committee, 31
  in charge of black propaganda, 31
  on pornography, 81-2
  on propaganda, 185
Liberia, 36
Libya, 110
Lie, Trygve, 54-6
Lille, 139

Littlestone, 95
London, 41, 81
London Controlling Section and Deception Staffs, 107
London Political Warfare Co-ordinating Committee, 41
Lord President, *see* Anderson
Low Countries, 70
Lloyd, Lord, 10, 15, 179
Lübeck, 81, 88
Luftwaffe, 71, 171
Luxembourg, 14, 152
Lyons, 139

Mack, W. H. B., 136
'M' Balloon Unit, 94-5
McClure, Brigadier-General Robert A., 39, 40, 131, 154, 155
McClachlan, Commander Donald, 152
MacMillan, Lord, 17, 21, 45, 46, 161
Madagascar, 36, 58
Mahomet, 84
Malingering, 99, 172
Mallet, Victor (later Sir Victor), 63
'Mandrill III', 86
Manston, 94
Marne, 122
Marseilles, 121, 139
Marylands, 35
Mediterranean, 19, 39, 57, 110
Mein Kampf, 15, 170
Messina, 110
Middle East, 37, 142, 145
Military intelligence:
  MI 5, 33, 106
  MI R, 179
Monckton, Walter (later Sir Walter), 20
Monotype, 35
Monte Cassino, 97
Montreal, 28
Moore, Vice-Admiral Sir Henry, 144
Morrison, Herbert (later Lord Morrison), 144, 179n
Moscow, 66, 81, 173
Moulins, 121
Mouvement National Belge, 86
Morocco, 136
Munich, 11, 16, 17, 161
Mussolini, 138

Nachrichten für die Truppe, 99, 100, 171, 172
Nancy, 28, 94, 122

Naples, 40
Napoleon, 12, 84
National Physical Laboratory, 93
National Review, 107
National Socialism, 84
Nazi Party, 67, 69, 75, 79, 80, 95, 150, 156, 168, 169, 173
  attitude to agriculture, 113
'Nelly', 86
New Delhi, 40, 41
Newsome, Noel, 124, 183
New York, 38, 39
Nickels, *see* Leaflets
Normandy, 29
North Africa, 31, 57, 77, 98, 119, 134, 138, 139, 142
North Cape, 148
Norway, 47, 54, 63, 89, 90, 96, 105, 119, 149, 183
Norwegian army, 55
  government, 54, 55
  Press Bureau, 55
  State Broadcasting, 56
Norwegians, 165

Oberramstadt, 157
Office of War Information (OWI), 38, 39, 40, 131, 136, 140, 165, 185
Office of Strategic Services (OSS), 38, 39, 136
Official Press Bureau (1914), 174
Operations
  Avalanche, 40
  Baytown, 40
  Braddock II, 128-33
  Cuckoo, 107
  Husky, 141-8
  Intruder, 53, 107, 153, 156-8
  Ironclad, 58
  Overlord, 130, 148-58
  Torch, 58, 134-41, 185
'Otello II', 86
Oxford University Press, 35

Paris, 28, 139, 160
Pas de Calais, 148
Pearl Harbour, 38
Peasants, 113-21
Peirse, Air Vice Marshal Sir Richard, 15
Perth, Earl of, 12n
Pfalz (Palatinate), 153
Poland, 45, 62, 70, 90, 105, 108, 160
Polish government, 54

Political survey officer, 43, 159
Political Warfare Executive (PWE)
  Central Intelligence Directorate, 33
  Central Planning Section, 33
  Committees
    Ministerial, 21-5, 31, 34, 132n, 180
    Propaganda, 34
    Services Consultative, 66-7
    Underground Propaganda, 109
    V, 125
  Director of Intelligence, 36
  Director of Political Warfare, 36
  Director of Production, 34
  formation of, 24, 31
  Missions
    Indian, 36-7
    Middle East, 37
    United States, 38, 39, 40, 136
    West African, 36
  Policy making, 49
  Press Cutting Library, 64
  Regional Directorates, 31-3, 34, 40, 51, 53, 54, 64, 65, 70, 105, 109, 117, 119, 125, 150
  relationship with SOE, 37-8, 182-3
  staff, 33-4
Portal, Air Chief Marshal Sir Charles (later Viscount Portal), 130
Portugal, 62, 63, 136, 138
Postage stamps, 35, 98
Powell, Sir Allen, 64
Press attachés, 10, 60
Prime Minister, *see* Chamberlain; Churchill
Prisoners of war, 29, 67, 130, 150, 159, 169, 174-5
  camps, 67, 68, 119
Propaganda
  black, 34, 49, 50, 69, 78, 81, 106, 117, 148, 151, 154, 186
  combat, 40
  consolidation, 40
  field, 140
  grey, 99, 169
  operational, 49-50, 51, 52, 53
  policy, 49
  preparatory, 49
  strategic, 40
  tactical, 40
  value of, 159-87
  white, 34, 54, 69, 78, 117, 148, 151, 154

INDEX

Propaganda Ministry (German), 71, 161-2
Propagandist's qualification, 42
Psychological Warfare Branch (PWB), see SHAEF
Pyrnees, 148

Quislings, 105

Radar, 88
Radio, 13, 28, 29, 100, 158
  'Aspidistra', 106-7, 131-3, 155-8, 170
  Freedom stations
    Arab Nation, 105
    Himalaya, 105
    New British Broadcasting Station, 105, 106
    Voix Chrétienne, 105
  'Research Units' (black radio), 54, 71, 78, 80-1, 82-3, 85, 103-5, 107, 111, 146
  Luxembourg, 14
RAF, 62, 77, 87, 88, 93, 99, 100, 108, 111, 160
  Bomber Command, 45, 87, 89, 90, 91, 92, 93
  Coastal Command, 89
  Operational Training Units (OTU), 88-9, 93, 94
Rationing, 51, 98, 100, 167-9
Rauschning, Dr Hermann, 12
Red Cross, 160
Reith, Sir John (later Lord Reith), 21, 46
Refugees, 61
Religion, 84-5
Resistance, 50, 119, 167
Reynaud, Paul, 30
Rheims, 28
Rhine, 153, 156
Ritchie, D. E., 101, 123n, 155
  and see 'Colonel Britton'
Rockets, 14
Romania, 105
Rome, 96
Roosevelt, Franklin D., 41, 77, 136, 137, 138, 139, 145
Rostock, 81
Roubaix, 139
Rouen, 122
Rowan, Leslie (later Sir Leslie), 47, 148
Royal Navy, 72, 95, 135

Ruhr, 44, 49, 93, 153, 155
Rumours, 36, 107-112, 115, 173
Rundstedt, General (later Field-Marshal) Gerd von, 172
Russia, 62, 66, 83, 110, 123, 151
Russians, 173

Sabotage, 50, 51, 52, 66, 111, 124, 125, 126-7, 128n, 129
  agricultural, 120
  undetectable, 51, 57-8
Sachs, Brigadier E., 65
St Lo, 174
St Nazaire, 134
Salerno, 40
'Samoyede III', 86
Sarrebourg, 94
Savoy, House of, 147
Scandinavia, 55, 70
Schlieben, General von, 170
Second Front, 135, 136
Secret Service, 14, 19, 33, 61, 81, 108, 109, 131, 161
  US, 184
Selborne, Earl of, 34, 129, 130, 133, 144, 183
Self-mutilation, 172
Serbs, 105
Sherwood, Robert, 41, 131
'Sibs', *see* Rumours
Sicily, 138, 141, 142, 144
Sikorski, General, 105
Silesia, 49
Simon, Sir John (later Viscount Simon), 15
Sinclair, Sir Archibald, 87
Singapore, 57
Skorpion West, 99-100
Slovenes, 105
'Socrates', 86
Sottens, 102
Spain, 62, 63, 95, 136, 138
Spanish Civil War, 14
Spears, Major-General Sir Edward, 73
Special Air Service, 152
Special Branch, 126
Special Operations Executive (SOE), 17-19, 24, 26, 30-1, 35-7, 43, 51-2, 80-2, 86, 91-2, 96-8, 100, 108-9, 124, 132, 136, 139, 144, 149, 151
  charter, 180
SO1, 24, 30, 31, 50, 122, 125
  co-operation with PWE, 150-1

SO2, 30, 50
and *Braddock II*, 128-9, 130-1
Sport Palast, 13
State Department, 142
Steinbeck, John, 129n
Stockholm, 62, 63, 165, 183
Stationery Office, 35
Strasburg, 94
Strikes, 151
Struye, Paul, 162, 164
Stuart, Sir Campbell, 16, 28-30, 38, 42, 45, 56-7, 69, 70-1, 74, 105, 177
  appointed to 'EH', 17
  opposed to Tallents, 178
  prniciples of propaganda, 44
Sun Engraving Co., 35
Supply Ministry (MOS), 23, 179
Supreme Headquarters, Allied Expeditionary Force (SHAEF), 130, 131, 153, 155, 165
  Psychological Warfare Division, 153, 154, 174, 186
  Voice of, 154, 171
Sweden, 62, 80, 95
Swiss, 112
Switzerland, 62, 63, 95

Tallents, Sir Stephen, 12-16, 100, 106, 177-9
Tallin, 160
Tangier, 136
The Hague, 162
Tokyo, 57
Toulon, 139
Tourcoing, 139
Training, 42-3
Travel and Industrial Development Association, 9-11, 14-15
Treasury, 10, 11, 33, 63, 177
Trichinosis, 110
Trier, 160
Tunisia, 97
'Tybalt', 86
Typhus, 108

Uberlingen, 112
U-boats, 67, 109, 111
'Ultra', 148
United Nations, 129, 146
United States, 36, 38, 40, 66-8, 72, 76-7, 80, 106, 134, 144
USAAF, 90, 91

VI, 112
Vansittart, Sir Robert (later Lord Vansittart), 9, 10, 11, 15, 60
'V' broadcasts, 51-3, 101, 121-8
VE-Day, 85
Vellacott, Paul, 37-8
Versailles, Treaty of, 74-5
Vichy, 31, 78, 79, 121, 139, 166
Vienna, 12, 157
Voigt, F. A., 32
Völkischer Beobachter, 10, 88

Walmer, 94
War aims, 47, 76
War Cabinet, 23, 24, 26, 29, 44-6, 54, 61, 69, 91, 144-5, 162
  Defence Committee 40, 90, 132n
  Office, 110, 139
  propaganda policy, 75, 146-7
War Department (US), 136
War Office, 13, 14, 22
War of Independence, American, 139
Warsaw, 45
Washington, 41, 136, 140, 144, 184
Waterlow's 35
Watford, 35
Wavell, General Archibold (later Field-Marshal Earl Wavell) advocates Fourth Arm, 57, 182n
Wehrmacht, 66, 70, 80-1, 162, 169n 169, 173
Wehrmachtsender, 105
Wesel, 156
West Africa, 36, 135
Western Desert, 137
Whispers, *see* Rumours
Wireless Telegraph Board, 106
Wilson, Sir Horace, 9, 44, 178-9
Woburn Abbey, 7, 17, 26, 31, 33-6, 43, 63, 64, 70, 96, 109, 180
Wolmer, Viscount, *see* Selborne

Yugoslav government, 54
Yugoslavia, 105

Zurich, 160